The First Edition of the New Testament

The First Edition of the New Testament

DAVID TROBISCH

OXFORD
UNIVERSITY PRESS
2000

OXFORD
UNIVERSITY PRESS

Oxford New York
Athens Auckland Bangkok Bogotá Buenos Aires Calcutta
Cape Town Chennai Dar es Salaam Delhi Florence Hong Kong Istanbul
Karachi Kuala Lumpur Madrid Melbourne Mexico City Mumbai
Nairobi Paris São Paulo Shanghai Singapore Taipei Tokyo Toronto Warsaw

and associated companies in
Berlin Ibadan

Published by Oxford University Press, Inc.
198 Madison Avenue, New York, New York 10016

Library of Congress Cataloging-in-Publication Data
Trobisch, David
[Endredaktion des Neuen Testaments. English]
The first edition of the New Testament / David Trobisch.
p. cm.
Includes bibliographical references and index.
ISBN 0-19-511240-7
1. Bible. N.T.—Canon. I. Title.
BS2320 .T7613 2000
225.1'2—dc21 99-048733

1 3 5 7 9 8 6 4 2

Printed in the United States of America
on acid-free paper

Contents

Abbreviations

ANRW	Aufstieg und Niedergang der römischen Welt
ANTF	Arbeiten zur neutestamentlichen Textforschung
APF	Archiv für Papyrusforschung und verwandte Gebiete
Baillet	J. Baillet, ed. Inscriptions grecques et latines des tombeaux des rois ou syringes
BEThL	Bibliotheca Ephemeridum theologicarum Lovaniensium
BHTh	Beiträge zur historischen Theologie
Bib.	Biblica. Roma
BNTC	Black's New Testament commentaries
BTB	Biblical theology bulletin
BZ	Biblische Zeitschrift
CBQ	Catholic biblical quarterly
CChr. SL	Corpus Christianorum. Series Latina
CIG	Corpus inscriptionum Graecarum
CSEL	Corpus scriptorum ecclesiasticorum Latinorum
DAI	Documenti antichi dell' Africa italiana. Bergamo
DBAT	Dielheimer Blätter zum Alten Testament
EWNT	Exegetisches Wörterbuch zum Neuen Testament
FS	Festschrift
GTA	Göttinger theologische Arbeiten
HAW	Handbuch der Altertumswissenschaft
HKAW	Handbuch der klassischen Altertumswissenschaft
HNT	Handbuch zum Neuen Testament
HNT. EB	Handbuch zum Neuen Testament. Ergänzungsband
HThK	Herders theologischer Kommentar zum Neuen Testament
HThR	Harvard theological review
ICC	International critical commentary

IGRR	Inscriptiones graecae ad res Romanas pertinentes. Paris
JAC. E	Jahrbuch fur Antike und Christentum. Ergänzungsband
JBL	Journal of biblical literature
JThS	Journal of theological studies
KEK	Kritisch-exegetischer Kommentar über das Neue Testament
LXX	Septuagint
NT	Novum Testamentum. Leiden
NT. S	Novum Testamentum. Leiden. Supplements
NTD	Das Neue Testament Deutsch
NTG^{27}	Kurt Aland et al., eds. Novum Testamentum Graece. 27th ed (Stuttgart: Deutsche Bibelgesellschaft, 1993)
NTOA	Novum testamentum et orbis antiquus
NTS	New testament studies. London
OBO	Orbis biblicus et orientalis
PG	Patrologiae cursus completus. Accurante Jacques-Paul Migne. Series Graeca
PL	Patrologiae cursus completus. Accurante Jacques-Paul Migne. Series Latina
RAC	Reallexikon für Antike und Christentum
RB	Revue biblique
RBen	Revue bénédictine
RNT	Regensburger Neues Testament
SHAW. PH	Sitzungsberichte der Heidelberger Akademie der Wissenschaften Philosophisch-Historische Klasse
TANZ	Texte und Arbeiten zum neutestamentlichen Zeitalter
Th Rv	Theologische Revue
ThHK	Theologischer Handkommentar zum Neuen Testament
ThLZ	Theologische Literaturzeitung
ThR	Theologische Rundschau
TRE	Theologische Realenzyklopädie
TU	Texte und Untersuchungen zur Geschichte der alchristlichen Literatur
VigChr	Vigiliae Christianae
WUNT	Wissenschaftliche Untersuchungen zum Neuen Testament
ZAW	Zeitschrift für die alttestamentliche Wissenschaft
ZKTh	Zeitschrift für katholische Theologie
ZNW	Zeitschrift für die neutestamentliche Wissenschaft
ZPE	Zeitschrift für Papyrologie und Epigraphik
ZThK	Zeitschrift für Theologie und Kirche

The First Edition of the New Testament

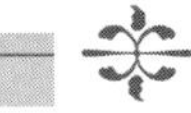

1

Introduction

Today the Christian Bible is a book that is printed, distributed, and sold very much like any other book. It consists of two parts. The second part bears the title "New Testament" and contains twenty-seven writings, beginning with the Gospels and ending with the Revelation of John. This "Canonical Edition," as I shall call it, is the subject of the following study.

Many if not most scholarly discussions of the New Testament concentrate on Jesus of Nazareth or on describing the time, location, and intentions of each of the New Testament's authors and their writings. This investigation, however, focuses on a time when the authors had long completed their work and when editors, publishers, and booksellers took on the task of satisfying the increasing demand of readers with the edition known to us as the "New Testament." I am interested in that specific moment in history when, for the first time, the collected writings of the New Testament were published in the form in which they are used today by the Christian churches.

HISTORICAL SOURCES

The historical sources on the early history of the New Testament may be divided into three categories. First, there is indirect evidence—quotations and allusions to texts of the New Testament from early Christian and non-Christian writers; second, there is the direct evidence of the extant manuscripts of the New Testament; and third, there is the redactional frame of the New Testament itself.

Indirect Evidence

Traditional studies on the history of the canon concentrated on indirect evidence. The authoritative collections and interpretations of these sources go back to the nineteenth century. They are closely associated with the work of four scholars in particular; B. F. Westcott[1] for English-speaking readers, A. Loisy[2] for the French, and Theodor Zahn[3] and Adolf von Harnack[4] for Germans. Despite considerable differences as far as details are concerned, these scholars agreed on a general outline of historical events and strongly influenced the twentieth-century consensus regarding the provenance of the Canonical Edition.

The shared assumption was that each of the New Testament's writings had been circulating separately for a considerable period before a lengthy and complicated collection process began. The process produced differing results in the various geographical regions. This eventually forced the emerging Catholic Church to issue authoritative lists of those writings that should be part of the Christian Bible and those that must be excluded.

Brevard S. Childs's 1984 analysis of contemporary research nicely illustrates that this widely accepted scenario was not seriously challenged during the second half of the twentieth century.[5] Childs's work highlights the theological and historical implications of the fact that at some point in history the Christian canon was closed and writings could neither be added to nor removed from the Christian Bible.[6] Childs summarizes the consensus's claim that by the year 200 Christian congregations recognized the four Gospels and a collection of Paul's letters and that they assigned the same authority to these writings as they did to the Jewish Scriptures. The process of determining which other apostolic writings should be accepted, however, continued to the end of the fourth century and was often carried out in heated debates.[7]

According to the accepted model, the canon evolved in three phases.[8] During the first phase numerous Christian writings emerged, each with a distinct claim to be authoritative.[9] In the second phase, which took place during the second and third century, Christian writings were combined into various collections.[10] The third and last phase, the actual canonization, took place in the fourth century, when the church finally established normative lists.[11] One question has always been of special interest to Christian theologians and remains theologically relevant beyond denominational boundaries: Which criterion became decisive in determining whether or not a specific writing was considered canonical?[12] So far, historical research has not yet provided a widely accepted answer.[13] The theological relevance of this question, however, remains undisputed.[14] And because the canon was not discussed at any of the ecumenical councils of the early church, a precise dating of the authoritative closing of the canon is simply not possible.[15]

Current research has established no consensus on whether the New Testament emerged gradually, carried by the intrinsic value of the writings,[16] or whether there was a historical event that forced the church to produce and publish and vigorously promote an edition of the Christian Bible.

Following Adolf von Harnack, advocates for the latter position often see the New Testament taking shape against the Bible of Marcion. Sometime at the beginning of the second century Marcion had edited and published a collection containing one anonymous gospel, which appears to have been closely related to the canonical Gospel of Luke, together with ten letters by Paul.[17] Even within this interpretive school, it remains an unresolved question whether the church produced the New Testament in reaction to Marcion's publication,[18] or whether Marcion edited and abridged the Canonical Edition,[19] or, indeed, whether the two editions originated independently of each other.[20]

Manuscripts

The discovery of many new manuscripts during the past seventy years has put the present generation of scholars in a much more favorable position than our predecessors. Today, we are able to examine copies of the New Testament dating from the second and third centuries. Unlike Westcott, Loisy, Zahn, and Harnack, we do not have to rely on reconstructions based on allusions and quotations in order to describe the contents and editorial features of early examples of the New Testament.

The Redactional Frame

I want to demonstrate that the redactional frame of the Canonical Edition of the New Testament constitutes a most valuable historical source, though one that is widely neglected. It complements the evidence from early manuscripts and the well-documented secondary references to the writings of the New Testament.

THESIS AND OUTLINE

The thesis of this study is that the New Testament, in the form that achieved canonical status, is not the result of a lengthy and complicated collecting process that lasted for several centuries. The history of the New Testament is the history of an edition, a book that has been published and edited by a specific group of editors, at a specific place, and at a specific time.

Because of the overwhelming number of publications related to the addressed topic—after all, I try to deal with the entire New Testament—I am very well aware that several important studies will have escaped my attention. Nevertheless, I have tried to survey as comprehensively as possible literature written between 1993 and 1996, when this study was first published in Germany. Instead of rewriting my book and incorporating the latest discussion, I decided to present a translation of the German work. More has to be done in the field, and I am well aware that this study will not be the final word.

Out of a personal interest in the intercontinental dialogue, I attempted to take both German and English publications equally into account. I resisted the temptation to compile references to easily accessible standard works, such as introductory books and commentaries, in the footnotes. Concerning the study of book production and publication in antiquity, however, I comprehensively documented the materials and sources I consulted. Among more recent publications, I want to draw the reader's attention to Harry Gamble's excellent monograph *Books and Readers in the Early Church* (1995), which was not accessible to me when I was writing the German manuscript. Gamble's book explores many of the same sources without reaching the same conclusions.

There are several questions I do not address, which may come as a surprise to the specialist in the field. First of all, I only marginally deal with the indirect evidence consisting of the secondary references of early Christian writers to New Testament passages, which usually form the heart of traditional investigations of the history of the canon. I studied them carefully and comprehensively but did not want to base my argument on them. The reader will have to consult the index in the appendix to find references to specific sources. I do not deal with source-critical theories concerning individual writings like the source Q, Proto-Mark, or Marcion's gospel, but not because I think that source-critical studies are irrelevant to the topic. I decided to focus on the final form of the *editio princeps* and not on the history of the incorporated writings. For the same reason, the obvious problem of pseudonymity of New Testament books is only briefly touched on in this study.

I have restrained myself from advancing a theory about exactly where and when and who published the Canonical Edition. However, I hope this study will serve as an important step toward finding valid answers to these questions. In addition, I do not intend to challenge the current consensus that none of the writings included in the New Testament originated significantly later than 150 C.E.

The book consists of three parts. The first part attempts to prove the existence of a uniform final redaction of the New Testament. The second part focuses on the editorial concept of this redaction, a term that will be explained in detail. The third part demonstrates a close link between this editorial concept and 2 Peter, 2 Timothy, and the Gospel of John. One particular passage, Jn 21:25, may even be interpreted as an editorial note to the readers of the Canonical Edition.

In conclusion, I will propose modifications for printed editions of the Christian Bible. The study ends with suggestions on dating and locating the first readers of the Canonical Edition.

2

Evidence for a Final Redaction

THE FINAL REDACTION OF THE NEW TESTAMENT IS NOT normally treated in introductions to the New Testament. This creates the impression that a final redaction never occurred. However, the evidence provided by the extant manuscripts indicates that the history of the New Testament is the history of an edition.

TERMINOLOGY

In this study, I introduce the term *canonical edition* of the New Testament. To avoid misunderstandings I want to clarify how the term will be used.

The word *edition* refers to "the form or version in which a text is published."[1] This form is the result of an editing process that will be called the "final redaction." The final redaction of a publication can be described by looking at external characteristics, such as the publications' size or binding, as well as by analyzing editorial changes that might express the publishers' interests and intentions.

The term *canonical* refers to editions that are regarded as authoritative by an interpreting community. For example, in the eyes of today's Christian churches in Europe and the Americas the Canonical Edition of the New Testament is defined by the exact number of twenty-seven specific writings and not by the exact wording of these writings, since it is considered legitimate to use different translations.

In this sense, the Canonical Edition is defined in terms of the history of its reception. Only if an edition is widely accepted by a community of readers can it become canonical, that is, normative for the group. Therefore, this study will not only focus on the intentions of the publishers and editors but will also try to describe the edition as it is seen and understood from the readers' perspective.

WHAT DOES "FINAL REDACTION" MEAN?

The term *final redaction* will be used in this study with regard to anthologies only. The term designates editorial elements that serve to combine individual writings into a larger literary unit and are not original components of the collected traditional material.

Textual Elements

The well-known *Theologische Realenzyklopädie*[2] may serve as an example. This ambitious publishing project attempts to document the results of historical and theological scholarship in the second half of the twentieth century. Today, more than two decades after the publication of its first volume, this encyclopedia is still not completed.

Articles beginning with the first letters of the alphabet therefore will represent a state of research less current than the articles of the last volumes. Furthermore, style, vocabulary, and breadth may vary considerably from author to author and therefore from article to article. However, the layout, a result of the final redaction, is consistent. At the top of every page of each volume, a centered header gives the title of the current article. Along the left margin, line numbers have been added to facilitate precise quoting. Not only the layout is uniform; all the abbreviations minutely correspond to the list published as one of the volumes of this encyclopedia. Bibliographical information and quotations are always formatted the same way. Reference symbols are included in the text and point to related entries. Such references will be called "cross-references" in this study because they work in both directions. They are a product of the final redaction.

Nontextual Elements

Elements of the final redaction of the *Theologische Realenzyklopädie* (*TRE*) are not restricted to textual changes. The size and type of fonts used, which vary between the text body and the title page; the page layout described above; the blue color of the book cover, with its gold letters; the inscriptions on the back of each volume (displaying the initials *TRE*, the volume number, and the beginning and ending lemmas, conveniently positioned above the publisher's logo); and the number and construction of the quires are standardized. All these characteristics were not part of the original articles; they result from the editors' and publishers' decisions. To the users of the edition, these nontextual signals are sometimes just as important as the textual elements. Because of them, readers will quickly recognize the well-known dark blue volumes even in an unfamiliar library.

How to Identify Redactional Elements

Elements of an anthology's final redaction can be identified by their late date, their unifying function, and the fact that they reflect a consistent editorial design.

Elements of the final redaction usually do not originate with the authors of the works published in an anthology. Even in the unlikely case that authors act as collectors and publishers of their own writings, the elements of the final redaction are still created at a *later date* than the original text.

Most redactional changes during the final editing process of a collection fulfill the *function* of creating a larger literary work out of diverse individual writings. Unifying signals are determined during the final redaction of anthologies. Responsibility for the final redaction rests with the editors and publishers.

Editors of modern anthologies like the *TRE* tend to collaborate more closely with the publisher who produces and distributes the work than the authors of the articles typically do. Often the publishers will take the initiative and participate in the conception and development of such projects.

Such projects usually involve a group of editors. The members of an editorial board may change over the years, without altering the underlying concept of the project. The *editorial concept* determines the criteria for commissioning articles from specific authors, the arrangement of the articles, the nontextual formal elements, and the redactional frame. Furthermore, the editorial board who developed the concept need not be identical with the editors who prepare the text for publication. The actual redactional tasks may be delegated to others.

For the bookseller, features that distinguish a specific edition from competing publications are very important. They may be more important than the unifying signals within the individual anthology. Therefore, the close collaboration between the editorial board and the publisher, who is responsible for the distribution of the final product, favors the development of distinctive literary features, which can be easily identified by the potential customer. After all, books are made to be sold.

The New Testament contains both textual and nontextual elements of a final redaction. Some of the more obvious of these elements are described in the following section.

THE NOTATION OF THE *NOMINA SACRA*

Provenance

Students of the Christian Bible who hold a manuscript of the Greek New Testament in their hands for the first time and try to read a few lines will soon make an interesting discovery. It does not matter when or where the manuscript was written, whether it is a majuscule or a miniscule, whether the text was written on papyrus or on parchment; and it does not matter whether the text is taken from the Gospels, the Letters of Paul, or the Revelation of John. Any manuscript of the New Testament will contain a number of contracted terms that have to be decoded by the reader: the so-called *nomina sacra*, sacred names.

Notation

The two leading studies on the phenomenon of the *nomina sacra* were published by L. Traube (1907)[3] and by A.H.R.E. Paap (1959),[4] who collected and evaluated the data that was available at the time.

There are approximately fifteen words that usually appear in manuscripts as *nomina sacra*. The Greek words and their usual notations are given in parentheses:[5] God (Θεος θ̅ς̅); Lord (κυριος κ̅ς̅); Jesus (Ιησους ι̅ς̅); Christ (Χριστος χ̅ς̅); spirit (πνευμα π̅ν̅α̅); man (ανθρωπος α̅ν̅ο̅ς̅); cross (σταυρος σ̅ρ̅ο̅ς̅) in $\mathfrak{P}^{46}$, but as a combination of the letters *tau* and *rho* σ̅⳨̅ο̅ς̅ in $\mathfrak{P}^{45}$, $\mathfrak{P}^{66}$, and $\mathfrak{P}^{75}$;[6] father (πατηρ π̅η̅ρ̅); son (υιος υ̅ς̅); redeemer (σωτηρ σ̅η̅ρ̅); mother (μητηρ μ̅η̅ρ̅); heaven (ουρανος ο̅υ̅ν̅ο̅ς̅); Israel (Ισραηλ ι̅η̅λ̅); David (Δαωειδ δ̅α̅δ̅ or δ̅δ̅); and Jerusalem (Ιερονσαλημ ι̅λ̅η̅μ̅).

Papp adds a few more to this list, words that were noted as *nomina sacra* only once or twice in the evaluated manuscripts: Moses, Isaiah, prophet, king, kingdom, blood, flesh, John, world, fish, daughter, angel, peace, salvation, and a few others.[7]

When forming the *nomina sacra*, the scribes apparently would write at least the first and the last character of the word, sometimes adding one or two letters from within the word as well. Then they would draw a horizontal line across the top of the contracted word.

Although the text witnesses all display the same system of noting the *nomina sacra*, there are variations in its application.

For example, the number of terms contracted in this way may differ from manuscript to manuscript. The suggestion that the number of *nomina sacra* would increase over time is not supported by the manuscript evidence.[8] A clear connection between the age of the text witness and the number of *nomina sacra* found within it cannot be established. According to G. Rudberg, the Codex Bezae Cantabrigiensis (D 05) of the fifth century displays only Θεος, κυριος, Ιησους and Χριστος consistently as *nomina sacra*, while occasionally contracting σταυρος, πατηρ, and πνευμα. Other terms, which are often contracted in other manuscripts, are written out in full.[9] On the other hand, the Bodmer Papyrus of the Gospel of John, $\mathfrak{P}^{66}$, which is dated about 250 years earlier (to the early third century), frequently adds ανθρωπος (in 35 of 50 incidents) and υιος (in 30 of 49 incidents) to its list of *nomina sacra*.[10]

And even within the same text witness, sometimes a term will appear as a *nomen sacrum* and on another occasion, for no apparent reason, it will be written out in full. Occasionally one has the impression that a term like *father* was contracted only when referring to God; however, this does not hold in all cases.[11] In the oldest extant copy of the Letters of Paul, $\mathfrak{P}^{46}$, dated toward the end of the second century, Paap finds eight instances where the nominative singular πατηρ is used in reference to God.[12] In two cases the word is contracted to $\overline{\pi\rho}$, twice it appears as $\overline{\pi\eta\rho}$, and four times it is fully written out as πατηρ.

Finally, the same word may be contracted in different ways, sometimes even within the same manuscript. Of the text witnesses examined by Paap,[13] fifteen display Χριστος 228 times as $\overline{\chi\rho\varsigma}$, whereas forty-nine other manuscripts contract it 223 times as $\overline{\chi\varsigma}$. And there are even instances where a *nomen sacrum* is written out in full with a superscript line.[14]

Of the terms listed above, only Θεος, κυριος, Ιησους and Χριστος apparently are regularly noted as *nomina sacra* in extant manuscripts of the New Testament.[15]

Table 1. Variations in the Notation of *Nomina Sacra*

Word	*Notation*	*Number of Witnesses*	*Occurrences*
υιος		143	
	Not contracted without supralinear line	123	
	n.s. with a sacred meaning	15	74
	n.s. without a sacred meaning	5	17
	$\overline{υς}$ $\overline{υυ}$ $\overline{υω}$ $\overline{υν}$	19	74
	$\overline{υις}$ $\overline{υιυ}$ $\overline{υιν}$	3	17
	Not contracted but with supralinear line	3	3
σωτηρ		28	42
	Not contracted without supralinear line	22	30
	$\overline{σηρ}$ $\overline{σρς}$ $\overline{σρι}$ $\overline{σρα}$	4	8
	$\overline{σωρ}$ $\overline{σωρς}$ $\overline{σωρι}$	3	4

SOURCE: Data from A. H. R. E. Paap, *Nomina Sacra in the Greek Papyri of the First Five Centuries A.D.* (Leiden: Brill, 1959), 110–12.

Research on the *nomina sacra* since L. Traube has mostly either disproven or failed to substantiate several theories regarding their provenance and meaning.

The Tetragram of the Jewish Bible

L. Traube saw a correlation between the *nomina sacra* and the notation of the tetragram in the Hebrew Bible. In the Hebrew Bible the name of God is represented by four consonants, the so-called tetragram JHWH (יהוה). However, it is vocalized and pronounced as *adonai* (אדני), Lord.[16] This observation led Traube to suspect a correlation between *adonai* and the Greek equivalent for Lord, κύριος, which is regularly written as a *nomen sacrum* in manuscripts of the New Testament. Traube carried the argument a step further, contending that the notation of the *nomina sacra* follows the Hebrew model in writing only the consonants of the name of God.[17] This explains why Θεος was noted as $\overline{Θς}$.

The connection to the Hebrew Bible may appear remarkable at first, but it soon meets with major obstacles. During the early Christian era, the entire text of the Hebrew Bible—not just the tetragram—was written without vocalization—that is, encoded signs within the text indicating how it should be read aloud. The vocalization of the Bible text was introduced centuries later by the Masoretes. The special treatment of the tetragram in the Hebrew Bible was therefore based not on a rule that had to be followed as the text was written down but on a rule that had to be observed as the text was read aloud. Because it was not permissible to pronounce the name of God, the tetragram was replaced by the term *Lord* while reading the Bible. This convention, by the way, created a considerable technical problem when copies of the Hebrew Bible were produced by dictation.[18] Christians, on the other hand, felt free to pronounce the words written as *nomina sacra* (Lord, God, Jesus, Christ, Father, etc.), so the Hebrew and Christian practices would not seem to be parallel.

The notation of *nomina sacra* should not be interpreted as an attempt to simply reduce words to their consonants, since consonants were omitted as well: the *nomen sacrum* χριστος reads $\overline{\chi\varsigma}$ and not $\overline{\chi\rho\sigma\tau\varsigma}$, as it should when simply recording the consonants. And the vowels are clearly included when the *nomen sacrum* is used in another case than the nominative singular; for example, the dative Θεος is recorded as $\overline{\Theta\omega}$.[19]

Another attractive explanation for the phenomenon of the *nomina sacra* relates them to the treatment of the tetragram in Greek editions of the Jewish Bible. The manuscripts of the Christian Old Testament usually render the Hebrew tetragram either as $\overline{\Theta\varsigma}$ or, more often, as $\overline{\kappa\varsigma}$.[20] But how did Jewish editions reproduce the name? Most fortunately, the discovery of the Dead Sea Scrolls has increased the number of text witnesses, so we are now in a more favorable position to describe pre-Christian Jewish practices than scholars were several decades ago.[21] These Jewish copies of the Greek Bible use neither *nomina sacra* nor κύριος to represent the tetragram.[22] Unlike their Christian colleagues, the Jewish scribes preserved the tetragram without seeking a Greek rendition.[23] They did it in a wide variety of ways, however. The tetragram is reproduced within the Greek text using characters of the Hebrew,[24] Aramaic,[25] or paleo-Hebrew[26] script (figure 1), or it is transliterated with Greek characters as πιπι[27] or ιαω.[28]

The Hebrew and Aramaic manuscripts discovered at Qumran and its vicinity display the same lack of uniformity concerning the representation of the tetragram as the early Greek editions of Jewish Bibles do. Next to the tetragram written in paleo-Hebrew script (e.g., 1QpHab), אל (e.g., 1Q14:27; 4Q180.183), צבאות, אדוני and אלוהים are occasionally noted in paleo-Hebrew characters as well.[29] Whereas the tetragram is frequently used

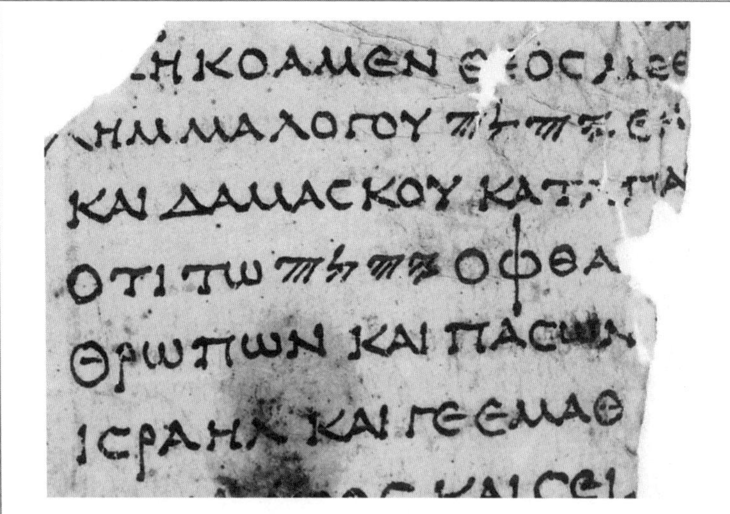

Figure 1. Tetragram in paleo-Hebrew characters, displaying text from Zech 8:23b–9:2. Photo courtesy of the Israel Antiquities Authority, Jerusalem.

within quotations from the Hebrew Bible, it is apparently avoided in the commentary and is often replaced by אל (e.g., 1QpHab 10:6–7.9–13 = Hb 2:13; 1QpHab 11:10.12–15 = Hb 2:16). Another representation of the tetragram outside the Dead Sea Scrolls is the notation of three Yod ייי (e.g., Ben Sira, Cairo Geniza MS B).[30] Although the Aramaic מרא (Hebrew אדוני) somehow corresponds to the usage of κύριος in the Christian Bible, it is not applied on a regular basis in the extant fragments of the targumim to represent the tetragram.[31]

Probably around the beginning of the second century C.E. an influential edition of the Hebrew Bible was published that eventually became the *textus receptus* of rabbinical Judaism and very successfully replaced competing editions.[32] At the same time, rules and regulations were developed on how to deal with scribal errors concerning the name of God.[33] This standard edition of the Hebrew Bible was then translated into Greek, resulting in the editions of Aquila,[34] Theodotion, and Symmachus. Unlike their Christian colleagues, however, these Greek editors did not translate the tetragram; instead, they retained the Hebrew letters, thus demonstrating that they regarded the tetragram as an essential editorial element of the Hebrew original.[35]

Given that editors and publishers of Jewish manuscripts had finally standardized the representation of the tetragram by writing it in Hebrew letters within Greek manuscripts of the Jewish Bible, it is significant that the Christian editions of the Greek Old Testament do not follow the same practice. Instead, the tetragram is rendered either as $\overline{\Theta\varsigma}$ or as $\overline{\kappa\varsigma}$.

Perhaps the *nomina sacra* were simply space-conserving abbreviations of certain often-used terms? Abbreviations in antiquity are typically found on coins or on signposts, where little writing space was available. Abbreviations were also made during dictation (when a text needed to be recorded rapidly) or the composition of lists with recurring expressions.[36]

In his monograph Paap discussed the studies of G. Rudberg[37] and E. Nachmanson,[38] who tried to explain the *nomina sacra* in the light of abbreviations found on Greek ostraca and inscriptions. However, Paap demonstrated convincingly that the evidence will not support this theory.[39] The most significant inconsistencies are:

- In antiquity, terms were normally abbreviated by writing the first letters and omitting the end, not by omitting the letters within the word.[40] Occasional exceptions, in which a *nomen sacrum* is abbreviated by omitting the end of the word, merely prove the rule.[41]
- A special notation of the last character or last characters usually marks omissions. In general, the final characters are either raised or lowered; or they are qualified by adding a specific symbol, such as a period, a horizontal line, a vertical line, a diagonal line, a cross, or an *S* symbol (also horizontal or reversed).[42] A continuous, horizontal line above the abbreviation is very rare, but it appears occasionally.[43]
- Although the selection of terms noted as *nomina sacra* varies in the manuscripts, their number is somewhat limited, whereas the number of words that could be abbreviated in inscriptions and ostraca is unrestricted.
- Nonliterary texts generally abbreviate words to save space. Saving space, however, is not a satisfactory explanation for the use of *nomina sacra*, since it would appear more practical to abbreviate either particularly long words or the terms that are used most often. The frequency and length of words were obviously not criteria for the selection of *nomina sacra*.

- An effort to save time during the writing process does not explain the phenomenon either. The time required to insert a line across the top of Θεος and κυριος, for example, is not significantly shorter than the time required to write the word in full.
- Although the notation of the *nomina sacra* is not uniform in the manuscripts, the general principle of contracting the first and final characters and marking them with a superscript line has created a certain standard.[44] Compared to this procedure, the abbreviations in inscriptions and ostraca display stronger variations.

There is another significant difference between abbreviations and *nomina sacra*. As an integral part of the Canonical Edition, the *nomina sacra* are elements of a literary text that has been reproduced and distributed in copies. Inscriptions and ostraca, however, are documents that exist only in one single exemplar. Numerous biblical manuscripts exhibit marginal notes that were added for personal purposes by the readers of the manuscript. Their nonliterary character is obvious. Whereas the Bible text will contain *nomina sacra*, these marginal glosses may contain both *nomina sacra* and abbreviations. The abbreviations often were added without following a specific system and usually are not easily decoded by modern readers. Since these abbreviations do not contain superscript lines, they are easily distinguished from the *nomina sacra* (figure 2).

In the seventh century, when the publishing industry finally adopted the practice of producing books using miniscule script, a system of abbreviating ligatures was gradually introduced. This system was designed to save both production time and valuable vellum space. The criteria for selecting words to be abbreviated were their length and their frequency in the text. The abbreviation system affected all literature, not just Christian publications.

The use of written shorthand is well documented in much earlier periods.[45] Shorthand scribes were employed for writing letters, which were dictated to them, as well as for more challenging literary assignments.[46] Sophisticated techniques for rapid and dependable text production were well established before the New Testament originated. Such techniques, however, have nothing in common with the notation of the *nomina sacra*.

Literary texts were generally reproduced in the manuscripts without spaces between the words. The superscript line above the *nomina sacra* in Biblical manuscripts provided some help for reading the *scriptio continua*.[47]

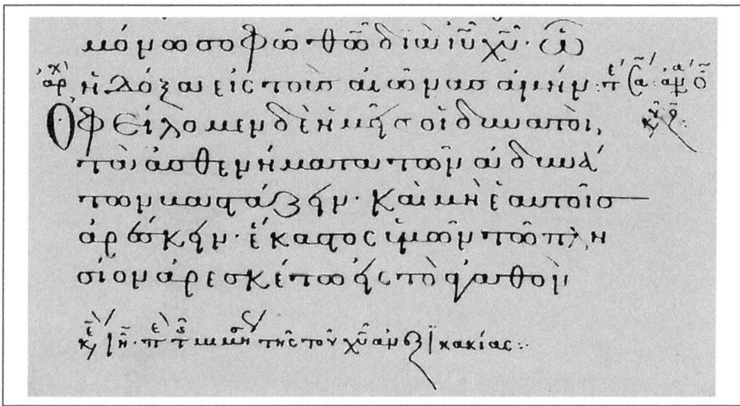

Figure 2. *Nomina sacra* and abbreviations on one page, showing Rom 16:26 + 15:1–2. The top line contains nomina sacra (Θω, ιυ, χυ); abbreviations are on the left (αρχ(η)), the right, and the bottom margins (περι της μιμησεως του χυ ἀνεξικακιας). Miniscule 223; Ann Arbor Univ. Michigan Ms. 34, section from f.144r. Photo courtesy of the University of Michigan Library, Ann Arbor.

In non-Christian texts, such as magical invocations, terms that were incomprehensible to readers as well as listeners were often separated from the rest of the text by dots.[48] A customary exercise for students learning to read and write was to mark the word boundaries with short strokes.[49] Paap noted that occasionally horizontal lines were used instead of dots or short strokes.[50] How helpful the superscript line can be becomes clear when you try to read fluently a New Testament passage that contains several *nomina sacra*—for example, Jude 25a:[51]

ΜΟΝΩΘΩΣΗΡΙΗΜΩΝΔΙΑΙΥΧΥΤΟΥΚΥΗΜΩΝ.

The benefits of the superscript line as a reading aid, however, do not sufficiently explain the introduction of the notation system. Actually, the early Christian editors were only solving a problem they themselves had created.

Elements of the Final Redaction

Two problems in particular have not yet found a satisfactory explanation: the selection of words noted as *nomina sacra* and the technique of contracting the first and last letters and marking them with a superscript line.[52] Because the *nomina sacra* cannot be interpreted as a routine convention, however, they are very valuable in the context of this study. They seem to reflect a conscious editorial decision made by a specific publisher.[53]

Nomina sacra are not only found in the New Testament but are used in the first part of the Canonical Edition, the Christian Old Testament, as well. Obviously, the notation system could not possibly have originated with the individual authors of the Jewish scriptures contained in the Old Testament. And because the Canonical Edition represents the tetragram differently from other Greek editions of the Jewish Bible, the *nomina sacra* apparently are a characteristic editorial feature of this Christian edition, which clearly distinguishes this edition from competing publications.

THE USE OF THE CODEX FORM

Aside from the characteristic notation of *nomina sacra* there is another fascinating observation concerning the Canonical Edition: from the very beginning, New Testament manuscripts were codices and not scrolls.

Provenance

The following statistics demonstrate that the codex form was rarely used for non-Christian literary texts during the first centuries C.E. In the first and second centuries, one hundred scrolls would be produced for every two codices; in the third century, every eighth manuscript was a codex; in the fourth century, more than half of the manuscripts were codices; and at the end of the fifth century, only one in ten manuscripts was produced as a scroll. By the end of antiquity, codices had thus almost completely replaced scrolls as the dominant literary medium (table 2).

These statistics have to be treated with caution because fragments of ancient manuscripts usually cannot be dated with certainty. New manuscripts are still being discovered or published for the first time. In addition, the number of text witnesses is not distributed evenly over time. As a consequence, the percentage figures for one century cannot necessarily be accurately compared to those for other centuries. Nevertheless, past studies using less material and dating the material differently have basically reached the same conclusion: from the fourth century on, codices largely replaced scrolls in the publishing business.[54]

Table 2. The Scroll and Codex Ratio For Non-Christian Texts

Century	*Scrolls*	*Codices*	*Total*	*% Scrolls*	*% Codices*
1	252	1	253	99.60	0.40
1–2	203	4	207	98.07	1.93
2	857	14	871	98.39	1.61
Sum	1312	19	1331	98.57	1.43
2–3	349	17	366	95.36	4.64
3	406	93	499	81.36	18.64
Sum	755	110	865	87.28	12.72
3–4	54	50	104	51.92	48.08
4	36	99	135	26.67	73.33
Sum	90	149	239	37.66	62.34
4–5	7	68	75	9.33	90.67
5	11	88	99	11.11	88.89
Sum	18	156	174	10.34	89.66

SOURCE: Data from Colin Henderson Roberts and T. C. Skeat, *The Birth of the Codex* (London: Oxford University Press, 1983), 37.

NOTE: The statistical data given by T. Kleberg, *Buchandel und Verlagswesen in der Antike* (Darmstadt: Wissenschaftliche Buchgesellschaft, 1967), 83–84, is outdated. For an older collection of data, see R. A. Pack, *Greek and Latin Literary Texts from Greco-Roman Egypt*, 2nd ed. (Ann Arbor: University of Michigan Press, 1965).

Fortunately, it is not difficult to determine whether a fragment originally was part of a scroll or a codex. If it was part of a codex, then the back side was used for writing as well, whereas a scroll fragment displays text on one side only.[55]

In contrast to non-Christian literary texts, the New Testament has been passed on to us almost exclusively in codex form; the oldest extant fragments reach back to the second century.[56] In a representative count, C. H. Roberts and T. C. Skeat evaluated 172 Greek manuscripts and fragments of the Christian Bible dating from the first four centuries, and they found that 158 originated from codices and only 14 from scrolls.[57] Five of the 14 scroll fragments are opisthographs, in which biblical texts were written on the backside of a discarded scroll in order to save paper. These copies were most probably not produced to be sold but were for private use only. Three of the remaining nine scroll fragments are almost certainly, and two are quite probably, of Jewish origin. The remaining four manuscripts contain odd characteristics and do not display typical features of scrolls, or they are too fragmentary to be evaluated.[58]

There is plenty of evidence, especially of Roman provenance, that the codex form was popular in pre-Christian times. Booklets were typically used to keep personal notes and diaries, for example, or for writing exercises in school, but they were not used for publications. The codex form is discussed in more detail in the next chapter.

Element of the Final Redaction

As was the case with the *nomina sacra*, the codex form is characteristic of both parts of the Christian Bible. Since the codex was not normally used for literary texts in the first two centuries, it is unlikely that the Greek master copies of the Jewish Bible, as well as all of the works of the New Testament authors, were initially published and available to editors in codex form. Therefore, it is very improbable that several publishers working independently of one another would produce their New Testament texts in codices. Thus two criteria for determining the codex form as an element of the final redaction are fulfilled: it affects all the writings of the collection, and someone other than the authors introduced it.[59]

ARRANGEMENT AND NUMBER OF WRITINGS IN THE MANUSCRIPTS

Methodological Considerations

The arrangement and the number of New Testament writings in the oldest extant manuscripts of the Christian Bible provide the most important evidence for describing the history of the canon. Methodologically, varied sequences of the writings in the manuscripts demonstrate that the writings circulated separately at first and were combined to form different collections later. This statement may also be reversed: if the same number of Gospels, Letters of Paul, General Letters, etc., are presented in the manuscripts in the same order, it follows that these manuscripts are based on an established collection. So the answer to the question of whether the New Testament developed over a certain period of time or whether there was a first edition that is represented by the extant manuscript tradition depends on what the manuscript evidence looks like.[60]

The editions of the apostolic fathers offer an example of a collection of writings that circulated separately for an extended period of time prior to their appearance within a single book. Although collections published under this title are mentioned as early as the sixth century by the Monophysitic bishop Severus of Antioch, they do not share a common manuscript tradition. The history of the edition used today actually only starts with J. B. Cotelier, a French patristic scholar, who published the work in two volumes in 1672.[61]

This edition included the Letter of Barnabas, the First Letter of Clement, the Shepherd of Hermas, the Letters of Ignatius, and the Letter of Polycarp, as well as the Martyrdom of Clement, the Martyrdom of Ignatius, and the Martyrdom of Polycarp. Without changing the title of the collection, the selection of included writings was continually modified in subsequent years. In 1765 A. Gallandi extended the collection by adding the Letter of Diognet, the Fragments of Papias, and the Fragment of Quadratus. And when the Didache was discovered in 1873, it was usually added to the canon of the apostolic fathers as well.[62] In his 1950 edition, E. J. Goodspeed included *De doctrina apostolorum*, which is extant only in a Latin version.[63] On the other hand, R. M. Grant (1964) left out the Letter of Diognet and the Quadratus fragment and instead added the Martyrdom of Polycarp.[64] M. W. Holmes (1992) in return deliberately excluded the Fragment of Quadratus from his edition.[65] The German patristic scholar J. A. Fischer (1956) even narrowed the collection down to the First letter of Clement, the Letters of Ignatius, the Letter of Polycarp, and the Quadratus fragment.[66] Not only does the list of writings included in each edition vary; there are variations in the arrangement of the writings as well (table 3).

Finally, the redactional concepts of the editors differ from edition to edition: Cotelier, for instance, in his effort to produce a comprehensive edition of all existing writings, included inauthentic writings and said as much in the title: "opera vera et suppositicia." Fischer, on the other hand, wanted to incorporate only those authors who were either actually in contact with the witnesses of the apostolic age or whose teaching was nearest to the spirit of the New Testament.[67] He even went beyond the manuscript evidence and, following a widely accepted source-critical theory of the time, divided the traditional text of the letter of Polycarp into two

Table 3. Number and Arrangement of Writings in the Editions of the Apostolic Fathers

Bihlmeyer	Did	Barn	1 Clem	2 Clem	Ign	Pol Phil	Mart Pol	Papias	Quadratus Diogn
Bauer	Did		1 Clem	2 Clem	Ign	Pol Phil	Barn		Herm
Fischer			1 Clem		Ign	Pol Phil			Quadratus Diogn
Wengst	Did	Barn		2 Clem					
Grant	1 Clem	2 Clem	Did.	Barn.	Ign	Pol Phil	Mart Pol	Papias	Herm

SOURCE: Data from K. Bihlmeyer, ed., *Die Apostlischen, Väter*, Neubearbeitung der Funkschen Ausgabe, vol. 1, 2nd ed. (Tübingen: Mohr, 1956).

"original" letters and published these as Polycarp's two letters to the Philippians.[68]

As far as methodology is concerned, I will assume the following: If the number and the arrangement of individual writings in the manuscripts are the same, then these manuscripts are copies of a common archetype. On the other hand, if the number and arrangement of writings within a collection vary considerably from one edition to the next, and if discernably different editorial concepts are present, then the corpus grew slowly and this process bore different results at different historical locations. This methodological principle is, to my knowledge, not disputed.

In the following I would like to demonstrate briefly that the oldest extant editions of the whole New Testament, which were produced during the fourth and fifth centuries, share the same number of New Testament writings and present them in the same arrangement. Therefore we may safely assume a common archetype. In addition I will look at the witnesses older than these complete editions and demonstrate that these witnesses do not provide any compelling evidence of an alternative selection or arrangement of writings.

Complete Editions

The four oldest extant manuscripts, which at the time of their production presented a complete edition of the New Testament, were produced during the fourth and fifth centuries.

The oldest complete exemplar is the *Codex Sinaiticus* (א 01).[69] The parchment manuscript contains all twenty-seven writings and was probably written during the fourth century. The sequence of the New Testament writings is as follows: the Gospels (Matthew, Mark, Luke, John), the Pauline Letters (Romans, 1 and 2 Corinthians, Galatians, Ephesians, Philippians, Colossians, 1 and 2 Thessalonians, Hebrews, 1 and 2 Timothy, Titus, Philemon), the Praxapostolos (Acts, the Letter of James, the two Letters of Peter, the three Letters of John, the Letter of Jude), and Revelation, followed by two early Christian writings, the Letter of Barnabas and the Shepherd of Hermas.

The other extant manuscript from the fourth century is the Codex Vaticanus (B 03).[70] The arrangement of the writings varies from the Codex Sinaiticus in that the Praxapostolos is placed between the Tetraeuangelion and the Corpus Paulinum. The manuscript breaks off in the middle of the Letter to the Hebrews (Heb 9:14), which follows 2 Thessalonians. The pastorals, the Letter to Philemon, and the Revelation of John are missing, due to the loss of the last part of this manuscript.

Two other parchment manuscripts, the Codex Alexandrinus (A 02)[71] and the Codex Ephraemi Rescriptus (C 04),[72] date from the fifth century. Originally they also contained all of the twenty-seven writings. The arrangement of the writings in the Codex Alexandrinus corresponds to the arrangement of the Codex Vaticanus. Unfortunately, the fragmentary character of the Codex Ephraemi does not permit a detailed reconstruction of the original sequence of writings. Its pages had been detached, washed off, reused for the writings of the Syrian church father Ephraem, and then rebound.[73]

It seems that none of these four manuscripts served as a master copy for any of the others and that they were produced independently.[74] Furthermore, each of these four manuscripts constitutes a complete edition of the Christian Bible. They all contain the writings of the Old Testament followed by the New Testament.

The Place of the Letter to the Hebrews and the Book of Acts

The arrangement of these writings varies in two aspects from most modern editions of the Christian Bible. The Book of Acts and the General Letters are presented as part of the same collection, and the Letter to the Hebrews is placed as the last of Paul's letters to congregations, following 2 Thessalonians and preceding 1 Timothy, right in the middle of the Pauline letter collection. Most German and English translations, and both standard editions of the Greek text,[75] follow the arrangement found in the majority of late Byzantine manuscripts, which place the letter to the Hebrews at the end of Paul's letters, and Acts between the Gospels and the Corpus Paulinum.[76] In the sixteenth century, Erasmus of Rotterdam, who used late Byzantine text witnesses to produce the first printed edition of the Greek New Testament, followed this sequence. From there it made its way into our modern editions. Even if contemporary editors of the Greek text claim to be indebted to the older Alexandrine manuscript tradition, their editions still reflect the arrangement of the late Byzantine manuscripts.

Four Collection Units

By comparing the sequence of the writings in the four oldest extant editions of the New Testament, the four collection units of the manuscript tradition are easily identified: The Four-Gospel Book, the Praxapostolos, the Letters of Paul, and the Revelation of John. The differences[77] between Codex Sinaiticus (Gospels, Letters of Paul, Praxapostolos, Revelation) and the Codices Vaticanus and Alexandrinus (Gospels, Praxapostolos, Letters of Paul, Revelation) indicate that the sequence of these units may vary.[78]

Dividing the New Testament into four collection units is consistent with the analysis of the remaining manuscripts. Only about 59 of the approximately 5,300 extant manuscripts include all four collection units of the New Testament. The overwhelming majority of manuscripts (98.87 percent) combine fewer units (table 4).

However, almost without exception, these editions contain a subset of the four above-mentioned units. A manuscript consisting of only one Gospel, one letter of Paul, and two General Letters, for example, would represent quite an oddity.

This is why the compilers of the appendix to the *Novum Testamentum Graece* were able to describe the contents of most manuscripts by using only four letters: *e* = gospels, *a* = Praxapostolos, *p* = the Letters of Paul, *r* = Revelation of John.[79] The editors refer to Acts and the General Letters using a single notation (*a*). If a significant number of manuscripts containing the Book of Acts without the General Letters or the General Letters without the Book of Acts existed, this notation would not suffice.

Because most of these manuscripts were produced after the fifth century, at a time when the number of the twenty-seven canonical writings had been firmly established, the division of the New Testament into collection units does not attest to different stages of the canon. The reason for such a division is probably a purely practical one. Smaller books were easier to bind, transport, and read. In case of loss or destruction, only the affected volume had to be replaced. Moreover, readers were not equally interested in each of the four units; some were clearly more popular than others. The 2,328 extant manuscript witnesses of the Four-Gospel Book known today outnumber by far the 779 copies of the Letters of Paul, the 655 copies of the Praxapostolos, and the 287 extant copies of the Book of Revelation.[80]

Table 4. Distribution of Collection Units in the Manuscripts

Papyri	*Majuscules*	*Miniscules*	*Number*	*Contents*
43	184	1,896	2,123	e
	8	265	273	ap
26	58	138	222	p
5	7	118	130	r
18	29	40	87	a
	1	75	76	apr
	3	56	59	eapr
		11	11	er
2	1	8	11	ea
		6	6	pr
		5	5	ep
		3	3	ar
		2	2	ear

SOURCE: Barbara Aland and Kurt Aland, *The Text of the New Testament: An Introduction to the Critical Editions and to the Theory and Practice of Modern Textual Criticism*, 2nd ed. (Grand Rapids, Mich.: Eerdmans; Leiden: Brill, 1989), 78–79.

NOTES: e = 2,361; a = 662; p = 792; r = 287.

If a literary work is published in several volumes, the literary unity of the collection is usually still apparent. The Bodmer Papyrus 𝔓[66] is a good example. This codex is exceptional because it contains only the Gospel of John. The pagination begins with Jn 1, which proves that no other gospels preceded it in the same volume. The title εὐαγγέλιον κατὰ Ἰωάννην, however, which is preserved on the first page, identifies the Gospel as part of the Canonical Edition. With the help of this title, any reader familiar with the Four-Gospel collection can recognize the Gospel as a part of this collection.[81] These very rare cases of individually bound writings neither prove nor disprove existing collection units.

In an effort to shed some light on the history of these four collection units prior to their inclusion in the four manuscripts mentioned above, I evaluated the data given in the *Novum Testamentum Graece* concerning all manuscripts up to and including the seventh century. I chose this time frame to avoid the distorting effect of late Byzantine editions on text witnesses, although I also did not want to overlook later exemplars, which could potentially have been copies of manuscripts older than the fourth century.[82]

Furthermore, I took care to consider only those exemplars that complied with the standards of ancient book publishers, that is, those that were produced to be sold. I excluded privately produced copies and peculiarities, such as personal excerpts (for instance, 𝔓[43] and 𝔓[62]); writing exercises; and talismans holding biblical texts that were rolled up and worn as charms (for instance, 𝔓[50] and 𝔓[78]).[83]

Excluded Manuscripts

Manuscripts containing the text of only one of the New Testament's writings were also excluded from further investigation. In addition to most of the New Testament papyri, which were taken into account up to number 99 and are not separately listed here, the witnesses listed in table 5 were not included.

The following manuscripts contain text from more than one writing of the New Testament. However, due to their fragmentary character, the sequence of the writings remains indeterminable: 𝔓[4] (Mt Lk, 3);[84] 𝔓[34] (1 Cor 2 Cor, 7);[85] 𝔓[53] (Mt Acts, 3);[86] 𝔓[92] (Eph 2 Thes, ca. 300);[87] Q 026 (Lk Jn, 5);[88] T 029 (Lk Jn, 5);[89] 067 (Mt Mk, 6);[90] 070 (Lk Jn, 6);[91] 078 (Mt Lk Jn, 6; see note 90); 083 (Mk Jn, 6–7);[92] 087 (Mt Mk Jn, 6); 088 (1 Cor Ti, 5–6); 093 (Praxapostolos, 6); 0102 (Mt Lk, 7)[93]; 0104 (Mt Mk, 7);[94] 0107 (Mt Mk, 7); 0171 (Mt Lk, ca. 300);[95] 0208 (Col 1 Thes, 6);[96] 0209 (1 Cor 2 Cor 2 Pt, 7).[97]

Arrangement of the Canonical Edition

The following manuscripts contain the writings in the sequence of the Canonical Edition: 𝔓[30] (1 Thes 2 Thes, 3);[98] 𝔓[61] (Rom 1 Cor, Phil Col 1 Thes, Ti Phlm, 7–8);[99] 𝔓[74] (Praxapostolos, 7)[100]; 𝔓[75] (Lk Jn, 3);[101] H 015 (Letters of Paul, 6) and I 016 (Letters of Paul, 5);[102] N 022 (Four-Gospel Book, 6); Σ 042 (Mt Mk, 6); Φ 043 (Mt Mk, 6); 048 (Praxapostolos, Letters of Paul, 5);[103] 064 (Mt Mk, 6)[104]; 0166 (Acts Jas, 5; see figure 3); 0247 (1 Pt 2 Pt, 5–6);[105] 0251 (3 Jn Jude, 6);[106] 0285 (Heb 1 Tim, 6).[107]

Table 5. Manuscripts Excluded from Further Investigation

Century	*Manuscript* (*Contents*)
2–3	0189 (Acts)
3	0220 (Rom)
3–4	0162 (Jn)
4	058 (Mt); 0169 (Rv); 0185 (1 Cor); 0188 (Mk); 0206 (1 Pt); 0207 (Rv); 0221 (Rom); 0228 (Heb); 0230 (Eph); 0231 (Mt); 0242 (Mt)
4–5	057 (Acts); 059 (Mk); 0160 (Mt); 0176 (Gal); 0181 (Lk); 0214 (Mk); 0219 (Rom); 0270 (1 Cor)
5	061 (1 Tm); 062 (Gal); 068 (Jn); 069 (Mk); 077 (Acts); 0163 (Rv); 0165 (Acts); 0172 (Rom); 0173 (Jas); 0174 (Gal); 0175 (Acts); 0182 (Lk); 0201 (1 Cor); 0216 (Jn); 0217 (Jn); 0218 (Jn); 0226 (1 Thes); 0227 (Heb); 0236 (Acts); 0240 (Ti); 0244 (Acts); 0252 (Heb); 0254 (Gal); 0261 (Gal); 0264 (Jn); 0267 (Lk); 0274 (Mk)
5–6	071 (Mt); 072 (Mk); 076 (Acts); 0158 (Gal); 0170 (Mt); 0186 (2 Cor); 0213 (Mk); 0232 (2 Jn)
6	E 08 (Acts) O 023 (Mt); R 027 (Lk); Z 035 (Mt); Ξ 040 (Lk); 060 (Jn); 065 (Jn); 066 (Acts); 073 (Mt); 079 (Lk); 080 (Mk); 081 (2 Cor); 082 (Eph); 085 (Mt); 086 (Jn); 089 (Mt); 091 (Jn); 094 (Mt); 0143 (Mk); 0147 (Lk); 0159 (Eph); 0184 (Mk); 0187*; (Mk); 0198 (Col); 0222 (1 Cor); 0223 (2 Cor); 0225 (2 Cor); 0237 (Mt); 0241 (1 Tm); 0245 (1 Jn); 0246 (Jas); 0253 (Lk); 0260 (Jn); 0263 (Mk); 0265 (Lk); 0266 (Lk); 0282 (Phil)
6–7	0164 (Mt); 0199 (1 Cor)
7	096 (Acts); 097 (Acts); 098 (2 Cor); 099 (Mk); 0100 (Jn); 0103 (Mk); 0106 (Mt); 0108 (Lk); 0109 (Jn); 0111 (2 Thes); 0145 (Jn); 0167 (Mk); 0183 (1 Thes); 0200 (Mt); 0204 (Mt); 0210 (Jn); 0239 (Lk); 0259 (1 Tm); 0262 (1 Tm); 0268 (Jn); 0275 (Mt)

NOTES: The dates are taken from *Novum Testamentum Graece*, 27th ed.

*See Adolf Deissmann, *Die Septuaginta-Papyri und andere altchristliche Texte der Heidelberger Papyrus-Sammlung*, Veröffentlichungen aus der Heidelberger Papyrus-Sammlung, no. 1 (Heidelberg: Winter, 1905), 80–84. I had access to the original.

Other Sequences

Manuscripts displaying a different arrangement and number of writings than the Canonical Edition are discussed individually.

The Chester Beatty Codex 𝔓[46] (ca. 200) presents the letters of Paul in a singular sequence: Romans, Hebrews, 1 Corinthians, 2 Corinthians, Ephesians, Galatians, Philippians, Colossians, and 1 Thessalonians. The remainder is missing due to the loss of the outer leaves of the codex, which was bound in one quire.[108] The peculiar sequence probably results from the letters' being arranged according to their length. This arrangement is not reflected in later manuscript tradition.[109]

The Bodmer Papyrus 𝔓[72] (third–fourth centuries) is the oldest presently known witness of the two letters of Peter and the Letter of Jude.[110] The unusual selection of writings in this codex and their peculiar arrangement are not easily explained. The Third Letter to the Corinthians follows the Nativity of Mary, succeeded by the Eleventh Ode of Salomon, the Letter of Jude, Melito's Homily on the Passover, a fragment of a hymn, the Apology of Phileas, and the canonical Psalms 33 and 34, and it concludes with both letters of Peter. The same hand (scribe B) copied the New Testament writings. Fortunately, these pages have retained an older pagination (table 6).

The pagination demonstrates that the Bodmer Codex combines two older codices. This exemplar has little in common with the Canonical Edition, and neither did the manuscript it was copied from. The Letter of Jude does not follow the letters of Peter in either case. This is a unique exemplar that did not try to preserve an older collection, which is especially evident in regard to the two Psalms.

The Codex Washingtonianus W 032 (fifth century)[111] arranges the Gospels in this order Matthew, John, Luke, and Mark.[112] A new quire was used for each Gospel. The sequence therefore is based solely on the continuous pagination of the quires, which was added by the original scribe and served as a guide for the bookbinder.[113] The reason for this sequence probably lay in the editorial intent to have the apostles' Gospels precede the Gospels of the apostles' students.

This sequence may have been an oddity from the very beginning. On the first page of each Gospel, peculiar spots are visible: twenty on the first page of Matthew, sixteen on John, five on Luke, and four on Mark. The most badly stained page is found at the beginning of John.[114] Henry A.

Figure 3. The Heidelberg Fragment (Gregory 0166) P.Heid G 1357 (fifth century) demonstrates nicely that even very small fragments may reveal the arrangement of whole collection units. The verso contains the end of Acts (Acts 28:30–31), and the second column of the recto contains text from the beginning of the Letter of James (Jas 1:11). Deissmann, ed., *Septuaginta-Papyri*, 85. Photo courtesy of Papyrologisches Institut, Heidelberg.

Sanders examined these spots in detail and found that they were not ink but were caused by drops of wax or oil from either a candle or a lamp. Presumably, the manuscript was taken out under poor light and these pages were opened repeatedly to demonstrate this curious arrangement of the Gospels to visitors.[115] When the manuscript was later rebound, the evangelists were pictured on the wooden cover in the arrangement of the manuscript: Matthew, John, Luke, and Mark.[116]

The famous Greek-Latin Codex Bezae Cantabrigiensis D 05 (fifth century) displays the same arrangement of the Gospels: Matthew, John, Luke, and Mark. Following the Gospels, the first preserved page contains the end of the Third Letter of John in Latin and, on its back side, the beginning of Acts in Greek. At some point in the history of this exemplar, the sixty-six pages between Mark and Acts were torn out and are now lost.[117] The unusual arrangement of the Gospels is paralleled by the unusual sequence of the writings of the Praxapostolos. J. Chapman calculated that the gap would be large enough to accommodate Revelation of John and the three letters of John.[118] Furthermore, the scribe inserted marks to indicate an alternative stichometry for the Gospels of Matthew and Mark and for the first chapters of John, but not for the Gospel of Luke, the Third Letter of John, and Acts. This stichometry was probably adopted from the master copy. Chapman assumes that the archetype of

Table 6. Arrangement of Writings in 𝔓[72]

Writing	*Page Number*
Nativity of Mary	Different hand and pagination
3rd Corinthians	50–57
11th Ode of Salomon	57–62
Letter of Jude	62–68
Melito's Homily on the Passover, a fragment of a hymn, Apology of Phileas, Ps 33, Ps 34	Different hand and pagination
1 Peter, 2 Peter	1–36

this stichometry was arranged in this order: Matthew, Mark, John, Luke, . . . 3 John, Acts. The scribe, however, chose not to continue to record the alternative stichometry when he copied the Gospel of John. If the analysis is correct, the producers of this bilingual codex probably followed the pattern of some Latin manuscripts. However this might be, the unusual arrangement of the writings that follow the Gospels suggests strongly that the odd sequence of the Gospels is not based on tradition either but results from deliberate editorial activity. The canonical sequence is the *lectio difficilior* and therefore the preferred order.

The Chester Beatty Codex 𝔓[45] (third century) contains parts of the four Gospels and of Acts.[119] Two consecutive sheets, which still preserve their center, illustrate that each page had been folded individually when the codex was bound. Therefore the sequence of the writings cannot be determined.[120] The manuscript ends with Acts 17:17, and, most fortunately, the page number of this sheet—199—is preserved.[121]

According to the calculations of the first editor, Sir Frederic Kenyon, the end of Acts would have been on page 218. Since one folded sheet constitutes four pages, the number of all the pages had to be divisible by four. Kenyon therefore concludes that there were two empty pages at the end.[122]

Although almost all reference books on the subject have adopted this conclusion, it is not indisputable.[123] The general layout of the manuscript allows for about 2,500 characters per page, so the General Letters would require exactly 20 pages, or 5 sheets. The final number of

Figure 4. *Subscriptio* for the Praxapostolos in the Codex Alexandrinus. The top line represents the conclusion of the letter of Jude. The *subscriptio* combines Acts and the General Letters to a single collection unit:

πραξεις των αγιων

αποστολων

και καθολικαι.

Photo courtesy of the British Library.

pages would consequently amount to 240 pages or 60 sheets, a size that was technically possible. The Chester Beatty Papyrus IX–X, from the middle of the third century, consists of 59 sheets; the Bodmer Papyrus $\mathfrak{P}^{74}$, from the seventh century, is made from 66 sheets.[124] In the context of the present investigation it is important to note that $\mathfrak{P}^{45}$ does not provide sufficient evidence for us to assert with certainty that this exemplar contained the Book of Acts without the General Letters. In the light of the later manuscript tradition it seems unlikely that such a collection unit ever existed.

The bilingual (Latin and Greek) Codex Claromontanus D 06 (fifth–sixth century) preserves the same arrangement of the Letters of Paul as the Canonical Edition, but the sequence of Colossians and Philippians is reversed. Following the Letter to Philemon and three originally blank pages, the manuscript contains the Letter to the Hebrews. The scribe probably intended to copy the Letter to the Laodiceans, which he knew from Latin manuscripts, onto the three empty pages but could not find a Greek text. Later the Catalogus Claromontanus filled the space. The peculiar arrangement of Colossians and Philippians in this bilingual edition may reflect the sequence in some Latin manuscripts.[125]

Conclusion

With the exception of five documents, all of the evaluated manuscripts of the first seven centuries may be interpreted as copies of the same edition. $\mathfrak{P}^{46}$ and D 06 (Letters of Paul), W 032 (Gospels), and D 05 (Gospels, Praxapostolos) may be understood as a deliberate redactional rearrangement of the same material. The selection and sequence of $\mathfrak{P}^{72}$ may best be explained as an irregular and singular exemplar, one that left no traces in the later manuscript tradition.

All the other evaluated manuscripts display the following features: (a) within the Letters of Paul they present Hebrews following 2 Thessalonians and preceding 1 Timothy; (b) the Book of Acts is combined with the General Letters to form the *Praxapostolos*;[126] and (c) the Gospels are given in this sequence: Matthew, Mark, Luke, and John.

The Revelation of John constitutes an independent unit in the manuscript tradition. This writing was copied either individually or in various combinations with one or more of the other three collection units.[127]

Reflections

The consensus of the discipline is that there was wide variation in both the size and the arrangement of the canon until well into the fourth century. My investigation arrives at precisely the opposite conclusion.

In this study I analyzed historical aspects of the Canonical Edition as a literary unit, while more traditional studies of the canon have focused on the history and development of Christian doctrine. My literary interest led me to select different sources and to emphasize strongly the manuscript evidence. I was forced to conclude that the extant manuscripts demonstrate little variation.

Traditional studies treating the birth of the Christian Bible as an unfolding doctrine are confronted with an odd paradox. On one hand, the Christian church strongly affirms the Christian Bible. On the other hand, to this very day there is no actual consensus on which writings are part of the Holy Scripture. Modern editions differ considerably with respect to which books are included in the Old Testament. Catholic editions usually follow the selection and arrangement of the Greek and Latin Bible, whereas Protestant Bibles will represent the selection of the Hebrew Bible and exclude some so-called apocryphal writings. History presents us with another puzzle: none of the great ecumenical councils of the early church ever conferred about the canon.[128]

The authority of specific writings was questioned as early as the second half of the second century. Many older studies of the history of the canon, in my opinion, have drawn the wrong conclusion from this observation. The traditional interpretation asserts that these discussions reflect a debate about which writings should be included in the Christian Bible. But with the uniform manuscript evidence in mind, the critical remarks of the church fathers can be better interpreted as a historical critical reaction to an existing publication. Their debate as to the authorship and authority of the individual writings continues among biblical scholars to this very day, and then, as now, the publication to which they referred was the Canonical Edition of the Christian Bible.

I would like to illustrate this point with an analysis of Theodor Zahn's argument. According to Zahn, an anonymous anti-Montanist writer at the end of the second century asserted that any additions to or deletions from the Holy Scripture were intolerable.[129] Zahn then turns to Tertullian, a Montanist, who only a few years later repeated exactly the same sentence about such additions and deletions during a discussion with a theological opponent.[130] For Zahn there is little doubt that both authors refer to the final verses of Revelation.[131] Zahn then ironically remarks that one could conclude that these men had perused an exemplar of the New Testament, one that began with the Gospel According to Matthew and ended with the Revelation of John—an exemplar, that is, that looked very much like modern printed editions. As far as Zahn is concerned, such a conclusion would be a foolish error. His verdict strongly influenced most twentieth-century studies on the New Testament canon.[132]

How does Zahn argue his case? First he mentions the oldest authoritative document for the boundaries of the New Testament canon, the

Thirty-ninth Easter Letter of Athanasius, written in 367. Then he cites the Muratorian Fragment, traditionally considered the oldest list of canonical books, allegedly produced toward the end of the second century.[133] From there he moves to the famous disputes about the inclusion of the Letter to the Hebrews, which was not considered Pauline by all early Christians. Zahn reports similar arguments concerning the Letter of James and compares this discussion to the debate over the authorship of the Shepherd of Hermas, a Christian document from the early second century. Zahn concludes that this debate indicates that the canonical status of these writings was still in question.

The argument is not very convincing. After all, Origen discusses the authorship of the Letter to the Hebrews and concludes that Paul did not write it.[134] Martin Luther, in the introduction to his translation of the New Testament, disapproves of the Letter of James. He places it dismissively at the end of his edition, together with the Letter to the Hebrews and the Letter of Jude. Philipp Vielhauer, in his popular 1978 German introduction to the New Testament, discusses the Shepherd of Hermas together with the twenty-seven writings of the New Testament. There is no doubt that the Letter to the Hebrews was handed down to Origen as a letter by Paul[135] and that both Luther and Vielhauer were well acquainted with the number of writings and their arrangement in the Canonical Edition of the New Testament. But anyone convinced by Zahn's argument would be forced to assume that Origen and Luther encountered fewer writings in their copies of the Christian Bible, while Vielhauer found more.

The oldest authoritative document, the Thirty-ninth Easter Letter of Athanasius, establishes the conventional boundaries of the canon, at least for the New Testament.[136] This is why it is often used to date the establishment of the canon. It plays an important part in Zahn's argument. However, this document addressed the question only for the geographical area overseen by Athanasius, bishop of Alexandria. It did not have the same authority for other regions. By the second half of the fourth century, two complete editions of the Christian Bible are extant: Codex Vaticanus (B 03) and Codex Sinaiticus (א 01). Given the availability of these two complete text witnesses, why continue to speculate on the basis of the Easter Letter of Athanasius and other secondary sources? The other source Zahn refers to regularly is the Muratorian Canon. This text, however, does not intend to describe the boundaries of the Christian Bible and is better characterized as a set of introductory notes to the New Testament.[137] This document does not constitute but rather presupposes the New Testament; its traditional dating to the second century is highly disputable;[138] and its barbarous Latin raises more questions than it answers. There is no need to use such a document to reconstruct the New Testament when we have manuscripts from the same time period, the close of the second century, that nicely document each collection unit. There is no need to speculate about whether the Letter to the Hebrews was part of a collection of the Letters of Paul in the second century, because a second-century exemplar of the Pauline letter collection, 𝔓[46], containing the letter at issue, actually exists. Are we not forced by the evidence to interpret the discussion in the early church about the authenticity of certain biblical writings as a reaction to an already published book?

From this perspective, the same documented debates that are usually evaluated to demonstrate a gradual growth process of the canon serve instead as proof that the Canonical Edition of the Christian Bible was finished, published, and widely used.[139]

It is not Theodor Zahn's fault that he did not appropriately evaluate the manuscript evidence. The Codex Sinaiticus had just been discovered when Zahn published his work, and a reliable transcript of the Codex Vaticanus was not yet available.[140] The high value of both witnesses for the reconstruction of the original text was not yet established among scholars. The impressive number of papyri accessible to us today had not yet been discovered. Zahn certainly is not to be blamed. Today, however, New Testament research has to deal with and evaluate the rich new manuscript evidence.

More often than not, the history of the Christian Bible was treated as the history of a doctrine and not as the history of a publication. Researchers focused on the canon, not on the Canonical Edition.

This study, on the other hand, tries to describe the history of the Canonical Edition by analyzing the oldest existing copies and tracing the edition back to the time and place of its first publication. With this method, Greek manuscripts became more important witnesses than the lists of canonical writings, quotes from biblical literature, and debates about the authenticity of certain writings, translations, and so on.

The use of a text-critical approach in order to describe the history of the Canonical Edition raises the question of how to deal with gaps within the textual tradition. This study applied the generally accepted rule that the form presented in later extant exemplars should guide the interpretation of the earlier fragmentary evidence. Since fragments could be placed within the pattern set by the four oldest extant comprehensive manuscripts, these fragments were treated as witnesses to a common archetype.

THE TITLES OF THE WRITINGS

Examining the titles of the New Testament writings, one of the first observations is that they are transmitted with few variants. They structure the Canonical Edition in this way: Gospels, Praxapostolos, Letters of Paul, and Revelation of John.[141]

Gospels

The complete titles of the Gospels in the manuscripts read as follows: εὐαγγέλιον κατὰ Μαθθαῖον, εὐαγγέλιον κατὰ Μάρκον, εὐαγγέλιον κατὰ Λουκᾶν, εὐαγγέλιον κατὰ Ἰωάννην.[142] They consist of three elements: the first element, εὐαγγέλιον, designates the literary genre; the third element refers to the authorial source; and κατά connects the two. Each of these three elements is very unusual.

The term *Gospel* is used to refer to the content of the message as well as to the act of preaching in the New Testament. It is not used to indicate a specific literary genre. And so far no evidence has surfaced in pre-Christian literature, either, that the term can be used to refer to a literary genre.[143]

Indicating the authorial source by κατά and the accusative is extremely rare for book titles.[144] The closest parallel is found in the formula used by Christian authors when referring to various competing Greek translations of the Jewish Scriptures: κατὰ τοὺς Ἑβδομήκοντα, κατὰ Ἀκύλαν, κατὰ Σύμμαχον, κατὰ Θεωδοτίωνα.[145]

The third element of the titles, the name of the authoritative witness, cannot be derived with certainty from the text of the writings. The alleged authorship of the titles is not repeated in the text of Matthew, Mark, Luke, and John.

The possibility that the titles were independently formulated this way by the authors of the Gospels may be safely ruled out. It would be too much of a coincidence for two independently working publishers to have decided on the same unusual genre designation, the same authorial source, and κατά as the syntactical connector.[146]

Praxapostolos

The title of the Book of Acts, in the Canonical Edition, reads πράξεις ἀποστόλων.[147] The term πράξεις designates the literary genre; ἀποστόλων, however, does not follow the pattern of the Gospel titles, which refer to the authorial source, but rather designates the central characters of the narrative.[148] Both elements of the title are problematic. The Book of Acts does not conform very well to the ancient literary genre described as πράξεις.[149] The term *apostle* is used twenty-seven times in reference to the twelve disciples of Jesus, and in only one story—though whether this is deliberate or not is a matter of debate[150]—the term is used twice for Paul and Barnabas (Acts 14:4 and 14:14). Nevertheless, Paul, the missionary to the Gentiles, is obviously the protagonist of the second half of the book. It seems very unlikely that two publishers would independently come up with the same title, especially one that accurately describes only the first half of the work.

The titles of the General Letters consist of two parts as well. The first part describes the writings as ἐπιστολαί, and many manuscripts add καθολικαί,[151] thus furnishing the collection with its traditional title: General Epistles. The second element lists the name of the authors, Ἰακώβου, Πέτρου, Ἰωάννου, Ἰούδα, followed by the numbering α', β', γ' in the case of the Letters of Peter and John.[152]

The numbering and the titles are redactional and do not derive from the writers of the letters. That the First Letter of John is a "letter" is in no way self-evident; it contains neither sender nor addressee in the prescript, nor greetings at the end.[153] And as far as the name of the letter writer is concerned, the Johannine authorship mentioned in the title is not repeated in the text of the three writings.

Letters of Paul

The titles of the fourteen writings that form the collection of Pauline Letters in the Canonical Edition indicate the addressees of the specific letter: πρὸς Ῥωμαίους, πρὸς Κορινθίους, and so on. To get the complete title, the readers would have to add Παύλου ἐπιστολή, because the full title of the letter to the Romans is Παύλου ἐπιστολὴ πρὸς Ῥωμαίους,[154] "Paul's Letter to Romans." The titles consist of two elements: the genre designation "Letter of Paul" forms the first part and furnishes the title of the collection; the second part, the addressee, serves to distinguish the writings within the collection.

Since the addressees of the Letters to the Ephesians[155] and Hebrews[156] are not mentioned in the text, the reason for the uniform titles in all the manuscripts is not self-evident. Two other letters of Paul are worth mentioning in this context. Second Corinthians is addressed not only to the Corinthians but also to "the saints in all of Achaia" (2 Cor 1:1). Likewise, the Letter to Philemon is addressed not only to Philemon but also "to Apphia our sister, Archippus our fellow soldier," and the congregation meeting in Philemon's house (Phlm 2). It is at least conceivable that independently working editors might have produced different titles for these writings than the ones used in the Canonical Edition.[157]

Furthermore, it became necessary to number letters to the same addressee (Corinthians, Thessalonians, and Timothy) only when they were combined and published in the same collection. The numbering therefore is clearly an element of the final redaction.[158] On a literary level, the contents of the two Letters to the Thessalonians does not allow us to determine with certainty which of the two letters was written first.[159]

Since the name Paul does not appear within the text of the Letter to the Hebrews, there is no evidence to support its genre designation, "Letter of Paul." Common features of letters are missing from Hebrews, such as the names of the senders and addressees. Elements so characteristic of a letter by Paul, such as his wish of grace and the passage of thanksgiving, are notably absent. The address is extraordinarily vague and lacks any geographical content; the idiom Ἑβραῖοι is used only three times in the New Testament.[160] As each one of these four words—Παύλου ἐπιστολὴ πρὸς Ἑβραίους—is highly problematic, it seems very improbable that two independently working publishers would have suggested the same title for this writing.

Revelation of John

The title of the last writing of the New Testament, the Revelation of John, is noted in the manuscripts as ἀποκάλυψις Ἰωάννου.[161] The title clearly reflects the first words of this writing, "The Revelation of Jesus Christ, . . . which he made known to his servant John" (Rv 1:1). Both the designation ἀποκάλυψις and the author's name, John, are repeated in the first sentence. It is not difficult to imagine that independently working editors would come up with the same title.

The Grouping of Writings

The titles serve to group the individual writings into collection units. The organizing function is clear for those letters that are numbered: the Letters to the Corinthians, Thessalonians, and Timothy, and the Letters of Peter and John.

Three additional groups are easily discerned: the four Gospels, the seven General Letters, and the Letters of Paul. The titles of the remaining two writings, Acts and Revelation, contain a genre designation in their first part, just like the titles of the three groups do:[162] εὐαγγέλιον and ἐπιστολαί (Παύλου/καθολικαι) corresponding with πράξεις and ἀποκάλυψις (see figure 5).

Conclusion

The uniform structure of the titles points beyond the individual writing to an overall editorial concept and was not imposed by the authors of the individual writings. The titles are redactional. In most cases the genre designations, the alleged authorship, and the structure of the titles cannot be derived from the text with certainty. This strongly suggests that the present form of the titles was not created by independently working editors but that they are the result of a single, specific redaction.

Reflections

Martin Hengel strongly rejects the idea that the uniformity of the Gospel titles, which he readily agrees existed toward the end of the second century, might be explained as the result of a centralized redaction promoted by the influence and power of the church (see note 163). And many historians will wholeheartedly agree with Hengel. The Christian church of the second century had not yet developed the structures that would later be used to promote and enforce specific practices and creeds. There was no central personality who could have exercised so much power. Hengel argues that even if it could be conceded for a moment that a widely successful effort actually had been made to declare a certain

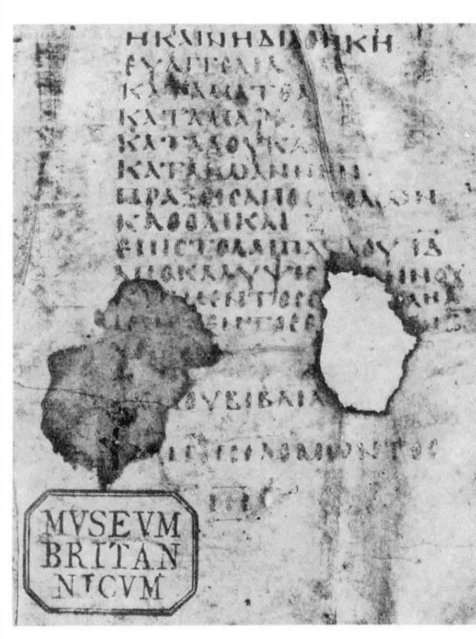

η καιη διαθηκη·
ευαγγελια [δ´]
κατα ματθα[ιον]
κατα μαρκ[ον]
κατα λουκαν
κατα ιωαννην.
πραξεις αποστολων
καθολικαι ζ´
επιστολαι παυλου ιδ´
αποκαλυψις [Ιωα]ννου
κ[λη]μεντος ε[πιστο]λη α´
κλημ]εντος ε[πιστολ]η β´

ομ]ου βιβλια [

Ψ[αλ]μ[ο]ι σολομωντος

ιη´[

Figure 5. List of contents of the Codex Alexandrinus, New Testament section. Photo courtesy of the British Library, London.

selection of writings as authoritative for all, it would be all the more surprising that not one record of this event has survived, not even in the form of a legend.

Hengel's close study of the Gospel titles covers the available evidence comprehensively and has helped focus the attention of scholars on a long-neglected problem. However, the conclusion he reaches is the exact opposite of the conclusion reached in this present study. Why? There are at least three reasons.

First, although it is accurate to state that the observance of dogmas and creeds was later enforced by certain hierarchical and centralized structures of the church, this did not hold true concerning early Christian literature. The Canonical Edition was not the only work of the second century distributed specifically to Christians. There were Polycarp's edition of the

Letters of Ignatius; Marcion's Bible; the Greek editions of Jewish Scripture published under the names of Theodotion, Aquila, and Symmachus; the Didache; the Letter of Barnabas; the Shepherd of Hermas; the Acts of Paul; and the Gospel of Thomas, to name only a few. They did not need an authoritative endorsement by the church to be produced, sold, bought, or read all over the Christian world. Hengel's presupposition is that an edition of alleged apostolic writings could be distributed successfully among Christians only if backed by a central church authority. But this is clearly disproved by the evidence of the rich Christian literature of the time. In my view, the fact that there is no record of a global church decision indicates that the *editio princeps* of the Canonical Edition was probably just one more ambitious Christian publication of the second century, one that faced strong competition.

Second, the focus of Hengel's study is clearly on the "precanonical" state of the gospels, whereas my study concentrates on the final form of the collection. Hengel presupposes that the uniform titles are based on tradition.[163] I argue that the awkward elements and structure of the titles are better explained as the result of editorial decisions by the collectors, who were trying to unify the dissimilar material. As these collectors selected a certain number of writings, then edited and arranged them, they had a deliberate redactional strategy in mind. This strategy, which will be discussed in the following chapter, harmonized Peter and Paul and endorsed the authority of the Jewish Scriptures, among other things. It is likely that no other redactional measure expressed the editors' intention so clearly, or could achieve the desired effect on the readers so successfully, as the design of the titles.

Finally, Hengel treats the Gospel titles individually and does not place them in context with the other titles of the New Testament. Yet the cross-references between the Gospels According to Mark and Luke and the Letters of Paul and the Praxapostolos cannot easily be discarded. His focus on the individual title is the primary reason that Hengel arrived at results so very different from mine.

THE TITLE OF THE CANONICAL EDITION

The archetype of the collection most probably was entitled ἡ καινὴ διαθήκη, "The New Testament."[164] Due to their fragmentary character, the oldest manuscripts do not preserve the title page. The uniform evidence of the extant tradition, however, strongly suggests that this was the title of the archetype.

The term *New Testament*, as it is used in second-century Christian literature, may very well refer to the Canonical Edition. At the end of the second century, Melito of Sardis, on behalf of a friend, compiles "extracts from the Law and the Prophets concerning the Savior, and concerning all our faith." In the introduction to this work, Melito informs his friend that he "learnt accurately the books of the Old Testament," especially "how many they are in number, and what is their order."[165] Even if the term *New Testament* is not explicitly used, it is implied by the designation *Old Testament*, which is introduced without explanation.

At approximately the same time the previously mentioned anonymous treatise against the Montanist movement seems to use the term *New Testament* in reference to a written source. The author explains that he was initially very reluctant to write at all. He did not want to create "the impression that he was adding anything to the word of the gospel of the New Testament [τῷ τῆς τοῦ εὐαγγελίου καινῆς διαθήκης λόγῳ]; since no one, who decided to live according to the gospel, can add to it or take away from it."[166]

When Clement of Alexandria,[167] Irenaeus,[168] and—in the early third century—Tertullian and Origen[169] refer to the second part of the Canonical Edition, they use the term *New Testament.*

All of these elements—the notation of the *nomina sacra*, the codex form, the uniform arrangement and number of writings in the manuscript tradition, the formulation of the titles, and the evidence indicating that the collection was called "New Testament" from the very beginning—are evidence of a careful final redaction. These editorial features did not originate with the authors of the individual writings. They serve to combine disparate material into a collection and to create the impression of a cohesive literary unit for readers of the work. Furthermore, these elements are so idiosyncratic that they cannot be credited to several independently operating editors but must be the work of a single editorial entity.

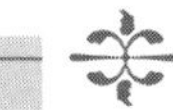

3

The Editorial Concept

THE FINAL REDACTION OF AN ANTHOLOGY ALWAYS REFLECTS a specific editorial concept. When editors publish material they guide readers to interpret it in a specific way by setting certain signals within a redactional frame. From a critical perspective their interpretation may or may not be inherent in the traditional material.[1]

THREE PERSPECTIVES: READER, MACROSTRUCTURE, TRADITIONAL MATERIAL

In the following I shall try to describe the editorial concept of the Canonical Edition by looking at it from three different perspectives.

First, I will examine the edition from the readers' point of view. I will follow the implied reading instructions provided by redactional signals and assume that this reading experience was intended by the editors and that it expresses an important component of the editorial concept.

Second, I will analyze the edition's macrostructure. The editors designed a "user interface" to guide their readers. I will interpret this as a deliberate attempt to find an appropriate form for the content of the collection.

And last, I will study the edition from the perspective of the traditional material. By focusing on apparent redactional interpretations that do not fit the traditional material very well, I hope to gain further insight into the intentions and tendencies of the editors.

For example, the names of the alleged gospel authors Mark and Luke refer the *readers* to passages in Acts, 1 Peter, and to the letters of Paul, which indicate harmony and cooperation between the Jerusalem authorities and Paul. The same message is conveyed by the macrostructure of the collection, which presents writings of the Jerusalem authorities, James, Peter, and John, side by side with the letters of the apostle Paul. When viewed from the perspective of the *traditional material*, however, the Letter to the Galatians sharply contradicts that image of harmony. The redaction suggests that the clashing parties had reconciled later, an interpretation that is not supported by the text of Galatians. All three perspectives therefore demonstrate an obvious interest on the part of the final editors to present the early Christian missionaries as working together in unity and harmony.

The naming of authors in the titles of specific writings is another editorial feature that illuminates the editorial concept. From the *readers' perspective* these famous names seem to guarantee the reliability of the Canonical Edition. As far as the *macrostructure* is concerned, the authoritative names are part of a carefully woven web holding together the disparate parts of the New Testament. And seen from the perspective of the *traditional material*, the Fourth Gospel clearly did not intend to disclose the name of the "beloved disciple." The final editors, however, presented it as the work of John. All three perspectives therefore display a strong editorial interest in conveying the names of the prominent authors to the readers. This concern demonstrates another element of the editorial concept.

In the following chapter I will use these three perspectives to analyze a number of editorial elements of the Canonical Edition. I will begin by interpreting the titles and implied authorship, then move to the selection of authors, the title of the edition, the *nomina sacra*, and the codex form.

IMPLIED AUTHORSHIP

Each book of the New Testament bears a title. Each title informs the readers, expressly or implicitly, about the author of the document. However, the author cannot be identified with certainty as long as the writing is read only by itself. Given the background of the entire anthology, however, the names mentioned in the titles stimulate the curiosity of the readers and direct them to specific text passages in other writings of the Canonical Edition.

Because literature always addresses the public, it depends heavily on credibility. If a text has passed through the professional hands of the author, editor, publisher, and bookseller, the readers will assume with good reason that the editorial frame and, in particular, the alleged authorship is accurate. From the readers' perspective it will not seem necessary to explicitly affirm the authenticity of a book. Most readers will be comfortable as long as the text does not confront them with obvious inconsistencies concerning its authorship.

I will start out by assuming the point of view of sympathetic readers, who are interested in identifying the authors mentioned in the titles. They will carefully study other text passages of the collection that contain these names.[2] For the readers it is like untangling a riddle that has already been solved by the editors. To demonstrate that no philological finesse is required, I will quote the relevant text passages from the New Revised Standard Version.

Gospel According to Matthew

The alleged authorship in the title of the Gospel refers the readers to the story of a tax collector, Matthew, who was called by Jesus to follow him.

> Mt 9:9
> As Jesus was walking along, he saw a man called Matthew sitting at the tax booth; and he said to him, "Follow me." And he got up and followed him.

When the twelve disciples are listed in this Gospel, Matthew is qualified as "Matthew the tax collector" (Mt 10:3). The readers therefore will feel confident that the two passages refer to the same person. And from the readers' perspective this is all that is necessary to establish the reliable narrator and presumed author of this book as one of the twelve.[3]

The readers will feel confirmed in their conclusion when they come across the two parallel narratives in the Gospels of Mark and Luke, which give the name of the tax collector as "Levi" (Mk 2:14; Lk 5:27). Christian interpreters have often offered the very satisfying answer that the name change from Levi to Matthew is an autobiographical note included by the writer of the First Gospel, who corrects an inaccurate tradition.[4] This autobiographical interpretation presupposes that the readers are familiar with the parallels; it constitutes a link between Matthew and the Gospels of Mark and Luke.

Gospel According to Mark

Reading the title of the Second Gospel, readers may ask, "Who is Mark?" In order to find an answer, they will have to consult other writings.[5] Not once is the name Mark used in the four canonical Gospels. It is mentioned in Acts, first in connection with Peter (Acts 12:12) and shortly thereafter in connection with Paul (Acts 12:25), revealing an important function of the alleged authorship: Mark constitutes a link between Peter and Paul.

> ⇨Acts 12:12 and 12:25
> As soon as he [Peter] realized this, he went to the house of Mary, the mother of John whose other name was Mark, where many had gathered and were praying. . . . Then after completing their mission Barnabas and Saul returned to Jerusalem and brought with them John, whose other name was Mark.

The next time Mark is mentioned is when Barnabas and Paul quarrel; their quarrel leads to a dissension and finally separation of these two early Christian missionaries. The cause of the strife was Mark.

> ⇨Acts 15:37–41
> Barnabas wanted to take with them John called Mark. But Paul decided not to take with them one who had deserted them in Pamphylia and had not accompanied them in the work. The disagreement became so sharp that they parted company; Barnabas took Mark with him and sailed away to Cyprus. But Paul chose Silas and set out, the believers commending him to the grace of the Lord. He went through Syria and Cilicia, strengthening the churches.

On the one hand, this report contains disturbing information; on the other hand, the readers learn that Mark belonged to the first Christian missionaries and that at the very beginning he was a companion of Paul. Whatever the true cause of this quarrel,[6] it was not enough for Barnabas to end his collaboration with Mark. And from the Letter to the Colossians the readers of the Canonical Edition will learn that Mark is a cousin of Barnabas (Col 4:10).

However, following Acts the early readers of the Canonical Edition found not the Letters of Paul but the General Epistles. In his first letter Peter refers to Mark as “my son.”

> ⇨1 Pt 5:13
> Your sister church in Babylon, chosen together with you, sends you greetings; and so does my son Mark.

Three times Mark is mentioned in the letters of Paul. Because the Letter to the Colossians associates Mark with Barnabas, the readers have good reason to believe that the John Mark mentioned in Acts is identical with the Mark referred to in the Letters of Paul. And the readers will learn that Paul and Mark have finally made peace again because Paul recommends Mark to the congregation and asks them to welcome him.[7]

⇨Col 4:10
Aristarchus my fellow prisoner greets you, as does Mark the cousin of Barnabas, concerning whom you have received instructions—if he comes to you, welcome him.[8]

This conclusion is confirmed the next time Mark is mentioned. "Only Luke is with me. Get Mark and bring him with you, for he is useful in my ministry" (2 Tm 4:11).[9] The quarrel is over. In the Letter to Philemon, at last, Mark greets in the same sentence in which Luke extends his greetings through Paul. Paul describes Mark as his coworker (Phlm 24).

Of course, the assumptions that the Mark of Acts is identical with the Mark of Paul's letters and the First Letter of Peter are not without problems, even for naive readers.[10] Taking into account, however, that the other authors of the New Testament are identified the same way—that is, by evaluating references to them in other writings of the collection—this synthesizing reading technique is consistent.[11]

The title "Gospel According to Mark" therefore links the three large collection units of the New Testament: Four-Gospel Book, Praxapostolos, and Letters of Paul.

Gospel According to Luke, Acts

The Letters of Paul mention Mark and Luke in the same sentence on two separate occasions (Phlm 24; 1 Tm 4:11). For readers of the Canonical Edition the proximity of these two names is not a surprise. The Gospel of Luke follows Mark's Gospel. And in the very first sentence Luke indicates that he knows of others who had set out to write a similar narrative.

Lk 1:1–2
Since many have undertaken to set down an orderly account of the events that have been fulfilled among us, just as they were

> handed on to us by those who from the beginning were eye-witnesses and servants of the word . . .

The expression "as they were handed on to us by those who from the beginning were eyewitnesses and servants of the word"[12] indicates that these colleagues—very much like Luke himself—were not eyewitnesses. They did not write from their own experience with Jesus. Because Matthew and John are written from the perspective of an eyewitness, the readers of the Canonical Edition will have to conclude that Luke refers to Mark.[13] Peter's reference to Mark in 1 Peter corroborates the conclusion that Mark is the disciple of a disciple.

Nowhere in the text of the Four-Gospel Book is the name Luke mentioned. Acts, however, presents itself as Luke's second book. The first sentence refers to Theophilus, who is mentioned at the beginning, and to the Ascension of Jesus, which is narrated at the end of Luke's Gospel.

> Acts 1:1–2
> In the first book, ❶*Theophilus*, I wrote about all that Jesus did and taught from the beginning until the day when he was ❷*taken up to heaven*, after giving instructions through the Holy Spirit to the apostles whom he had chosen.

> ⇨Lk 1:3
> I too decided, after investigating everything carefully from the very first, to write an orderly account for you, most excellent ❶*Theophilus* ...

> ⇨Lk 24:51–53 (end of the Gospel)
> While he was blessing them, he withdrew from them and was ❷*carried up into heaven*. And they worshiped him, and returned to Jerusalem with great joy; and they were continually in the temple blessing God.

The readers of the Canonical Edition learn of Jesus' Ascension only from Luke. Matthew, the original short ending of Mark, and John mention neither the Ascension nor Theophilus. The connection between Acts and Luke's Gospel is obvious, making Luke the alleged author of Acts.

The use of first person plural in the so-called we-passages in Acts implies that the author is a companion of Paul and that he reports these specific events from personal experience.[14] So the readers learn that the author of Acts traveled with Paul from Troas in Asia Minor to Philippi in Greece (Acts 16:10–17), that he accompanied him from Philippi back to Milet in Asia Minor (Acts 20:5–15) and from there to Jerusalem (Acts 21:1–18), and finally that he stayed with Paul during his last long voyage from Caesarea in Palestine to Rome (Acts 27:1–28:16).[15]

Although the readers by now may have a vague sense of Luke's identity, the name Luke was not mentioned anywhere in the text of the Gospels or in the Book of Acts. However, their attention will be directed to passages referring to Luke in the Letters of Paul.

> ⇨Col 4:14
> Luke, the beloved physician [Λουκᾶς ὁ ἰατρὸς ὁ ἀγαπητός], and Demas greet you.

> ⇨2 Tm 4:11
> Only Luke is with me. Get Mark and bring him with you, for he is useful in my ministry.

> ⇨Phlm 23–24
> Epaphras, my fellow prisoner in Christ Jesus, sends greetings to you, and so do Mark, Aristarchus, Demas, and Luke, my fellow workers [οἱ συνεργοί μου].

Luke, who sends his greetings through Paul in Phlm 24, is called a fellow worker. In Col 4:14 he is characterized as "Luke, the beloved physician." Both instances portray Luke at Paul's side. They repeat the two essential pieces of information that the readers learned concerning the author of the Book of Acts in a very satisfying way: that his name is Luke and that he accompanied Paul on his travels.[16]

This identification is further supported by a remark in 2 Timothy. According to Acts, Luke traveled with Paul to Rome (Acts 27:14–16). In 2 Timothy, which Paul wrote from Rome (2 Tm 1:17), all except one of Paul's companions had left him; "only Luke is with me" (2 Tm 4:11a). The last sentences of Acts, read on the background of 2 Timothy, reveal that Luke, Paul's faithful companion, is the narrator of the Book of Acts.[17]

These links are significant. The name Luke is puzzling when first encountered as part of the Gospel title. Only after realizing that Acts is another book written by Luke and after combining the information given in Acts with the references to Luke in the Letters of Paul is the reader able to identify the author of the Third Gospel. In analogy to Mark, the title "Gospel According to Luke" connects the three major collection units of the New Testament: Four-Gospel Book, Praxapostolos, and Letters of Paul.[18]

Gospel According to John

Reading the title of the Fourth Gospel, again the readers may ask, "Who is John?" The name John is mentioned twenty times in this Gospel, sixteen times in reference to John the Baptist and four times in reference to John, the father of Peter.[19] Neither one can be regarded as the author, because the death of John the Baptist is reported in the text (10:40–41) and because Peter's father would be a very unlikely candidate to write the Gospel.

The last chapter expressly addresses the authorship, however, without giving a name. The "disciple who is testifying to these things" (Jn 21:24) is identified with the disciple "whom Jesus loved" and who "was the one who had reclined next to Jesus at the supper and had said, 'Lord, who is it that is going to betray you?'" (John 21:20).

On the one hand, the readers are told by an unidentified voice that the beloved disciple wrote the Gospel and that it is now—maybe for the first time—presented to the public. (See the next chapter for a more detailed treatment of John). Both the title and the final remarks refer to the authorship. They enclose the book like brackets. From the readers' point of view the title does not necessarily have to be formulated by the author. On the contrary, the readers may readily accept the publisher's comments at the end as an explanation for the strange wording "According to John" in the title. They indicate that John is not the author of this book in its present form but that John's original manuscript was edited for publication by someone else. From the readers' perspective editorial activity is not problematic.

On the other hand, the readers are invited to go back to a specific passage and read it again. The reference to "the supper" alludes to Jn 13.

Jn 13:23–25
❶*One of his disciples*—❷*the one whom Jesus loved*—was ❸*reclining* next to him; Simon Peter therefore motioned to him to ask Jesus of whom he was speaking. So while ❸*reclining* ❹*next to Jesus*, he ❺*asked* him, "❻*Lord, who is it*?"

⇨Jn 21:20
Peter turned and saw ❶*the disciple* ❷*whom Jesus loved* following them; he was the one who had ❸*reclined* ❹*next to Jesus* at the supper and had ❺*said*, "❻*Lord, who is it* that is going to betray you?"

Jn 13:23–25
ἦν ἀνακείμενος ❶εἷς ἐκ τῶν μαθητῶν αὐτοῦ ἐν τῷ κόλπῳ τοῦ Ἰησοῦ, ❷ὃν ἠγάπα ὁ Ἰησοῦς· νεύει οὖν τουτῳ Σίμων Πέτρος πυθέσθαι τίς ἂν εἴη περὶ οὗ λέγει. ❸ἀναπεσὼν οὖν ἐκεῖνος οὕτως ❹ἐπὶ τὸ στῆθος τοῦ Ἰησοῦ ❺λέγει αὐτῷ, ❻Κύριε, τίς ἐστιν;

Jn 21:20
Ἐπιστραφεὶς ὁ Πέτρος βλέπει ❶τὸν μαθητὴν ❷ὃν ἠγάπα ὁ Ἰησοῦς ἀκολουθοῦντα, ὃς καὶ ❸ἀνέπεσεν ἐν τῷ δείπνῳ ❹ἐπὶ τὸ στῆθος αὐτοῦ καὶ ❺εἶπεν, ❻Κύριε, τίς ἐστιν ὁ παραδιδούς σὲ;

⇨Jn 21:24
This is the disciple who is testifying to these things and *has written* them, and we know that his testimony is true.

However, there is a way the readers can corroborate the suggestion of the publishers that John the son of Zebedee is the beloved disciple. All the readers will have to do is consult the other three Gospels. The preceding synoptic Gospels inform the readers that Jesus occasionally chose to confide in only three of the twelve disciples; these were Peter and the two sons of Zebedee, John and James (Mt 17:1 par.; 26:37 par.; Mk 5:37). If the readers suspect the beloved disciple to be one of these three preferred disciples, they should be able to conclude with confidence that the beloved disciple is identical with John, son of Zebedee. Peter is eliminated as the possible author of the Fourth Gospel since he is mentioned next to the beloved disciple in the final chapter and in the scene depicting the Last Supper, to which the readers are referred. James can be excluded from further consideration because according to Acts 12:2 the Zebedee James died early, before the first missionary trip of Paul; Jn 21, however, presupposes that the beloved disciple outlived all the other disciples.[20] One way readers may identify the author of the Fourth Gospel, therefore, is to eliminate two names from the circle of the three disciples who were especially close to Jesus.[21]

That John outlived the other disciples is inferred from a comment in Jn 21, which corrects a rumor based on a prediction of Jesus that the beloved disciple would live to witness Jesus' Second Coming.

> Jn 21:23
> So the rumor spread in the community that this disciple would not die. Yet Jesus did not say to him that he would not die, but, "If it is my will that he remain until I come, what is that to you?"

On the one hand, this comment indicates that the beloved disciple had died before this text was written. On the other hand, the argument works best if the beloved disciple had reached a considerable age when he died, thus disappointing hopes that had been nourished in the course of time.

Seen from this angle, the name of the author in the title creates a cross-reference between the Gospel of John, the synoptic Gospels, and Acts.

Yet another view on what the editors intended to do and how they proceeded opens up when we look at the fact that the traditional material used by the editors of John's Gospel very probably did not disclose the name of the author. How do the editors deal with the anonymity of their source?

In Jn 21 the readers are informed that the book they just finished reading has a manuscript history. The title of the book tells them that it was written by John, and the editors deliberately point them to Jn 13 in an effort to help them identify the author.[22] This has been demonstrated above.

After finding out—by way of comparison with the synoptic Gospels—that the John mentioned in the title is in fact Zebedee's son, the readers are now able to interpret the text on two levels. Jn 1–20 may now be understood as based on a manuscript written by John, and the title together with the final passages (Jn 21) may now be understood as an editorial addition. Tensions between the two levels may actually enhance the reading experience. A substantial difference lies, for example, in the fact that the author of Jn 1–20 seems very interested in remaining anonymous, whereas the redactional frame assists the readers in uncovering the identity of the beloved disciple.

This situation has two effects. On the one side, it may stimulate the curiosity of the readers and invite them to look for other instances where a nameless disciple appears in the Gospel: for example, when Jesus calls his very first followers. After the prologue and John the Baptist's testimony about Jesus ("This is the Son of God!" Jn 1:34), they find the story of how Jesus calls two of John the Baptist's disciples (Jn 1:35–40). However, only one of the two is mentioned by name—Andrew, Peter's brother (Jn 1:40); the other disciple remains anonymous. Why? Did the evangelist not know the name of the disciple? Or is the other disciple—(as readers may suspect) the author, John the Zebedee, who prefers to remain anonymous?[23]

On the other hand, the anonymity of the Fourth Gospel has an effect on how the readers interpret the other three Gospels. The synoptic Gospels, too, display some tension between the authors mentioned in the title and the text of the Gospels, where the authors are either not mentioned at all (Mark, Luke) or are not introduced as the narrator (Matthew). Anonymity becomes a trademark of a "true" Gospel. In a way the editors of John's Gospel respect the anonymity by not mentioning the author's name in Jn 21. They refer the readers to specific text passages, but the name John is given only in the title.[24]

Letters of John

Since 1 John gives the name of the letter writer in the title, and since no distinction is made with the author of the Fourth Gospel, the readers may assume that it is the same person.[25] Both writings are part of the same publication, and each time the author is simply called "John." Readers will infer that if the editors had wanted to make a distinction between two authors with the same name, they would have done so.

That the same person authored both writings is corroborated in the first lines of 1 Jn, which emphasize that the writer is an eyewitness. Terms that are often used in John's Gospel, like *beginning*, *word*, *life*, are repeated. Even the structure of the opening sentences is very similar.[26]

> 1 Jn 1:1
> We declare to you what was ❶*from the beginning*, what we have heard, what ❷*we have seen* with our eyes, what we have looked at and touched with our hands, concerning the ❸*word* of ❹*life* . . .

> Jn 1:1.4.14
> (1) ❶*In the beginning* was the ❸*Word*, and the Word was with God, and the Word was God.

(4) In him was ❹*life*, and the life was the light of all people.

(14) And the Word became flesh and lived among us, and ❷*we have seen* his glory, the glory as of a father's only son, full of grace and truth.

Furthermore, in 1 John the readers may find confirmation of their assumption that John must have been an old man when he died. Frequently the recipients of this writing are addressed as "my little children," which is appropriate if an older person is speaking.[27]

Once the author of 1 John is identified, there is little doubt about who wrote 2 John and 3 John. The other numbered letters of the New Testament (Corinthians, Thessalonians, Timothy, Peter) also imply that they were written by the same person.

Revelation of John

Since John is mentioned as the author in the title as well as in the text[28] of Revelation, and since no distinction is made between this author and the author of the Gospel or the respective letters, readers will assume in good faith that all these books were written by the same John whom they identified as the beloved disciple and son of Zebedee.

Letter of Jude

The writer of this letter is introduced with the words "Jude, a servant of Jesus Christ and brother of James" (Jude 1). There is only one pair of brothers, James and Jude, mentioned in the Canonical Edition, the brothers of Jesus.

Mt 13:55
Is not this the carpenter's son? Is not his mother called Mary? And are not his brothers James and Joseph and Simon and Judas?[29]

This conclusion is corroborated by the peculiar way Jude refers to himself. Whereas Paul and Peter introduce themselves as apostles of Jesus Christ, Jude and James write "Jude, servant of Jesus Christ" (Jude 1) and "James, a servant of God and of the Lord Jesus Christ" (Jas 1:1).

Letter of James

The readers can identify the author of the letter of James in several independent ways. The Canonical Edition mentions five persons by the name of James. (1) James, the son of Zebedee[30] and brother of John;[31] (2) James, son of Alphaeus;[32] (3) James, the brother of the Lord;[33] (4) James the younger,[34] who is often thought to be identical with the previously listed brother of Jesus; and (5) James, the father of the disciple Jude.[35]

The cross-reference to the Letter of Jude, which was demonstrated above, will direct the readers to choose James, brother of Jesus.

Another way to decide which James is the author of the letter is to concentrate on a central passage: "You see that a person is justified by works and not by faith alone" (Jas 2:24). Read at face value, this statement bluntly opposes Paul, who writes, "For we hold that a person is justified by faith apart from works prescribed by the law" (Rom. 3:28).[36] When looking for someone who knows Paul and who occasionally opposed him, the readers will inevitably come across the James who is mentioned in the Letter to the Galatians. In his account of the Antioch incident Paul refers to opponents as "people from James" (Gal 2:12), "the Lord's brother" (Gal 1:19).

Another way to identify James is to look at the Jerusalem Council in Acts 15. The narrative recounts that James, the brother of Jesus, signed a resolution and handed it to a delegation, which was led by Paul. This event establishes not only that Paul and James knew each other well but also that James had experience in writing letters to a broader public. A general letter addressed "to the twelve tribes in the Dispersion" (Jas 1:1) would fit the person nicely who sent out the apostle's decree (Acts 15:23–29) to Christians outside Palestine.

Finally, the immediate literary context, the Praxapostolos, encourages the readers to make the same identification. Whoever wondered which James wrote the letter found this letter immediately following the Book of Acts. And from Acts readers would know about the Jerusalem authorities. The Praxapostolos contains letters from Peter and John; to include an epistle from the Lord's brother James, the third prominent leader of the Jerusalem congregation, makes perfect sense. Some readers may even realize that the editors arranged the letters in accordance with Paul's list of Jerusalem "pillars" in his Letter to the Galatians.[37]

> Gal 2:9b
> And when *James* and *Cephas* and *John*, who were acknowledged pillars, recognized the grace that had been given to me, they gave to Barnabas and me the right hand of fellowship, agreeing that we should go to the Gentiles and they to the circumcised.

Letters of Peter

The author of 1 and 2 Peter introduces himself as "Peter, an apostle of Jesus Christ" (1 Pt 1:1) and as "Simeon Peter, a servant and apostle of Jesus Christ" (2 Pt 2:1). Peter is one of the main characters featured in the Canonical Edition. He is mentioned in the Gospels, Acts, 1 Corinthians, and Galatians altogether more than 150 times. His prominent place within other writings is the reason why readers of the Canonical Edition will have little trouble identifying the writer of these two letters.

Letters of Paul

Similarly, readers identify Paul the letter writer through information found in other writings. Although the letters contain some personal information, it is the Book of Acts that interprets Paul's role in the expanding mission and his relations with the Jerusalem apostles, thus explaining to the readers why Paul's letters are part of this collection of apostolic writings. The readers learn from Acts—not from the Letters of Paul—that Paul came from Tarsus; that he was a Roman citizen; that he became a follower of Christ while persecuting Christians in Damascus; that the congregation of Antioch sent him and Barnabas out as missionaries; and that a conflict in Jerusalem triggered the events leading to his imprisonment in Rome.[38] Acts provides the readers with biographical details that help place Paul's individual letters in time and space.

As far as the literary history of these texts is concerned, however, Paul's letters represent the oldest stratum of Christian publications incorporated by the editors in the Canonical Edition.[39] The Letters of Paul needed no introduction; the source and authorship of the other writings had to be explained.

Letter to the Hebrews

The title "To Hebrews" conveys to the readers that this writing is not part of the Praxapostolos, which names the letters by their authors, not by their addressee. Hebrews belongs to the Pauline letter collection. So the title of the anonymous Letter to the Hebrews implies the name of the author, Paul.[40]

Summary

From the readers' perspective it is possible to identify the authors of every New Testament writing by linking the names of the titles to passages in other writings of the Canonical Edition mentioning the same names.

THE SELECTION OF AUTHORS

Eight Authors

The preceding treatment of the titles demonstrated that the Canonical Edition of the New Testament presents itself to the readers as a collection of twenty-seven writings originating from eight authors: Matthew, Mark, Luke, John, Paul, James, Peter, and Jude. The titles, with their carefully constructed cross-references between authors and specific text passages, connect the collection units and function as the user interface of the edition. They are the result of a deliberate redactional effort typical for anthologies to direct the interest of the readers to what the editors feel is the central message of the collection. If the names of the authors are so important to the editors, the question arises, how is the selection of authors explained to the readers in the text of this anthology? Again, I will begin by looking at the Canonical Edition from the readers' perspective.

Twice the readers of the Canonical Edition learn about a meeting of several of the eight New Testament authors, in Gal 2:2–10 and in Acts 15. The two accounts agree that they met in Jerusalem but differ in who exactly participated. In Galatians Paul mentions himself, Peter, John, and James; Luke's account does not expressly mention John by name. The other four authors of the New Testament can easily be related to these names. Matthew, like Peter and John, is one of the twelve disciples; Jude and

James, as the Lord's brothers, belong together; Luke goes with Paul; and Mark nicely connects Peter and Paul.

From the readers' perspective the selection of authors forms an interesting cross-reference between the Antioch incident (Gal 2:11–21; Acts 15:1) and the Jerusalem Council (Acts 15:6–29). The arrangement of the General Letters corresponds with Paul's list of the "pillars" in Galatians (2:9) and further accentuates this connection (see note 37).

The Arrangement of the Edition

The assumption that the editors were interested in establishing links between the brothers of Jesus, the twelve disciples, and Paul becomes more plausible when the overall design of the New Testament is taken into account. Next to the Letters of Paul the editors placed a collection of the Letters of James, Peter,[41] John, and Jude[42] and arranged them in the order they are mentioned in Galatians. In the Gospel collection Paul is represented by Luke, the Jerusalem apostles are represented by Matthew and John, and Mark conveniently forms a link between the two groups. Paul and his fellow workers are consistently placed next to the authorities of the Jerusalem congregation.

Authenticity

This investigation does not deal with the interesting question of whether or not the names of the authors provided by the titles are accurate. Many modern scholars would argue that only seven letters of Paul are authentic and that the authorship of the other twenty writings is very questionable on historical-critical grounds. But from a literary-critical point of view, which reads the collection at face value, I want to stress one observation that seems relevant in this context. If the editors are interested in demonstrating to their readers that after an initial discord there was undivided harmony between the Jerusalem apostles and Paul, they will have to insist that the documents promoted in their collection are authentic.[43]

Paul the Editor of His Letter Collection

The goal of the editors would be clearer if one could demonstrate that not all of the traditional material they promoted supported the harmonious view they wanted to express. I believe this is possible, at least for some of Paul's letters. Studying other letter collections published in antiquity, I was able to uncover typical patterns of how letter collections grow. I found that almost all of them originate with the author, who would often publish more than one collection of selected letters. After the author's death these original editions would typically be enlarged by appendices, and finally an editorial effort to combine smaller collections to form comprehensive editions is clearly discernible. It is possible to interpret the growth of the Pauline corpus as following this pattern.[44]

Under this theoretical assumption I suggested that the first four letters of the canonical collection preserved an older edition and should be read as a literary unit. In this case Paul himself would have edited Romans, Galatians, and 1 and 2 Corinthians, and he had a copy of this collection sent to the congregation in Ephesus. The cover note that accompanied the copy is preserved in Rom 16. In these four letters the collection for the poor in Jerusalem is portrayed as a conflict that—with the possible but not necessary exception of Matthew and Jude—directly involved all the New Testament authors. Paul had collected money from congregations in Galatia, Macedonia, and Achaia for the church in Jerusalem (1 Cor 16:1–4; 2 Cor 8–9). According to Paul he was simply fulfilling an agreement he had reached with the Jerusalem apostles (Gal 2:10). However, he fears that the saints in Jerusalem may reject this money (Rom 15:31).[45] The controversy about the collection exposed a deeper disagreement between Paul and the Jerusalem apostles, a conflict that could no longer be concealed. The significance of the Jewish law, in particular whether or not Gentile Christians should be circumcised, evoked heated debates. And there was open disagreement about how to finance missionaries. Paul outlines his position in direct opposition to "the other apostles and the brothers of the Lord and Cephas" (1 Cor 9:5), all of them prominent authors in the New Testament.[46]

The Letter to the Galatians is exclusively dedicated to this conflict, and Paul mentions his adversaries by name: Peter and the Lord's brother James (Gal 2:11–12). The controversy is not resolved in Paul's original compendium of four letters.[47] The final redaction of the Canonical Edition does not deny the conflict. But the editors insist that the later documents presented to the readers indicate that Paul and the Jerusalem apostles finally made peace and collaborated. If this reconstruction of the editorial process is correct, then the tendency of the traditional material was deliberately changed when the editors, who were responsible for the final redaction, incorporated Paul's compendium into the New Testament.

THE TITLE OF THE EDITION

"New Testament" is the title of the second part of the Canonical Edition. What did the editors want to express by choosing this title? Again, let us ask this question from the readers' point of view.

The function of the two words of the title is to simultaneously separate and combine. *Testament* connects the two parts of the Christian Bible; *New* distinguishes them.[48] This helps the readers to perceive the New Testament as a sequel to a much larger work, a Christian edition of the Jewish Bible. This observation may seem trivial to modern readers of the Christian Bible; during the second century, however, the question of whether or not the Jewish Scriptures were authoritative to the Christian community was a matter of heated debate. By including the "Old Testament" the editors of the Canonical Edition take an unambiguous position, and this is one of the strongest indicators we can use to place the edition historically.[49]

The designations "Old" and "New" probably express an essential component of the editors' concept. How do the two parts interact? How are they explained to the readers? One way of answering this question is that the Old Testament contains promises by God that are fulfilled by the christological events documented in the New Testament.

Septuagint

When combining the writings of the Jewish Bible with the collected Christian writings, the editors had to deal with several technical problems. Let us now look at some of the issues from the editors' point of view.

Both parts obviously were prepared to serve Greek readers. The Septuagint, which the editors used extensively, presented itself as a faithful translation, produced by seventy-two scholars.[50] The editors changed the title to "Old Testament," introduced the system of *nomina sacra*, established uniform names of the books, arranged them in a specific order, and checked competing editions of the Jewish Scriptures in Greek. Instead of using the Septuagint version of Daniel, for example, they incorporated the translation associated with Theodotion.[51] The publishers may have advertised their Old Testament as a revised edition of the Septuagint.

Structure

The editors clearly intended to standardize the user interface of the two parts. As I pointed out before, the first element in the title of each of the New Testament writings indicates a literary genre. This helps to group the writings into Gospels, Acts, General Letters, Letters of Paul, and Revelation. Why did the New Testament editors organize the writings according to their genre?

The Hebrew Bible displays three kinds of titles. (1) Some titles repeat the first words of the respective writing (Pentateuch, Proverbs מִשְׁלֵי Lamentations אֵיכָה). (2) Others carry the name of the most important characters or alleged authors (Joshua, Judges, Samuel, Kings, Prophets, Job, Ruth, Esther, Daniel, Esra, Nehemiah). (3) And the third group displays genre designations (Psalms, Song of Solomon, Chronicles).

Groups 2 and 3 were retained in the Greek edition with slight changes regarding the titles of Kings, which is called "Kingdoms," and Chronicles, which is changed from "Diaries" (דִּבְרֵי־הַיָּמִים) to "Omissions" (Παραλειπόμενα). However, the editors did not reproduce titles of the first group, which cite the Hebrew text. Nevertheless, the names of the books allude to a specific passage from the respective writing: Αὕτη ἡ βίβλος γενέσεως (Gn 2:4); ἐξόδος τῶν υἱῶν Ισραηλ ἐκ τῆς Αἰγύπτου (Ex 19:1); ἀριθμοί (Nm 1:2); γράψει ἑαυτῷ τὸ δευτερονόμιον τοῦτο εἰς βιβλίον (Dt 17:18); ῥήματα Ἐκκλησιαστοῦ υἱοῦ Δαυιδ (Ecc 1:1). The title "Leviticus" is not very obvious; the only time the word λευίτης is used is Lv 25:32–33. Proverbs quotes the genre designation παροιμίαι from Prv 1:1 (Παροιμίαι Σαλωμῶντος), and Lamentations refers to the genre designation in Lam 1:12 (Ιερεμιας . . . ἐθρήνησεν τὸν θρῆνον τοῦτον).[52]

The Hebrew Bible arranges the writings in three groups: Law, Prophets, and Writings.[53] Within these groups, the twelve Minor Prophets constitute another unit, and so do the five "scrolls" (Ruth, Song of Solomon, Ecclesiastes, Lamentations, Esther). The Greek prologue to Jesus Sirach uses this classification (SirachProlog 1–2, 6–7, 14–15).[54]

In contrast to the Hebrew editions, the oldest extant editions of the Christian Bible show a tendency to group the writings into historical, poetic, and prophetic writings.[55] The sequence of these blocks may vary.[56]

The Codex Vaticanus (B 03) places the poetic books before the prophetic writings. That sequence is the most common one in the manuscript traditions.[57] The Codex Sinaiticus (א 01) and the Codex Alexandrinus (A 02), however, have placed the prophetic writings before the poetic books. The arrangement of the Codex Ephraemi (C 04) is not clear.[58]

Although the number of books and their arrangement is not as consistent for the Old Testament as for the New Testament, the old Bible uncials may be interpreted as a combination of five collection units with three appendices (table 7).

The three parts of the Christian Old Testament may be reflected in the New Testament: the Gospels and Acts correspond to the historical books, the General Letters and the Letters of Paul to the poetic writings, and Revelation to the Prophets.

Let us now return to the initial question: Why did the editors of the New Testament organize the writings according to their genre? The arrangement of New Testament writings according to genre may very well reflect the organizing principle used in the Old Testament. The editors created a unified user interface for both parts of the edition.[59]

Textual Reference to 2 Corinthians 3

The title "New Testament" also refers the readers to a specific text passage. Readers who are willing to follow the signals provided by the titles will inevitably encounter 2 Cor 3, the only passage of the New Testament that uses the terms *Old Testament* and *New Testament* in the same context (see note 48). Paul uses the designation "Old Testament" to refer to the Holy Scriptures as a literary work from which the Jews read aloud, and Paul calls himself a "servant of the New Testament."[60]

2 Cor 3:6 and 3:12–16

[6] [God,] who has made us competent to *be ministers of a New Testament*, not of letter but of spirit; for the letter kills, but the Spirit gives life.	[6] ὃς καὶ ἱκάνωσεν ἡμᾶς διακόνους καινῆς διαθήκης, οὐ γράμματος ἀλλὰ πνεύματος· τὸ γὰρ γράμμα ἀποκτέννει, τὸ δὲ πνεῦμα ζῳοποιεῖ.

[12–14a]
Since, then, we have such a hope, we act with great boldness, not

Table 7. Arrangement of the Old Testament Writings in B 03, ℵ 01, A 02

B	1 + a	2	3	4	5
ℵ	1 + a	3 + b	5	4	2
A	1	4	5	3 + a + b	2 + c

SOURCE: Henry Barclay Swete, *An Introduction to the Old Testament in Greek*, (Cambridge: Cambridge University Press, 1900; rev. R. R. Ottley, reprint, New York: Ktav, 1968), 201–2.

NOTES:

1 = Gn Ex Lv Nm Dt Jos Jgs Ru 1 Sm 2 Sm 1 Kgs 2 Kgs 1 Chr 2 Chr
2 = Pss Prov Eccl Cant Job Wis Sir
3 = Esth Jdt Tob
4 = Hos Am Mi Jl Ob Jon Na Hb Zep Hg Zec Mal
5 = Is Jer Bar Lam EpJer Ez Dn
a = Ezra Neh
b = 1 Macc 2 Macc 3 Macc 4 Macc
c = PssSol.

ℵ 01 is defective and does not contain: Ex Lv; Dt Jos Jgs Ru 1 Sam 2 Sam 1 Kgs 2 Kgs; 2 Chr Ezra; EpJer Ez Dn; Hos Am Mi. Bar did not follow Jer and is not preserved.

like Moses, who put a veil over his face to keep the people of Israel from gazing at the end of the glory that was being set aside. But their minds were hardened.

[14b–15] Indeed, to this very day, when they hear *the reading of the Old Testament*, that same veil is still there, since only in Christ is it set aside. Indeed, to this very day whenever Moses is read, a veil lies over their minds; [16] But when one turns to the Lord, the veil is removed.

[14b–15] ἄχρι γὰρ τῆς σήμερον ἡμέρας τὸ αὐτὸ κάλυμμα ἐπὶ τῇ ἀναγνώσει τῆς παλαιᾶς διαθήκης μένει μὴ ἀνακαλυπτόμενον, ὅτι ἐν Χριστῷ καταργεῖται· ἀλλ᾽ ἕως σήμερον ἡνίκα ἂν ἀναγινώσκηται Μωϋσῆς κάλυμμα ἐπὶ τὴν καρδίαν αὐτῶν κεῖται·

From the first page of the Canonical Edition readers are aware that the term *Old Testament* is the name of a book. This book relates the story of God with Israel before God sent Christ into this world. That "the Old

Testament comes to an end in Christ" from a literary point of view seems very obvious. And since Paul is one of the main authors, the readers may interpret the statement that Paul is a "servant of the New Testament" literally as well. In addition to the Letters of Paul, the New Testament contains writings of two of his coworkers, Mark and Luke.

Certainly the traditional material did not intend a literary meaning of the term *testament*. But the editors of the Canonical Edition, who very deliberately picked "Old and New Testaments" as the title of their work and who consistently point the readers from the titles of the single writings to specific text passages, probably liked and provoked this "misunderstanding".[61]

The spirit of the New Testament gives life and overcomes the letter of the Old Testament, which kills.[62] When people turn to the Lord, the veil that causes them not to fully understand the Old Testament will be removed. The New Testament is the fulfillment and conclusion of the Old Testament.

Because the title of the work refers the readers to this Pauline passage, I suspect that it expresses the editors' theological concept.

NOMINA SACRA

Tetragram

As I already indicated, the extant Greek copies of the Jewish Bible from the first century deliberately avoid representing the tetragram with κύριος. Instead, they use various techniques when they note the name of God, often writing the tetragram in Hebrew letters (see the previous chapter for more on the tetragram). This is what the exemplars Paul used probably looked like. In their effort to standardize the way the name of God was noted, the editors of the Canonical Edition might have introduced the *nomina sacra*. What worked fine for the Old Testament, however, created ambiguity in numerous New Testament passages that was not present in the traditional material.[63]

Paul sometimes bases his argument on a quote from the Jewish Bible and carefully makes a distinction between JHWH and Christ. After the *nomina sacra* are introduced, however, both may be represented as $\overline{\kappa\varsigma}$ and may be interpreted as synonyms by the readers. The meaning of the passage may thus change considerably.[64] I want to demonstrate the shift using the passage quoted above from 2 Corinthians. The text continues, "But when one turns to the Lord, the veil is removed." It can easily be documented that Christian readers tend to interpret "Lord" as a reference to the Lord and Savior Jesus Christ.[65] Assuming that 2 Cor 3:16 alludes to the wording of Ex 34:34,[66] and assuming that the exemplar of the Jewish Bible in Greek that Paul used contained the tetragram, it may safely be concluded that the following verses contained the tetragram as well.[67] If κύριος is preceded by an article, the word probably refers to Christ, but in all other instances Paul's original letter showed the tetragram.

2 Cor 3:16–18 (own translation)
But when one turns to *JHWH*, the veil is removed. Now the Lord [Christ] is the Spirit [of *JHWH*], and where the Spirit of *JHWH* is, there is freedom. And all of us, with unveiled faces, seeing the glory of *JHWH* as though reflected in a mirror, are being transformed into the same image from one degree of glory to another; for this comes from *JHWH*, the Spirit.

(16) ἡνίκα δὲ ἐὰν ἐπιστρέψῃ
πρὸς יהוה, περιαιρεῖται τὸ
κάλυμμα. (17) ὁ δὲ κύριος τὸ
πνεῦμά ἐστιν· οὗ δὲ τὸ *πνεῦμα*
יהוה, ἐλευθερία. (18) ἡμεῖς δὲ
πάντες ἀνακεκαλυμμένῳ
προσώπῳ τὴν δόξαν יהוה κατοπτριζόμενοι τὴν αὐτὴν εἰκόνα
μεταμορφούμεθα ἀπὸ δόξης εἰς
δόξαν, καθάπερ ἀπὸ יהוה
πνεύματος.

According to this reconstruction, identifying Christ as the spirit of JHWH establishes the connection between JHWH and Christ. Turning to JHWH in the Old Testament is the same as turning to Christ now. Because the "names of God" are represented by *nomina sacra*, the readers of the Canonical Edition arrive at the same conclusion faster. For them 2 Cor 3:16 means that as soon as Jews turn to the Lord (Jesus), the veil is removed from their reading of the Old Testament.[68]

The editors did not mind this misrepresentation of Paul.[69] The effect on Christian readers—that Jesus and JHWH become synonyms—was probably intended.

Emergence

Anyone in charge of the final redaction of an anthology like a letter collection, a Festschrift, or a journal knows about the editorial decisions that have to be made in order to give the publication a harmonious appearance. I suspect that primarily technical aspects motivated the introduction of the *nomina sacra*. Three stages may still be discernible.

First of all, the editors obviously had to decide how to deal with the tetragram when they worked on the Old Testament. They voted to contract and note with a superscript line the Greek representations κύριος, "Lord," and Θεός, "God."[70] Whether this was an original idea of the editors or whether they found it in one of their traditional sources remains unclear. I assume that they had several options to choose from. Not to use a foreign alphabet but to stick to Greek characters was a very pragmatic solution and certainly reduced confusion during the process of book production.[71]

Second, when the editors started to work on the New Testament they had to be consistent. The words, *Lord* and *God* function differently in the New Testament because they do not necessarily refer to the Hebrew tetragram. As I demonstrated above, κύριος in the New Testament may refer not only to God but to Jesus as well. And if the name *Jesus* is treated as a *nomen sacrum*, *Christ* should be included as well. The four common words contracted in the New Testament—*God*, *Lord*, *Jesus*, and *Christ*—are all *nomina divina*.[72]

During the third stage the scribes copying the Christian Bible were not aware anymore of the special treatment of the tetragram in the Jewish community. They note other words, too, as *nomina sacra*, such as *spirit*, *man*, *cross*, *father*, *son*, *savior*, *mother*, *heaven*, *Israel*, *David*, *Jerusalem*, and so on.

Group-Defining Function

More important than particulars concerning its emergence are the effect the system of *nomina sacra* had on the Christian community. With one glance Christian readers were now able to recognize the Canonical Edition and distinguish it from Jewish-Hellenistic publications[73] and other competing editions of apostolic writings. The Canonical Edition thus gradually became a significant criterion for identifying a specific, internationally organized Christian movement.

The emerging Catholic Church appears to have used the system of *nomina sacra* very early in its publications.[74]

CODEX

Selected Sources

The codex form was popular before Christians discovered it for their purposes. In the following I will discuss selected sources that shed some light on the history of the codex prior to the publication of the New Testament, and I will point out its advantages and disadvantages compared to the scroll. This comparison will illustrate why the codex as a medium served so well for the Canonical Edition.[75]

Lucius Anneus Seneca,[76] a Roman philosopher, poet, and contemporary of Paul, makes fun of irrelevant questions asked by scholars of his time. As an example Seneca mentions a study that attempts to decide whether Claudius Caudex, a consul in 164 B.C.E., had been named after the word *codex*: "since at that time several tablets bound together were called 'caudex,' which is why we refer to public tablets as 'codices.'"[77] I do not want to reverse the question and ask if the codex was named after Claudius Caudex, a discussion Seneca would certainly have regarded as just as futile. However, it is worth mentioning that Seneca could presuppose that his contemporary readers were familiar with the term *codex*. He uses *codex* to explain the unfamiliar word *caudex*. And he illustrates his point by referring to public tablets, *publicae tabulae*, which he assumes are examples of codices the readers will know.

When the Roman poet Martial (38/41 to 103/104)[78] advertised a new edition of his poems (ca. 84–86 C.E.), he announced that the first two books were now available in one codex. He even mentioned the address of his publisher, Secundus.[79]

> Martial, *Epigrams* 1:2[80]
> You who want my little books to keep you company wherever you may be and desire their companionship on a long journey, buy these, that parchment compresses in small pages. Give book boxes to the great, one hand grasps me.
>
> But in case you don't know where I am on sale and stray wandering all over town, you will be sure of your way under my guidance. Look for Secundus, freedman of lettered Lucensis, behind Peace's entrance and Pallas' Forum.

Martial praises the advantages of the codex form. It is more convenient when you travel, it needs less space in the library, and a codex is easier to handle than a scroll because you do not need both hands to open it: "Scrinia da magnis, me manus una capit."

Martial points out that other authors like Homer, Virgil, Ovid, Cicero, and Livius are available in codex form as well. Whether codices were a success from an economical point of view or not, however, is not certain. Martial's boisterous advertising slogans suggest that customers had to be talked into buying familiar texts in codices.[81]

Sueton (ca. 70–140), Martial's younger contemporary, writes in his biography of Caesar, "Some letters of his to the senate are also preserved. And he seems to have been the first one to copy them on several pages put together in the form of a journal. Previously consuls and generals sent their reports written on a scroll."[82] The question of whether Caesar was the first writer to abandon scrolls is not essential for our discussion. More significant is Sueton's casual assumption that his readers knew what "several pages put together in the form of a journal" looked like compared to the scroll. First-century Roman citizens seem to be familiar with codices. Whereas Martial refers to professionally produced and distributed publications, Sueton talks about a single document, the autograph of Caesar's letters.

Long before the codex had finally found its place in the thriving book industry of the fourth century, it was widely used by two professional groups: lawyers and physicians. One book written by the lawyer Neratius Priscus in the first century is called *liber sextus membranarum*;[83] *membrana* probably refers to the notes that were published in this work.[84] Galen (129–99), the physician of Emperor Mark Aurel, relates that he found a remedy against hair loss in a leather codex, ἐν πυκτίδι διφθέρα. The physician Claudianus wrote this codex, and Galen acquired it after Claudianus's death.[85]

Augustine reports that even in later times codices were closely associated with medical literature. A certain Donatus of Calama, who had been charged in 303 of having handed out Holy Scriptures to his persecutors during the Diocletian persecutions, defends himself and explains to his bishop, "Dedi codices medicinales [I handed over medical codices]."[86] To the Christian brothers who were listening to Donatus's defense, it made sense that illiterate soldiers could easily be tricked into taking medical books for Christian Bibles. Both were usually published in codex form.[87]

Although Jerome published his literary works in codices, he used scrolls for writing letters. When Augustine sends Jerome a letter in codex form, he apologizes for doing so. Apparently the codex was not appropriate for letters.[88]

Scroll

The scroll was particularly useful for filing documents that carried a date. The documents were simply glued together in the sequence they had been processed. Documents concerning the same matter could be filed sequentially, nicely displaying the dates when they were handed in and how they were processed. Gluing them together provided some protection against manipulation; similarly, in many countries nowadays notary publics are required to bind loose documents together using special knots and seals. To make changes one had to cut the scroll up, and this was easily detected.

This feature of scrolls offered certain advantages for literary texts as well. A bound codex eventually would wear out and would have to be rebound. It often happened that single pages or whole layers were mistakenly rearranged, as numerous New Testament manuscripts document.[89]

Normally, only one side of the scroll was used to write on. This way the scribes could use the better side, the recto, where the fibers of the papyrus run horizontal. Likewise, the inner side of leather is smoother and tends to be lighter than the side with the hair.

The back side of the scroll served as an effective protection, comparable to the wooden covers of codices. On the other hand, a scroll had to be unrolled and rolled up again after use, which might have worn out the material faster than the opening of codices.[90] Finally, writing on the back of an old scroll was easier than washing the ink off a codex to be recycled.[91]

Papyrus was delivered in bales. The scribes would simply cut off as much as they needed to produce a scroll.[92] This way the papyrus manufacturer was in full control of the production process. Many extant samples of papyrus were produced with great care and achieved high quality. The surface is smooth, and the places where the single sheets are glued together are barely visible to the inexperienced eye, thus allowing the scribe to lay out the columns following practical and aesthetic standards. Apparently the writing utensil did not get caught in the adhesion areas.

The scroll was a practical medium for literary texts intended to be read from the beginning to the end. Like chapters in a modern publication, longer texts were broken up into several "books," and each book filled one scroll. Authors would structure their works according to the practical length of a scroll, and this division helped the readers to quote and find specific passages. One could usually read the author, the title, and the book number without opening the scroll.[93]

Codex

The codex, however, provided significant advantages, particularly for reference works, because it could be opened randomly and did not have to be read sequentially. This may have been why physicians and lawyers preferred the codex to the scroll even before it became an acceptable medium for literary texts.

There is no word for *codex* in Greek.[94] The Latin *membrana* depicts the individual plates or leaves made of wood, leather, or papyrus, regardless of whether they are bound. Martial uses *membrana* to refer to the codex, "brevibus membrana tabellis" (*Epigrams* 1.2). The Greek term μεμβράναι clearly derives from the Latin, and it is used once in the New Testament in 2 Timothy, when Paul tells Timothy to bring the μεμβράναι that he had left with Carpus (2 Tm 4:13). Even after the codex finally became popular in the fourth century, the Greek language did not have a special word for it.[95] Often σωμάτιον is used, which corresponds to Latin *corpus* and signifies a literary unit, such as a multivolume work, and could be applied to scrolls as well.[96] The term πτυκτίον signifies "something folded" and is sometimes applied to codices because they are made from sheets folded into quires and bound. Occasionally the Latin word *codex* is simply transliterated with Greek characters.[97]

As mentioned earlier, papyrus was manufactured and sold in bales. The scribes themselves would then cut pieces off.[98] Producing a codex was more complicated. The scribes would write the text on single sheets, fold them, organize them in quires, bind the quires, and fit them between book covers. This process was demanding, and it took more time and required certain manual skills that were not necessary when scribes produced scrolls. The considerable cost of binding occurred only after the text had been copied.[99] To my knowledge this aspect has not yet been sufficiently documented in a study comparing scrolls and codices.

To produce a notebook, scribes would cut blank pages to size, fold the pile in the middle, and sew them together to form a single quire; the outer sheets served as covers. Notebooks were very practical for journals and other records, which had to be kept periodically. When one notebook was full, the next one was started. If they were made from leather, the ink was sometimes washed off so that the booklet could be used a second time. They were very popular in schools to record students' writing exercises.[100] On the other hand, these notebooks were not very practical if they had to hold the entire text of a communication and if the length of the text could not be anticipated in advance. Letters, for example, sometimes had to be written in a hurry because the messenger who had brought the letter wanted to return as soon as possible and waited for the response.[101]

Caesar's letters to the senate, mentioned above, were certainly not casually written documents; no doubt, their style was polished and they were carefully edited. Because the amount of text was known, the notebook could be produced to exactly accommodate the letters. To avoid empty pages at the end, it is essential to know how much text a codex will hold.[102] The same is true for the other example, Augustine's letter to Jerome. Augustine apologizes because the bound form of his written response clearly indicates that the text was written and edited with a broader public in mind; it is more than just a private letter to Jerome. In other words, Augustine responds to Jerome's letter with a "printed" brochure.[103]

The codex form is more profitable to the publisher if books are produced in larger numbers.[104] A scribe probably could manufacture a single copy of a scroll without great technical difficulties. In order to copy a codex, however, the amount of text and the layout of each page had to be carefully calculated in advance to determine the exact number of sheets and quires needed. No doubt, this is more time-consuming and calls for more experimentation than the production of a scroll would. But for the next copy these calculations could be used again. Whenever books were reproduced by dictation, the number of copies depended on the number of scribes taking the dictation.[105] The preproduction costs would not have such an impact, and specialized workers like bookbinders could be used more efficiently, if codices were produced in numbers.

I think Martial's comments should be interpreted in this context. The other works he refers to as being published in codex form are not first editions; they are "reprints" of well-known books. This may indicate that the targeted audience for the codex were clients thinking about buying a second copy of the same book because they wanted to take it with them on a trip and codices were easier to handle, or simply because they were cheaper than scrolls. Others may have known those titles from school but never acquired a private copy and now were tempted to buy because of the reasonable price. To mention the bookstore would only make sense if Secundus carried the advertised titles in stock, indicating that standard works were probably reproduced in adequate numbers and could be purchased at a fixed price. Publishers like Secundus may have acted as both book producer and bookseller.

There has been a lively debate about whether codices were sold at a lower price than scrolls.[106] I suspect that it depended on whether a book could be reproduced in large numbers. If so, the higher labor costs incurred as a result of binding the codices could be offset by the fact that codices used both sides of the pages and therefore needed less writing material than scrolls. And a lower price probably would be passed on to the customers.

For publishers of collections the codex form offered distinct advantages. As I indicated earlier, there is a natural practical limit to a scroll's length. On the other hand, a scroll needed a certain length and could not be used very well for very short texts. Among the writings of the New Testament, the Letter to Philemon, the Letter of Jude, and the Third Letter of John[107] are too short to fill a scroll. On the one hand, it probably did not seem feasible to publish the New Testament in twenty-seven separate scrolls. On the other hand, it is cumbersome to look up a specific writing if several writings are copied on one scroll. In addition, extant copies demonstrate that from the beginning codices were able to hold more text than scrolls.[108]

From the very beginning the codex was considered by many to be forgery-proof. It offered several features that indicated whether or not it was complete and made it more difficult to manipulate.[109] During the complex production process the quires would be numbered, and each page would be paginated. Codices with more than one writing could display a table of contents, typically giving the titles and the respective length of the writings.[110]

Many older indices of the canonical writings contain the length of the books listed in *stichoi*, which constitute a widely accepted measurement (one *stichos* represents roughly sixteen syllables). These figures were important to booksellers, scribes, and customers alike because length formed a significant factor in determining the purchase price. If a book's length was known, incomplete copies were easier to detect. The author of the Canon Mommsen, which was written before 359, explains the need for such lists with these words: "Since the index of verses in the city of Rome is constantly changing, and elsewhere too through avarice of gain [*avaritiae causa*] they do not keep it correctly, I have gone through the books one by one, counting sixteen syllables to the Virgilian verse, and noted the number next to every book." The title of this list nicely demonstrates the two functions, recording writings' length (*indiculum versuum*) and an index of their canonical status (incipit indiculum veteris testamenti qui sunt libri cannonici sic). Immediately following the biblical books, the catalogue lists the writings of Bishop Cyprian of Carthage. This document is a nice example of consumer protection in antiquity.[111]

It was much more difficult to add or remove a writing from a bound codex than from a collection of individual scrolls. Last but not least, the reputation of the codex form as forgery-proof is documented by the fact that some publishers used the codex form to mislead their customers. Rufin reports that the Pneumatomachian heretics produced in large numbers codices that contained Novatian's treatise *De Trinitate* next to the popular letters of Saint Cyprian. They then sold these books below cost, apparently in an attempt to distribute Novatian's writings more effectively.[112]

Why did it take non-Christian publishers so long to adapt the codex form for literary texts if codices were easier to ship, more convenient to use and store, and probably cheaper to produce and could hold more text than scrolls?

One answer might lie in the fact that in antiquity people did not buy a book simply because it was offered at a low price; that holds true today as well.[113] If publishers were able to determine exactly what sells a book, they all would feature fewer titles and produce them in larger numbers. A book's success is based on a complicated mixture of contents, author recognition, and the use of a well-established genre. Compared to these factors, the specific price does not influence the decision to buy a particular book as strongly; aspects of aesthetics, quality, and authenticity are more important. Social recognition, on which the educated in antiquity could count, was significant as well. Books were a status symbol.[114] The codex, however, may have looked cheap. The place of bound books in everyday life was as notebooks or journals, used for exercises in school, and as a cheap medium for mass-produced standard literature.

Even centuries later, when printed books began to replace manuscripts, not everyone readily accepted the new and cheaper medium.[115] And in our century the enormous success of the paperback and of cheap pocketbook editions did not happen overnight. The first genres to adopt the pocketbook format were pulp fiction and mystery stories. Nowadays it is conceivable that just about any book, no matter how sophisticated and demanding the literary genre, may be published as a pocket book. It took decades for this form to become "socially acceptable."

Advantages of the Codex Form for the Canonical Edition

For the publishers of the Canonical Edition the codex form probably offered several distinct advantages.

First of all, codices are able to hold more text than scrolls. The four collection units of the New Testament—Four-Gospel Book,[116] Praxapostolos, Letters of Paul, Revelation of John—could be bound in four volumes.

To reduce production costs, publishers probably tried to produce codices in significant numbers. Large numbers helped with standardizing and distributing revisions of the Canonical Edition because publishers could concentrate on and improve a single archetype. The characteristic and consistent editorial features described in this chapter gave their publication high recognition value and created the notion among book buyers who were interested in early Christian literature that this was to be the authoritative edition.

Furthermore, the codex form warranted that no writing was left out; the very short documents, in particular, benefited from this protection. Content sheets and indexes of text length, adequately guaranteed the quality of a collection if published in a codex.

The publishers must also have liked the sociological function of the codex form. In contrast to the evolving Christian community, the Jewish community kept using scrolls for their Holy Scripture.[117] Like the distinctive system of *nomina sacra*, the codex form became a trademark of the Canonical Edition.[118]

Among the many objectives the editors and publishers of the Canonical Edition pursued, two are very obvious.

First, by combining the "Old Testament" and the "New Testament" in one work, they assert that the Jewish Bible is relevant to their audience.

Second, by placing the writings of the Jerusalem apostles next to the writings of the apostle Paul, they emphatically endorse both Paul and the Jerusalem authorities. Letters of the three Jerusalem pillars—James, John, and Peter—complement the Letters of Paul. The writings of Jesus' disciple Matthew and Jesus' brother Jude are placed next to the writings of Mark, who is portrayed as a coworker of Peter and Paul, and Luke, who is presented as Paul's travel companion and reports on Peter and Paul in Acts.

The particular contents of the Canonical Edition were supplemented by nontextual editorial characteristics like the *nomina sacra* and the use of the codex form. These features clearly distinguished the edition from its competition.

Furthermore, the authenticity of the writings is a significant element of the editorial concept. This is demonstrated by the careful construction of the titles, which allow the readers to identify the respective authors from the text of the Canonical Edition and enable them to determine whether an author is associated with Paul or with Jerusalem. From the editors' point of view the focus on the authors' names makes sense only if the writings are considered genuine.

This editorial concept expresses the self-understanding of a very specific group within the diverse early Christian community. Marcion of Sinope held the opposite view according to Tertullian, Irenaeus, and others who write at the end of the second century.[119] Marcionite congregations rejected the Jewish Bible as Holy Scripture. Following a literal reading of Paul's Letter to the Galatians, they considered Paul the only true apostle and guardian of the gospel and did not recognize the Jerusalem authorities. Consequently, Marcion's edition of Paul's letters began with Galatians, which describes the conflict between Peter and Paul in vivid detail. Because of the polemic character of the sources concerning Marcion, it is not possible to determine with certainty whether the emphasis on the conflict between Paul and the Jerusalem authorities was Marcion's original contribution. He may simply have expressed what many Christians believed.[120] Be that as it may, there is little doubt that the alleged Marcionite position was popular among second-century Christians.

If the New Testament can be traced back to a coherent publication, it follows that this question may and should be asked with urgency: Who published the Christian Bible? It is my hope that in the near future historical studies will narrow down the possibilities for who was involved and when and where the first edition appeared.

In the following chapter I want to demonstrate that at least four writings—Acts, 2 Peter, 2 Timothy, and John—may contain valuable clues to help us identify the editors and first publishers of the Canonical Edition.

4

A Note to the Readers of the Canonical Edition

EDITORS OF A COLLECTION DO NOT NECESSARILY HIDE THEIR identity. To address the reader openly is an acceptable and common practice, and editors do it frequently, in prefaces, appendices, commentaries, or annotations. I will use the phrase *editorial note to the reader*[1] to refer to such passages. Such a note will be clearly marked as redactional. Readers will be able to distinguish between the later work of the collectors and editors and the original material.

As we have seen, the New Testament contains such an editorial note to the readers of John's Gospel in Jn 21.[2] In the following, I will argue that some references of Jn 21 reach beyond this Gospel. Jn 21 can be seen as the conclusion not only to John's Gospel but also to the Four-Gospel Book. Since the collection of Gospels forms the heart of the Canonical Edition, this chapter may very well be understood as an editorial note to the readers of the entire New Testament.

Relative Chronology

Let us first establish the chronological order of the writings in relation to each other. Among other things, the New Testament displays a strong interest in the conflict between Peter and Paul. 2 Timothy and 2 Peter present themselves as the last writings of the two apostles and can be seen as a literary testament. Acts concludes in Rome, at a time when Paul is still alive, with these words: "He lived there two whole years at his own expense and welcomed all who came to him, proclaiming the kingdom of God and teaching about the Lord Jesus Christ with all boldness and without hindrance" (Acts 28:30–31).[3] The same situation is reflected in 2 Timothy, a letter Paul allegedly writes from Rome (2 Tm 1:16–17) waiting for his trial: "At my first defense no one came to my support" (2 Tm 4:16). Paul uses the situation to preach his gospel: "But the Lord stood by me and gave me strength, so that through me the message might be fully proclaimed and all the Gentiles might hear it. So I was rescued from the lion's mouth" (2 Tm 4:17).

Because Luke writes about Stephen's death (Acts 7:54–60) and the execution of James the Zebedee (Acts 12:2), readers of Acts have good reason to expect that Luke would have reported the deaths of Peter, John the Zebedee, James the Lord's brother, or Paul, if he had known about them. From a reader's perspective it looks as if Luke finished the Book of Acts before Peter and Paul died, at about the same time that 2 Timothy was produced.[4] Jn 21 appears to presuppose the death of Peter[5] and John;[6] it follows that Jn 21 was written some time after the Book of Acts.

Arrangement of the Gospels

From the readers' perspective, Acts helps to establish the chronological order of the synoptic Gospels. Since Acts presents itself as the second volume of a larger work, the reader infers that Luke's Gospel must be older. The introductory passage to the Gospel mentions earlier literary attempts by other writers: "Many have undertaken to set down an orderly account of the events that have been fulfilled among us" (Lk 1:1). This remark may easily be taken to refer to Mark's Gospel, which precedes Luke (see also the discussion of Mark in the previous chapter). It provides the readers with the key to understanding the sequence of the four canonical Gospels. Since John was published later than Luke, and Luke was written later than Mark, it is evident that the last three Gospels were arranged chronologically in the sequence of their original date of publication. Under the assumption that this organizational principle applies to the whole Gospel collection, it follows that Matthew's Gospel, which heads the collection, is presented as the oldest one.[7] In addition, it is very plausible that Matthew, one of the twelve disciples of Jesus, would have written earlier than Mark and Luke, who are disciples of the apostles. Furthermore, from the first to the very last sentence Matthew's Gospel presents itself as the literary product of the evangelist. John's Gospel, however, clearly indicates that someone other than the evangelist published it. From the readers' perspective these observations make the First Gospel appear to be older than the three following Gospels.

To sum up: the synoptic Gospels were written before Paul's death; and since Jn 21 looks back on the death of Peter and John the Zebedee, the canonical version of John's Gospel is younger than the letters of Peter, the letters of John, and the Book of Revelation.

How This Study Will Proceed

Next, I want to deal briefly with the Book of Acts, 2 Timothy, and 2 Peter and point out some apparent parallels to the editorial concept of the final redaction.

I will leave the question open as to whether these writings were part of the tradition and accepted without alteration, or whether they were heavily edited or even created by the editors of the Canonical Edition. All of these answers are possible and can be supported by ancient parallels.[8] Fortunately, my interpretation, which attempts to understand the text from the readers' perspective, would remain unaffected in any case. It can hardly be denied that the edition presents the separate writings as authentic.

I will end by reflecting on Jn 21.

ACTS OF THE APOSTLES

The final redaction of the Canonical Edition demonstrates an interest in minimizing the conflict between the Jerusalem authorities and Paul so vividly described in his Letter to the Galatians. Of all New Testament writings, it is the Book of Acts that most explicitly displays this harmonizing tendency.

Paul and Peter

This tendency is detectable in the apparent parallels between the accounts of the two apostles and their companions.

First there are the miraculous healings performed by Peter, which immediately recall some of the Jesus stories as they are narrated in the canonical Gospels. Peter's miracles find parallels in Paul's ministry. Just as Peter and John heal a man who was lame from birth at the gate of the temple (Acts 3:1–10), in Lystra Paul heals a man similarly lame from birth (Acts 14:8–10). The shadow of Peter is portrayed as sufficient to heal the sick in Jerusalem; in Ephesus Paul can do the same by means of handkerchiefs and aprons that had touched his skin (Acts 19:12). In Jerusalem Peter casts out unclean spirits (Acts 5:16); in Ephesus Paul successfully charges a spirit of divination to come out of a slave girl (Acts 16:18). Peter cured the sick who were brought from towns around Jerusalem (Acts 5:16). This is paralleled in the story of Paul's stay on Malta following the shipwreck, where he healed all the sick who were brought to him (Acts 28:9). Both are capable of bringing dead people back to life. In Joppa, Peter restores the woman disciple Tabitha to life (Acts 9:36–41), while in Troas, Paul raises young Eutychus, who sank into sleep during Paul's sermon and fell from a window to the ground three floors below (Acts 20:9–12). In Lydda, Peter heals Aeneas, who was paralyzed and had been bedridden for eight years (Acts 9:33–34). In very much the same way, Paul cures the father of Publius in Malta, who suffered from fever and dysentery (Acts 28:8).

In Samaria, the power of Peter and John is stronger than the power of the magician Simon (Acts 8:18–25). Together with Barnabas, Paul is in Paphos on the island of Cyprus, proclaiming the word of God to the proconsul Sergius Paulus, when he reproaches the magician Elymas in the presence of the proconsul. Elymas immediately becomes blind (Acts 13:6–12). In Ephesus Paul prompts a public burning of magic books (Acts 19:17–20).

Just as Cornelius falls down at the feet of Peter (Acts 10:25), Paul and Barnabas are worshiped as gods in Lystra (Acts 14:11–18, cf. 28:6). Peter and Paul reply with almost the same words: "I too am only a mortal" (Acts 10:26) and "We are mortals just like you" (Acts 14:15). In Samaria Peter and John lay their hands on people and they receive the Holy Spirit (Acts 8:14–17, cf. 10:44). In Ephesus, Paul lays his hands on the twelve disciples of John the Baptist, and the Holy Spirit comes on them (Acts 19:1–7). A vision causes Peter to accept Gentiles into the Christian community in Joppa (Acts 10, cf. 11:5–10), while Paul receives his vision on his way to Damascus and is transformed from enemy to minister of Christ's gospel (Acts 9:1–22, 22:6–11, 26:12–18).

Paul and the Jerusalem apostles resemble each other in more than their miraculous powers. They also share the same sufferings and persecutions. In Jerusalem the apostles are physically punished in front of the council (Acts 5:40); in Philippi the magistrates tear the garments off Paul and his companions and give orders for them to be beaten with rods (Acts 16:22–23). In Jerusalem, Stephen, who had been appointed by Peter and the apostles, is stoned (Acts 7:54–60); in Lystra of Galatia, Paul is stoned and his body is dragged out of the city, where he is left for dead (Acts 14:19–20). When the apostles are arrested in Jerusalem, an angel opens the prison doors at night (Acts 5:17–20). This happens again after the execution of James, son of Zebedee, by Herod, when Peter was sleeping between two soldiers in prison (Acts 12:6–11). In Philippi, Paul and Barnabas are put into the inner prison and their feet are fastened in the stocks. A great earthquake miraculously opens the doors and unfastens everyone's fetters (Acts 16:24–34).

Structure of Acts

Using the focus on Peter and Paul as a guide, Acts may be divided into two parts. Acts 1–12 describes the growth and influence of the Jerusalem congregation under the leadership of Peter and the other authorities, whereas Acts 13–28 reports on the activities of Paul. The two parts are intertwined. In the first part Paul is introduced as a witness to the stoning of Stephen (Acts 7:58) and as persecuting Christian communities (Acts 8:1–3). His vision of Christ on the road to Damascus is narrated (Acts 9:1–30), and the readers are informed that it was Barnabas who brought Paul to Antioch (Acts 11:25–26).

In the second part of Acts, the Jerusalem apostles play a significant role during the council at Jerusalem (Acts 15) and during Paul's last trip to Jerusalem (Acts 21).

Apostolic Council at Jerusalem

The selection of the eight authors featured in the New Testament points toward the conflict between Paul and Peter described in Galatians.[9] If minimizing this conflict was one of the major objectives of Acts, the Apostolic Council at Jerusalem (Acts 15:1–19) forms the heart of this book. From the perspective of the final redaction of the New Testament, the Apostolic Council at Jerusalem might even form the heart of the New Testament. No other passage documents the absolute accord between the circle around Paul and the circle around Peter so effectively as this report of a common meeting and resolution.

Paul and James

Paul is portrayed as in perfect agreement not only with Peter but also with James, the Lord's brother. According to the account in Acts, when Paul arrived in Jerusalem to deliver the collection, he was dragged out of the temple by an aroused crowd, publicly abused, arrested by the authorities, and sent to Rome as a prisoner (Acts 21:27–40; Acts 27–28). Before all these events take place, however, Paul has a private consultation with James. James is reported to warn him explicitly about "how many thousands of believers there are among the Jews, and they are all zealous for the law. They have been told about you that you teach all the Jews living among the Gentiles to forsake Moses, and that you tell them not to circumcise their children or observe the customs" (Acts 21:20–21).[10] The two apostles devise a plan to fool the naive Jewish converts without violating the apostolic decree for Gentile converts (Acts 21:18–26). In order to create the impression that Paul lives in strict observance of the law, James advises Paul to participate in the private ritual of Nazirite purification. Although the plan fails miserably, the readers are informed that James did not side with an anti-Pauline Jewish-Christian opposition but supported Paul, counteracting an impression the readers might have gathered from reading Galatians.[11]

Paul and Barnabas

While perusing Galatians, readers may make the discomfiting discovery that Paul publicly spoke out against Peter. "If you, though a Jew, live like a Gentile and not like a Jew, how can you compel the Gentiles to live like Jews?" (Gal 2:14). This is not the only time the readers are led to disapprove of Peter's behavior. In the Gospels, it is Peter whom Jesus sharply rebukes because he does not understand the necessity of Jesus' Passion ("Get behind me, Satan!" [Mk 8:33]), or because he struck the high priest's slave with a sword and cut off his right ear (Jn 18:10–11). It is also Peter who denies Jesus three times (Mt 26:69–75, Mk 14:66–72, Lk 22:54–62, Jn 18:17.25–27).[12] To a reader of the Canonical Edition, Peter leaves yet another scene with a blemish. As if to balance the poor impression readers might have of Peter from Galatians, two episodes immediately following the Apostolic Council cast a negative light on Paul, the apostle to the Gentiles: the dispute with Barnabas and the circumcision of Timothy.[13]

In his Letter to the Galatians Paul states that Barnabas was carried away by the hypocrisy of Peter and other Christian Jews who were present at Antioch (Gal 2:13). Acts also recounts a controversy between Paul and Barnabas but informs readers that Peter was hardly involved at all. The controversy centered on their coworker Mark, who had connections to Peter as well as to Barnabas and Paul. Paul refused to take Mark with him on their next missionary trip because Mark "had deserted them in Pamphylia and had not accompanied them in the work. The disagreement became so sharp that they parted company" (Acts 15:38–39). Acts presents the conflict as a disagreement between Barnabas and Paul, not between Peter and Paul. As has already been pointed out, readers of the Canonical Edition will find apparent hints that later this quarrel was peacefully settled (see also the discussion of Mark in the previous chapter).

Paul and Timothy

Immediately following this passage an act of Paul is reported that stands in absolute contrast to the decree of the Apostolic Council and to Paul's own convictions. "Paul wanted Timothy to accompany him; and he took him and had him circumcised because of the Jews who were in those places, for they all knew that his father was a Greek" (Acts 16:3). Paul is acting here in blunt contradiction to his own statements in Galatians, where he uses strong language to underline that he does not support the practice of circumcision for converts from the Gentiles.[14] Not only in their miraculous power but also in their weaknesses, the two apostles Peter and Paul have much in common.[15]

Cross-References

No other writing connects the collection units of the New Testament as well as Acts. It continues the narrative of Luke, which is part of the Four-Gospel Book. It also serves as an introduction to the General Letters, introducing in its first part the authors of these writings—James, Peter, and John. In its second part, Acts provides biographical information concerning Paul that helps readers better understand the background of the individual letters. Without Acts readers would never learn that Paul came from Tarsus (Acts 9:11, 22:3) and that he was born a Roman citizen (Acts 22:28).[16] Moreover, although Paul in his letters repeatedly and proudly mentions that he works for a living (1 Thes 2:9, 2 Thes 3:8), it is only from the Book of Acts that readers learn his profession of tent-making (Acts 17:3). The story of the journey related to Paul's collection for Jerusalem, which provides the background of Romans (Rom 15:25–28) and the Corinthian correspondence (1 Cor 16:1–4, 2 Cor 8–9), is continued in Acts by a report that this trip ended with Paul's arrest in Jerusalem (Acts 21–28). Readers are introduced to those congregations who received a canonical letter of Paul. Acts recounts Paul's activity in Philippi (Acts 16:11–40, 20:6), Thessalonica (Acts 17:1–15), and Ephesus (Acts 18:19–21, 18:24–19:40, cf. 20:16–38). There are several short references to Galatia as well (Acts 16:6, 18:23). The only congregation who received a canonical letter without being mentioned in Acts is the church at Colossae. According to the Letter to the Colossians, Paul had never visited them (Col 2:1).

2 TIMOTHY

Let us now turn our attention to 2 Timothy. The readers know Timothy from Acts (Acts 16:1–3, 17:14–15, 18:5, 19:22, 20:4). As demonstrated above, Paul's situation at the end of Acts is described in very much the same way as it is in 2 Timothy. Luke alone is with Paul as he waits for the trial (2 Tm 4:11.16). Expecting a death sentence, Paul writes to his co-worker: "As for me, I am already being poured out as a libation, and the time of my departure has come" (2 Tm 4:6).

The end of Acts strongly suggests to readers of the Canonical Edition that Luke had finished his book before Paul died. Therefore, it is quite plausible that Luke did not know the canonical collection of the Letters of Paul. Paul either had not yet written his last letter or had just mailed his last letter. Luke could not have used the letters if they were not collected and published. The readers of the Canonical Edition will read Acts and the Letters of Paul as parallel sources that describe the same events, not as documents using each other. It is the reading pattern they were taught to use when reading the canonical Gospel collection.[17]

Recommended Reading

It is worth noting that in their last letters Paul and Peter are very much in agreement as to what further reading they would recommend to their audiences. The coworkers Luke and Mark are presented in a very positive light: "Only Luke is with me. Get Mark and bring him with you, for he is useful in my ministry" (2 Tm 4:11). Paul recommends these two New Testament authors, endorsing in the eyes of the readers the credibility of their two Gospels as well as the Praxapostolos, which opens with Luke's Book of Acts. Furthermore, the text highlights Paul's opinion of the Old Testament. He praises it with the following words: "From childhood you have known the sacred writings [ἱερὰ γράμματα] that are able to instruct you for salvation through faith in Christ Jesus" (2 Tm 3:15). The text permits the implied conviction that the Jewish Bible is inspired to be easily extended by the readers to the writings of the New Testament as well: "All scripture is inspired by God [πᾶσα γραφὴ θεόπνευστος] and is useful for teaching, for reproof, for correction, and for training in righteousness, so that everyone who belongs to God may be proficient, equipped for every good work" (2 Tm 3:16–17).

Cross-References

As I demonstrated above, the interest of the final redaction is to bridge the gap between Peter and Paul. The authorship of the Gospels bearing the names of Mark and Luke serves this interest as well, with vital reinforcement from 2 Timothy (see the discussion of Mark in the previous chapter). 2 Timothy also supplies the decisive piece of indirect evidence for the date of Acts. Dating the Book of Acts finally permits placement of the four Gospels in a relative chronological order, which further suggests that the Gospels are arranged chronologically (see the introduction to this chapter).

2 PETER

Within the General Letters, 2 Peter functions very much the way 2 Timothy does for readers of the Letters of Paul. This writing is the literary testament of Peter. In his second letter, the apostle addresses "those who have received a faith very much like ours [ἰσότιμον ἡμῖν πίστιν]" (2 Pt 1:1). No geographical information and no names of specific persons are given. This makes it easier for readers of the Canonical Edition to identify with the addressee. They already know who Peter is from the stories of the Gospels and Acts. These stories provide the frame in which the brief references to

Peter in 1 Corinthians and Galatians may be understood. Readers will assume that these comments refer to the same person who authored 1 Peter.

Gospel According to John

Following the opening paragraphs, where "precious and very great promises" (2 Pt 1:4) are mentioned—a reference to the Jewish Scriptures—Peter reflects upon his personal situation: "I know that my death will come soon, as indeed our Lord Jesus Christ has made clear to me" (2 Pt 1:14). Readers are familiar with Jesus' prophecy to which Peter refers in Jn 21:18: "When you grow old, you will stretch out your hands, and someone else will fasten a belt around you and take you where you do not wish to go." Moreover, they know how the editors of the Gospel According to John expect them to understand this promise: Jesus "said this to indicate the kind of death by which he would glorify God" (Jn 21:19a).[18]

Gospel According to Mark

In the next sentence, Peter states that he wants to pass his message along to future generations. Aware of his impending death, he writes, "And I will make every effort so that after my departure you may be able at any time to recall these things" (2 Pt 1:15). The readers may safely assume that Peter is talking about a literary legacy, since the expression "that you should remember [ἔχειν ὑμᾶς τὴν τούτων μνήμην]" is repeated later as an explicit reference to Peter's writings: "In both letters . . . I am reminding you, that you should remember (ἐν αἷς διεγείρω . . . ἐν ὑπομνήσει . . . μνησθῆναι]" (2 Pt 3:1b-2a).[19] Since the Canonical Edition displays a special interest in the writings of the apostle Peter, readers may further assume that the writing referred to is part of the Canonical Edition, though obviously not published under Peter's name. Once these conclusions are reached, it is not difficult to identify the literary legacy of Peter as the Gospel According to Mark. Among the New Testament authors, Mark is the only disciple of an apostle who is linked to Peter in the text.[20]

Readers may feel that these conclusions are confirmed by two corroborating observations. The expression "I will make every effort [σπουδάσω]" (2 Pt 1:15) supports the notion that Peter did not write down his recollections himself but commissioned this work to someone else.[21] Concerning the contents of this legacy, in the following sentence Peter insists that he and others "did not follow cleverly devised myths [σεσοφισμένοις μύθοις] . . . but we had been eyewitnesses [ἐπόπται γενηθέντες] of his majesty" (2 Pt 1:16). This describes the claim of the canonical Gospel collection very precisely: it intends to narrate the ministry of Jesus based on the reliable testimony of eyewitnesses.[22]

The conjecture that Peter is referring to a canonical Gospel becomes certainty for readers of the Canonical Edition when Peter clearly recalls the account of the Transfiguration, which is reported in Mt 17:1–9, Mk 9:2–10, and Lk 9:28–36.[23]

2 Peter 1:17–18

For he received honor and glory from God the Father when that voice was conveyed to him by the Majestic Glory, saying, "This is my Son, my Beloved, with whom I am well pleased."[24] We ourselves heard this voice come from heaven, while we were with him on the holy mountain.	λαβὼν γὰρ παρὰ θεοῦ πατρὸς τιμὴν καὶ δόξαν φωνῆς ἐνεχθείσης αὐτῷ τοιᾶσδε ὑπὸ τῆς μεγαλοπρεποῦς δόξης, Ὁ υἱός μου ὁ ἀγαπητός μου οὗτός ἐστιν, εἰς ὃν ἐγὼ εὐδόκησα, καὶ ταύτην τὴν φωνὴν ἡμεῖς ἠκούσαμεν ἐξ οὐρανοῦ ἐνεχθεῖσαν σὺν αὐτῷ ὄντες ἐν τῷ ἁγίῳ ὄρει.

This reference to the account of the Transfiguration prepares the readers for another, very remarkable cross-reference to the first part of the Canonical Edition, the Old Testament.

Old Testament

Peter continues with the words "So we have the prophetic message more fully confirmed. You will do well to be attentive to this" (2 Pt 1:19). A classical theological statement about the inspiration of Scripture follows: "First of all you must understand this, that no prophecy of scripture is a matter of one's own interpretation [πᾶσα προφητεία γραφῆς ἰδίας ἐπιλύσεως οὐ γίνεται], because no prophecy ever came by human will, but men and women moved by the Holy Spirit spoke from God [ὑπὸ πνεύματος ἁγίου φερόμενοι ἐλάλησαν ἀπὸ θεοῦ ἄνθρωποι]" (2 Pt 1:20–21).

The meaning of the expression "prophecy of scripture [πᾶσα προφητεία γραφῆς]" (2 Pt 1:20) is defined by the immediate context. The following verse uses the term *prophecy* as a phenomenon of the past (2 Pt 1:21). It refers to the people and false prophets of that time (2 Pt 2:1), thus clearly marking the statement as a literary reference to Old Testament prophecy. The use of the key words προφητικὸς λόγος (1:19), προφητεία γραφῆς (1:20), προφητεία ποτέ (1:21), and ψευδοπροφῆται εν τῷ λαῷ (2:1) supports and strongly suggests this meaning.[25]

These comments on the prophecy of Scripture are introduced at a crucial point in the argument of 2 Peter. They form the transition to the warnings against false teachers that dominate the second chapter. The false teachers of the future (ψευδοδιδάσκαλοι) are paralleled to the false prophets of the past (ψευδοπροφῆται) mentioned in the Scriptures: "But false prophets also arose among the people, just as there will be false teachers among you" (2 Pt 2:1). This also implies a correspondence between the true prophets of the Old Testament and the true teachers of the present days. The connection between prophets and apostles is made more explicitly later in the letter: "You should remember the words spoken in the past by the holy prophets, and the commandment of the Lord and Savior spoken through your apostles" (2 Pt 3:2). Seen from this perspective, the inspired prophets are paralleled to the apostles who become inspired advocates of the tradition on Jesus.

After referring to the key word *prophecy* (2 Pt 2:1) in this way, the second chapter demonstrates the relevance of Old Testament passages by offering readers a list of representative examples. God did not spare the angels when they sinned (Gn 6:1–4), but he preserved Noah (Gn 6:5–10:32); he condemned Sodom and Gomorrah, but he rescued righteous Lot (Gn 19:1–29). These are reliable accounts, Peter argues, of how God acted in history. These actions have significance for the situation of the readers of 2 Peter.[26] Just as God acted in the past, he will act in the future.

Letter of Jude

2 Peter shares a parallel structure, content, and vocabulary with the Letter of Jude. The similarity is so striking it prompted Luther to say that Jude does not "contain anything special beyond pointing to the Second Epistle of Saint Peter, from which it has borrowed nearly all the words."[27] The source-critical question—which writing derived from the other—is not important to a reader-oriented interpretation as long as the texts themselves do not comment on the literary relationship. That is why the problem does not have to be solved in the context of this study. The numerous literary

parallels, however, seem significant in the context of the Canonical Edition. In particular, 2 Pt 2:1–18 and Jude 4–16 have very much in common.[28]

The two texts begin with a similar description of false teachers who will have to face God's coming judgment:

2 Pt 2:1–18 (*left*) and Jude 4–16 (*right*)

2 Pt 2:1–18	Jude 4–16
2:1 Ἐγένοντο δὲ καὶ ψευδοπροφῆται ἐν τῷ λαῷ ὡς καὶ ἐν ὑμῖν ἔσονται ψευδοδιδάσκαλοι, οἵτινες παρεισάξουσιν αἱρέσεις ἀπωλείας, καὶ τὸν ἀγοράσαντα αὐτοὺς ❶δεσπότην ❷ἀρνούμενοι, ἐπάγοντες ἑαυτοῖς ταχινὴν ἀπώλειαν.	**4** παρεισέδυσαν γάρ τινες ἄνθρωποι, οἱ πάλαι προγεγραμμένοι εἰς τοῦτο ❹τὸ κρίμα, ἀσεβεῖς, τὴν τοῦ θεοῦ ἡμῶν χάριτα μετατιθέντες εἰς ❸ἀσέλγειαν καὶ τὸν μόνον ❶δεσπότην καὶ κύριον ἡμῶν Ἰησοῦν Χριστὸν ❷ἀρνούμενοι.
2:2 καὶ πολλοὶ ἐξακολουθήσουσιν αὐτῶν ταῖς ❸ἀσελγείαις, δι᾽ οὓς ἡ ὁδὸς τῆς ἀληθείας βλασφημηθήσεται·	
2:3 καὶ ἐν πλεονεξίᾳ πλαστοῖς λόγοις ὑμᾶς ἐμπορεύσονται· οἷς ❹τὸ κρίμα ἔκπαλαι οὐκ ἀργεῖ, καὶ ἡ ἀπώλεια αὐτῶν οὐ νυστάζει.	

Three examples of God's judgment follow, two of which are shared by the texts: the sinful angels (2 Pt 2:4, Jude 6):

2 Pt	Jude
2:4 Εἰ γὰρ ὁ θεὸς ❶ἀγγέλων ἁμαρτησάντων οὐκ ἐφείσατο, ἀλλὰ σειραῖς ❷ζόφου ταρταρώσας παρέδωκεν ❸εἰς κρίσιν ❹τηρουμένους,	**5** Ὑπομνῆσαι δὲ ὑμᾶς βούλομαι, εἰδότας ὑμᾶς πάντα, ὅτι (ὁ) κύριος ἅπαξ λαὸν ἐκ γῆς Αἰγύπτου σώσας τὸ δεύτερον τοὺς μὴ πιστεύσαντας ἀπώλεσεν,
	6 ❶ἀγγέλους τε τοὺς μὴ τηρήσαντας τὴν ἑαυτῶν ἀρχὴν ἀλλὰ ἀπολιπόντας τὸ ἴδιον οἰκητήριον ❸εἰς κρίσιν μεγάλης ἡμέρας δεσμοῖς ἀϊδίοις ὑπὸ ❷ζόφον ❹τετήρηκεν·

and the example of Sodom and Gomorrah (2 Pt 2:6, Jude 7):

2:5 καὶ ἀρχαίου κόσμου οὐκ ἐφείσατο, ἀλλὰ ὄγδοον Νῶε δικαιοσύνης κήρυκα ἐφύλαξεν, κατακλυσμὸν κόσμῳ ἀσεβῶν ἐπάξας,

2:6 καὶ ❶πόλεις ❷Σοδόμων καὶ Γομόρρας τεφρώσας (καταστροφῇ) κατέκρινεν, ὑπόδειγμα μελλόντων ἀσεβέ(σ)ιν τεθεικώς,

7 ὡς ❷Σόδομα καὶ Γόμορρα καὶ αἱ περὶ αὐτὰς ❶πόλεις, τὸν ὅμοιον τρόπον τούτοις ἐκπορνεύσασαι καὶ ἀπελθοῦσαι ὀπίσω σαρκὸς ἑτέρας, πρόκεινται δεῖγμα πυρὸς αἰωνίου δίκην ὑπέχουσαι.

Next, Peter brings forth several accusations against false teachers. Two accusations, that they defile the flesh and reject authority, are found both in 2 Pt 2:10 and in Jude 8.

2:7 καὶ δίκαιον Λὼτ καταπονούμενον ὑπὸ τῆς τῶν ἀθέσμων ἐν ἀσελγείᾳ ἀναστροφῆς ἐρρύσατο·

2:8 βλέμματι γὰρ καὶ ἀκοῇ ὁ δίκαιος ἐγκατοικῶν ἐν αὐτοῖς ἡμέραν ἐξ ἡμέρας ψυχὴν δικαίαν ἀνόμοις ἔργοις ἐβασάνιζεν·

2:9 οἶδεν κύριος εὐσεβεῖς ἐκ πειρασμοῦ ῥύεσθαι, ἀδίκους δὲ εἰς ἡμέραν κρίσεως κολαζομένους τηρεῖν,

2:10 μάλιστα δὲ τοὺς ὀπίσω ❶σαρκὸς ἐν ἐπιθυμίᾳ ❷μιασμοῦ πορευομένους καὶ ❸κυριότητος καταφρονοῦντας. Τολμηταί, αὐθάδεις, ❹δόξας οὐ τρέμουσιν ❺βλασφημοῦντες,

8 Ὁμοίως μέντοι καὶ οὗτοι ἐνυπνιαζόμενοι ❶σάρκα μὲν ❷μιαίνουσιν, ❸κυριότητα δὲ ἀθετοῦσιν, ❹δόξας δὲ ❺βλασφημοῦσιν.

The next accusation, that the false teachers behave like irrational animals and that they revile matters of which they are ignorant, together with additional details, are shared by 2 Pt 2:12 and Jude 10.

2:11 ὅπου ἄγγελοι ἰσχύϊ καὶ δυνάμει μειζονες ὄντες οὐ φέρουσιν κατ´ αὐτῶν ταρὰ κυρίου ❶βλάσφημον ❷κρίσιν.

2:12 ❸οὗτοι δέ, ❹ὡς ἄλογα ζῷα γεγεννημένα ❺φυσικὰ εἰς ἅλωσιν καὶ φθοράν, ἐν οἷς ❻ἀγνοοῦσιν βλασφημοῦντες, ἐν τῇ φθορᾷ αὐτῶν καὶ ❼φθαρήσονται,

2:13–14 (⇨Jud 12)

9 ὁ δὲ Μιχαὴλ ὁ ἀρχάγγελος, ὅτε τῷ διαβόλῳ διακρινόμενος διελέγετο περὶ τοῦ Μωϋσέως σώματος, οὐκ ἐτόλμησεν ❷κρίσιν ἐπενεγκεῖν ❶βλασφημίας, ἀλλὰ εἶπεν, Ἐπιτμήσαι σοι κύριος.

10 ❸οὗτοι δὲ ὅσα μὲν ❻οὐκ οἴδασιν βλασφημοῦσιν, ὅσα δὲ ❺φυσικῶς ❹ὡς τὰ ἄλογα ζῷα ἐπίστανται, ἐν τούτοις ❼φθείρονται.

Finally, they are compared to Bileam both in 2 Pt 2:15–16 and in Jude 11.

2:15 καταλείποντες εὐθεῖαν ὁδὸν ἐπλανήθησαν, ἐξακολουθήσαντες ❶τῇ ὁδῷ ❷τοῦ Βαλαὰμ τοῦ Βοσόρ, ὃς ❸μισθὸν ἀδικίας ἠγάπησεν

2:16 ἔλεγξιν δὲ ἔσχεν ἰδίας παρανομίας· ὑποζύγιον ἄφωνον ἐν ἀνθρώπου φωνῇ φθεγξάμενον ἐκώλυσεν τὴν τοῦ προφήτου παραφρονίαν.

11 οὐαὶ αὐτοῖς, ὅτι ❶τῇ ὁδῷ τοῦ Κάϊν ἐπορεύθησαν, καὶ τῇ πλάνῃ ❷τοῦ Βαλαὰμ ❸μισθοῦ ἐξεχύθησαν, καὶ τῇ ἀντιλογίᾳ τοῦ Κόρε ἀπώλοντο.

Their carousing is criticized in both Jude 12a and 2 Pt 2:13. Two of the following images taken from nature (Jude 12b and 13) are found in 2 Pt 2:17 as well: waterless springs, and mists driven by the wind. The brief final sentence, indicating that for them the nether gloom of darkness has been reserved, has a literal parallel in Jude.

2:13 ἀδικούμένοι μισθὸν ἀδικίας· ἡδονὴν ἡγούμενοι τὴν ἐν ἡμέρᾳ τρυφήν, σπίλοι καὶ μῶμοι ἐντρυφῶντες ἐν ταῖς ἀπάταις αὐτῶν ❶συνευωχούμενοι ὑμῖν,

2:14 ὀφθαλμοὺς ἔχοντες μεστοὺς μοιχαλίδος καὶ

12 οὗτοί εἰσιν οἱ ἐν ταῖς ἀγάπαις ὑμῶν σπιλάδες ❶συνευωχούμενοι ἀφόβως, ἑαυτοὺς ποιμαίνοντες, νεφέλαι ❷ἄνυδροι ὑπὸ ἀνέμων παραφερόμεναι, δένδρα φθινοπωρινὰ ἄκαρπα δὶς ἀποθανόντα ἐκριζωθέντα,

ἀκαταπαύστους ἁμαρτίας,
δελεάζοντες ψυχὰς ἀστηρίκ-
τους, καρδίαν γεγυμνασμένην
πλεονεξίας ἔχοντες, κατάρας
τέκνα,

2:17 Οὗτοί εἰσιν πηγαὶ
❷ἄνυδροι καὶ ὁμίχλαι ὑπὸ
λαίλαπος ἐλαυνόμεναι, ❸οἷς ὁ
ζόφος τοῦ σκότους ❹τετήρηται.

13 κύματα ἄγρια θαλάσ-
σης ἐπαφρίζοντα τὰς ἑαυτῶν
αἰσχύνας, ἀστέρες πλανῆται
❸οἷς ὁ ζόφος τοῦ σκότους εἰς
αἰῶνα ❹τετήρηται.

The accusation, repeated several times, that they entice with licentious passions of the flesh (2 Pt 2:18) is found in Jude 16 as well.

2:18 ὑπέρογκα γὰρ ματαιό-
τητος φθεγγόμενοι δελεάζουσιν
ἐν ❶ἐπιθυμίαις σαρκὸς ἀσελ-
γείαις τοὺς ὀλίγως ἀποφεύγον-
τας τοὺς ἐν πλάνῃ ἀναστ-
ρεφομένους . . .

14 Προεφήτευσεν δὲ καὶ
τούτοις ἕβδομος ἀπὸ Ἀδὰμ
Ἑνὼχ λέγων, Ἰδοὺ ἦλθεν κύριος
ἐν ἁγίαις μυριάσιν αὐτοῦ,

15 ποιῆσαι κρίσιν κατὰ πάντων
καὶ ἐλέγξαι πᾶσαν ψυχὴν περὶ
πάντων τῶν ἔργων ἀσεβείας
αὐτῶν ὧν ἠσέβησαν καὶ περὶ
πάντων τῶν σκληρῶν ὧν
ἐλάλησαν κατ᾽ αὐτοῦ ἁμαρτωλοὶ
ἀσεβεῖς.

16 Οὗτοί εἰσιν γογγυσταί,
μεμψίμοιροι, κατὰ τὰς ❶ἐπι-
θυμίας ἑαυτῶν πορευόμενοι,
καὶ τὸ στόμα αὐτῶν λαλεῖ
ὑπέρογκα, θαυμάζοντες
πρόσωπα ὠφελείας χάριν.

Readers of the Canonical Edition are accustomed to parallels. While they do not use exactly the same words, the traditions shared by the four Gospels are understood as agreeing on the essential matter. In this way, they confirm the reliability of these writings. The same applies to the parallel accounts in the Letters of Paul and Acts, or to the Transfiguration on the mountain, which 2 Peter (1:17–18) describes differently from any of the Gospels. The cross-references of the titles link Jude and his brother James to the circle of Jerusalem apostles around Peter. Paul, who in 1 Cor 9:5 mentions Peter together with the brothers of Jesus, endorses this connection explicitly. The close parallels between Jude and 2 Peter may simply provide another confirmation of what readers of the Canonical Edition already know: the apostle Peter and Jude, the brother of Jesus, knew each other very well.

1 Peter

The next writing readers of 2 Peter are referred to is 1 Peter. "This is now, beloved, the second letter I am writing to you" (2 Pt 3:1), Peter reminds them, quoting the accurate title in the Canonical Edition: Second Letter of Peter. At the same time, he implies the title of 1 Peter, and he assumes that it is familiar to the readers. As far as the content is concerned, the two letters are treated as a unit: "In them [ἐν αἷς] I am trying to arouse your sincere intention by reminding you . . ." (2 Pt 3:1).

Letters of Paul

Another vital interest of the final redaction of the Canonical Edition is expressed in the third chapter of 2 Peter. The editors seek to harmonize Peter and Paul.[29]

> 2 Pt 3:15b-16
> So also our beloved brother Paul wrote to you according to the wisdom given him, speaking of this as he does in all his letters. There are some things in them hard to understand which the ignorant and unstable twist to their own destruction, as they do the other scriptures.

Peter refers to Paul with a positive connotation; he calls him their beloved brother (ὁ ἀγαπητὸς ἡμῶν ἀδελφός) and states that Paul is in complete agreement with him. Any difficulties are discarded as misrepresentations of "things hard to understand [δυσνόητά τινα]," promoted by people who are "unstable" and who twist "the other scriptures [τὰς λοιπὰς γραφάς]" as well. By using the expression "other scriptures," the author presupposes a limited number of writings. The collection the author has in mind evidently contained the Letters of Paul together with other books. Readers of the Canonical Edition will immediately think of the writings of the Old and New Testament.[30]

Peter takes it for granted that the people he is writing to are the same people Paul wrote his letters for (ἔγραψεν ὑμῖν). Moreover, his reference to "all his letters [ἐν πάσαις ἐπιστολαῖς]," taken literally, implies a comprehensive edition of Paul's letters. To readers of the Canonical Edition this reference should not cause a problem. They may safely assume that the New Testament collection entitled "Letters of Paul" represents just that comprehensive edition. And they would learn that 2 Peter had been written after the Book of Acts and 2 Timothy, at a time when the Pauline letter collection was complete and already published.

1 Thessalonians and Revelation of John

I should at least mention two more passages that might also serve to encourage readers to establish cross-references to other New Testament writings.

"The day of the Lord will come like a thief [Ἥξει δὲ ἡμέρα κυρίου ὡς κλέπτης]" (2 Pt 3:10) may recall 1 Thes 5:2, "For you yourselves know very well that the day of the Lord will come like a thief in the night [οἴδατε ὅτι ἡμέρα κυρίου ὡς κλέπτης ἐν νυκτὶ οὕτως ἔρχεται]."[31]

The second allusion is the promise of new heavens and a new earth, which recalls Rv 21:1, where this promise is repeated. However, it might just as well be understood as a reference to Is 65:17 or Is 66:12.

Cross-References

When 2 Peter is read as an integrated part of the Canonical Edition of the Christian Bible, the apparent cross-references to the collection units are quite astonishing. The Old Testament is quoted abundantly. Biblical prophecy is explicitly addressed, its relevance for the present time of the readers is demonstrated, and it is related to a theology of divine inspiration formulated in a manner easily applied to other New Testament writings as well. The letter clearly refers to the canonical Gospel collection by pointing to John (Jn 21), Mark, and the synoptic account of the Transfiguration. The references to 1 Peter and Jude serve as links to the Praxapostolos. It presupposes that the readers have access to a comprehensive collection of Paul's letters. In addition to these literary links, the treatment of Peter and Paul as equals is another trait 2 Peter shares with the editorial interest of the Canonical Edition.

I hope to have demonstrated that the interest of the editors of the Canonical Edition as derived from the editorial frame can be found in the text of Acts, 2 Timothy, and 2 Peter as well. This observation supports the view that the Canonical Edition represents a careful selection of writings. Passages that in some way harmonize the conflict between Paul and the Jerusalem authorities were included in the collection. In this context, it may be significant that the New "Testament" contains a literary "testament" of Paul and a literary "testament" of Peter.

GOSPEL ACCORDING TO JOHN

The Gospel According to John reaches a preliminary end at the close of chapter 20.

> Jn 20:30–31
> Now Jesus did many other signs in the presence of his disciples, which are not written in this book [οὐκ ἔστιν γεγραμμένα ἐν τῷ βιβλίῳ τούτῳ]. But these are written so that you may come to believe that Jesus is the Messiah, the Son of God, and that through believing you may have life in his name.

In addition, at the end of chapter 21 we hear a voice different from the author of the Fourth Gospel, who is referred to as "this . . . disciple."

> Jn 21:24
> This is the disciple who is testifying to these things and has written them [ὁ γράψας ταῦτα], and we know that his testimony is true.

From the readers' perspective there is little room to doubt that someone is talking about the author of the Gospel that has just been read. This voice explicitly points out that the author is not only an eyewitness, whose oral report has been used, but also the person who actually wrote this Gospel down. Now, if readers search for a point in the text where the written testimony of John ended, they will almost certainly consider Jn 20:30–31, the passage mentioned above. Readers might be encouraged to do so if they observe that John closes his other book, the Revelation of John, with a similar reference: "I warn everyone who hears the words of the prophecy of this book [τοῦ βιβλίου τούτου]" (Rv 22:18–19). In Jn 21, however, the publisher of the Gospel According to John is speaking.

Several questions regarding Jn 21 have given rise to lively controversy. Is Jn 21 simply an appendix to a finished Gospel? Or is this chapter so closely linked to the preceding work as to indicate text alterations in chapters 1–20?[32] These questions are crucial for any attempt to reconstruct the literary sources, but the answers make little difference if this Gospel is viewed from the perspective of the Canonical Edition. The fact that the uniform manuscript tradition of the Canonical Edition does not contain manuscripts without Jn 21 indicates that this chapter was part of the archetype of this edition. From the very beginning readers encountered this chapter as an integral part of the Gospel. And it is just as clear that readers were informed that these last passages of this Gospel were written by someone other than the beloved disciple. The publisher does not disguise himself as the author—a literary device that was quite common in pseudepigraphic literature. Rather, he introduces himself or herself to the readers. The last sentence of the canonical Gospel collection presents itself as an editorial note to the readers.

John 21:25, the Last Sentence of the Canonical Four-Gospel Book

The last sentence of the Gospel According to John reads:

> Jn 21:25
> But there are also many other things that Jesus did; if every one of them were written down, I suppose that the world itself could not contain the books that would be written.

For several reasons, this sentence is crucial for a reader-oriented interpretation of the New Testament.

1. The change from first person plural, "we know that his testimony is true," in 21:24 to first person singular, "I suppose," in 21:25 indicates that these two verses are not to be read in one breath. They seem to point to different subjects.[33]
2. The mention of multiple "books" (τὰ γραφόμενα βιβλία) as opposed to the one book in Jn 20:30 (ἐν τῷ βιβλίῳ τούτῳ) signifies that this sentence does not talk about John's Gospel alone but refers to several books.
3. The contents of what could be "written down" is referred to as "things that Jesus did [ἃ ἐποίησεν ὁ Ἰησοῦς]." In all modern

> editions of the New Testament, the Book of Acts follows Jn 21. The implied author, Luke, repeats this literary definition to point back to his own Gospel: "I wrote about all that Jesus did [λόγος περὶ πάντων ὧν ἤρξατο ὁ Ἰησοῦς ποιεῖν]" (Acts 1:1). From a reader's perspective this may create an important cross-reference between Jn 21:25 and Acts 1:1. Both texts seem to refer to canonical Gospels.

The close connection to the preceding sentence plus the strong resemblance in wording to Jn 20:30 suggest that the publishers of the canonical Gospel collection are identical with the publishers of the Gospel According to John. The first person singular ("I suppose") indicates that the publishers of the canonical Gospel collection assumed that they were well known to their readership. The *editio princeps* was not put out anonymously.

ℵ 01 and John 21:25

Some scribes copying New Testament manuscripts might have felt the break between Jn 21:24 and 21:25. The first hand of Codex Sinaiticus (ℵ 01) originally added a colophon and the subscription ευαγγελιον κατα ιωαννην. "Later on, however, the scribe washed the vellum clean and added the concluding verse, repeating the coronis and subscription in a corresponding lower position"[34] (see figs. 6 and 7).

Considering the uniform tradition of this text passage in the manuscripts, it seems very unlikely that Jn 21:25 was missing in the *Vorlage* of Codex Sinaiticus.[35] However, for some reason—whether external or internal—this scribe of the Sinaiticus originally did not seem to regard the verse as part of John's Gospel. This conjecture is supported by two miniscules[36] that conclude the Gospel with Jn 21:24 and place Jn 21:25 on a new page.

Cross-References

Earlier in this study a close link was established between the title of John's Gospel and its final chapter.[37] By following the references of Jn 21:24 to the synoptic Gospels of the Canonical Edition it became possible to identify the John mentioned in the title as John, son of Zebedee. This identification consequently informed readers about the

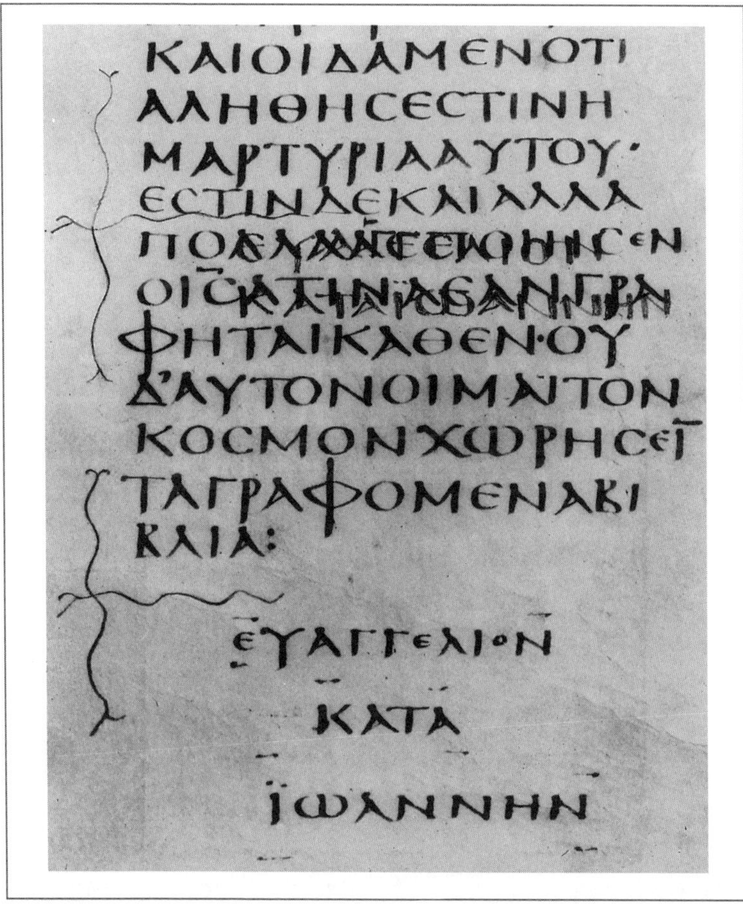
ΚΑΙΟΙΔΑΜΕΝΟΤΙ
ΑΛΗΘΗCΕCΤΙΝΗ
ΜΑΡΤΥΡΙΑΑΥΤΟΥ·
ΕCΤΙΝΔΕΚΑΙΑΛΛΑ
ΠΟΛΛΑΕΠΟΙΗCΕΝ
ΟΙCΑΤΙΝΑΕΑΝΓΡΑ
ΦΗΤΑΙΚΑΘΕΝΟΥ
ΔΑΥΤΟΝΟΙΜΑΪΤΟΝ
ΚΟCΜΟΝΧΩΡΗCΕΙ
ΤΑΓΡΑΦΟΜΕΝΑΒΙ
ΒΛΙΑ:
ΕΥΑΓΓΕΛΙΟΝ
ΚΑΤΑ
ΪΩΑΝΝΗΝ

Figure 6. Codex Sinaiticus, conclusion of the Gospel According to John, examined by ultraviolet light. Photo courtesy of the British Library, London.

authorship of the Letters of John and the Revelation of John. The authorship of John links the Gospels to the Praxapostolos and to the Book of Revelation.

Furthermore, the location of John's Gospel within the Canonical Edition makes sense for the Praxapostolos as a collection unit. At first glance, it is not obvious why Luke's Gospel and Luke's Acts of the Apostles should be separated by the Gospel of John. However, the placement of John seems

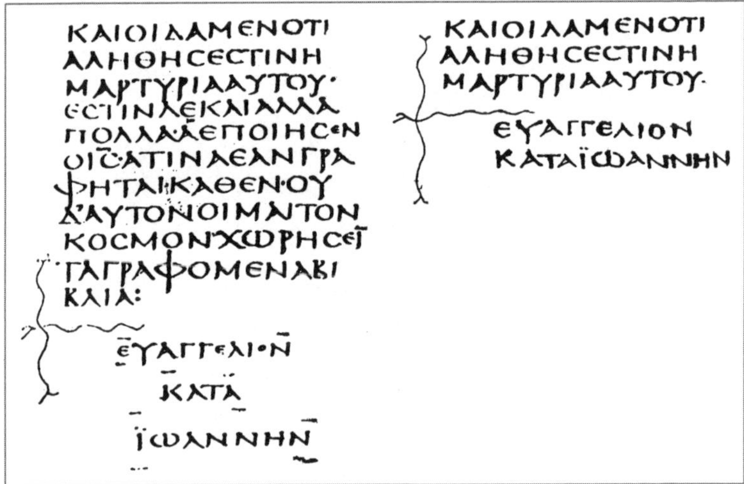

Figure 7. Corrected text (*left*) and reconstruction of the first hand (*right*), Codex Sinaiticus, conclusion of the Gospel According to John.

intentional if the editors of the four Gospels wanted to arrange them chronologically. By adding their editorial note to the Gospel According to John, they are presenting this Gospel as the most recent of the collection. The placement would also make sense if they wanted to connect Acts with the General Letters.

Jn 21 becomes the last text passage added to the Canonical Edition if one makes two assumptions, both of which are entirely plausible from a reader's perspective. The first is that Peter's martyrdom, which John's Gospel refers to as in the past, and Paul's martyrdom took place at roughly the same time.[38] The second assumption is that John had survived James and Jude, brothers of Jesus.

The most important formal feature of an editorial is that it presents itself as the last passage added to an edition. From the readers' perspective that is exactly what Jn 21 looks like. Moreover, if Jn 21:25 is understood as referring to the Four-Gospel Book, it may further be linked to the Canonical Edition as such, thus serving as an editorial note to the readers of what today is called the Christian Bible, consisting of the Old and New Testaments. By choosing the words *books* and *the world* and first person singular, the unnamed publisher alludes to his or her act of publication. And therefore the last sentence [Jn 21:25: ἐὰν γράφηται καθ᾽ ἕν, οὐδ᾽ αὐτὸν οἶμαι τὸν κόσμον χωρῆσαι τὰ γραφόμενα βιβλία] could very well be translated as:

> But there are also many other things that Jesus did; if every one of them were published, I suppose that the world itself could not contain the books that would be published.

5

Outlook

MODERN EDITIONS

How could the results of this investigation influence modern printed editions of the Christian Bible?

Although the text of the New Testament was considered sacred very early, it was not considered unethical to make changes. There is probably no one verse of the New Testament that has exactly the same wording in every one of the extant Greek manuscripts.

Proposed Goals of Text Criticism

The exact wording of both the Jewish Bible and the Koran are regarded as vitally important by their respective communities. Evidently, the early Christian community did not share this emphasis. Numerous variants in the Greek text and full acceptance of translations in the practice of the Christian church indicate that the exact wording of the text is not the most essential conceptual element of the Canonical Edition. In fact, as we have seen, the title *New Testament* points to 2 Cor 3, where readers are informed that the New Testament is not to be treated as sacred "letters." God "has made us competent to be ministers of a New Testament, not of letter but of spirit. For the letter kills, but the Spirit gives life" (2 Cor 3:6). The exact wording of the text is of little importance compared with other features of the Canonical Edition. The essential characteristics can still be described, and they should be reflected in modern printed editions of the Christian Bible. Modern textual criticism should strive to produce an edition of the Greek text that closely represents the *editio princeps* of the

Canonical Edition. The original intent should be respected not only as far as peculiarities of the text are concerned but also, more important, with regard to the redactional frame of this carefully designed work. With this goal in mind, I would propose that several changes be incorporated in modern editions of the Christian Bible.

New Testament

Modern printed editions of the Christian Bible should reflect the collection units and the arrangement of the writings in the *editio princeps*. For the New Testament, this means that the literary unit of the Four-Gospel Book, the Praxapostolos, the Letters of Paul, and the Revelation of John should be preserved. The titles of these units could be included in the table of contents, repeated on a separate page or at the end of each unit: ευαγγελιοι δ', πραξεις αποστολων και επιστολαι καθολικαι ζ', επιστολαι Παυλου ιδ', αποκαλυψις Ιωαννου. It seems especially important not to separate the Acts of the Apostles from the General Letters.

The arrangement of these four collection units varies in the manuscripts. Given the editorial concept of the Canonical Edition, it seems appropriate to start out with the Gospel collection because it contains the editorial note to the readers of the edition (Jn 21:25). The Praxapostolos and the Letters of Paul may follow, because of the close connection between the Gospels and because Acts introduces the readers to the authors of the General Letters in its first part and to Paul in its second part. Revelation of John fits the end nicely because of the concluding remarks (Rv. 22:18–22).

In this case, the writings of the Old Testament may be arranged in a corresponding way: historical writings, poetic writings, and prophetic writings. It might prove appropriate to use this arrangement for translations as well.

Furthermore, the Letter to the Hebrews should appear as the last letter of Paul to congregations, placed after 2 Thessalonians and before 1 Timothy.

Old Testament

It seems desirable to try to create an edition of the Greek Old and New Testaments showing the same final redaction. The New Testament is only the second, much shorter part of the Canonical Edition. The same editorial committee who worked on the New Testament should be given responsibility for an edition of the Greek Old Testament, containing the same abbreviations and the same apparatus and following the same editorial guidelines. Such an edition could help modern readers of the Canonical Edition experience the Christian Bible as a literary unit more than any other measures.

Furthermore, it should be made clear that a Greek Old Testament from the Canonical Edition is quite different from the Hebrew Bible and the Jewish Septuagint. Often this difference is not addressed or adequately reflected in today's academic practice. An obvious difference from the Hebrew Bible is that the Christian Old Testament contains more writings that are included without negative discernment. The Canonical Edition differs from the Septuagint by including Daniel in the translation attributed to Theodotion and by introducing the *nomina sacra.*

It is not my intention to reduce its value for scholarly studies of the Bible, but it must be acknowledged that the Masoretic edition of the Hebrew Bible does not represent the edition used by early Christianity. It is unlikely that the Masoretic archetype was created specifically to combat Christianity. Still, this text form was preserved and cherished by the Jewish community in contrast to, and in competition with, the Christian Old Testament ever since the Canonical Edition was published.[1] The Roman Catholic Church has preserved, through the Vulgate, the *editio princeps* of the Christian Bible more faithfully than their Protestant sisters and brothers as far as the number and arrangement of writings are concerned. The objective of Christian exegesis must be to take seriously the self-understanding of the Old Testament in its canonical form. At the same time, in order to assess its theological significance, we must acknowledge the historical fact that it has a twofold *Wirkungsgeschichte*, both Jewish and Christian.[2]

Nomina Sacra

For more than thirteen centuries the *nomina sacra* formed a characteristic redactional element of the Christian Bible and identified Christian literature. Modern editions should preserve this old tradition and represent the *nomina sacra*. They are a significant feature of the *editio princeps.* They do not obstruct the reading process. At least the four generally noted terms—$\overline{\kappa\varsigma}$, $\overline{\theta\varsigma}$, $\overline{\iota\varsigma}$, and $\overline{\chi\varsigma}$—and, in addition, the staurogram should be reintroduced into printed editions.

THE READERSHIP OF THE CANONICAL EDITION

I want to end this study with reflections on the readership of the Canonical Edition.

First, it is worth noting that, through references to geographical regions, the two literary testaments of Paul and Peter connect Rome and Asia Minor. 2 Peter is sent from Rome to all the congregations in Asia Minor; Paul writes 2 Timothy in Rome and sends this letter to Ephesus. Presupposing that the editors were trying to satisfy a specific interest on the part of their readers, we may look for a situation in the middle of the second century when the church in Asia Minor communicated with Rome. Two such situations are easily identified. In both regions the churches struggled with and finally rejected the movement formed under the leadership of Marcion, first in Asia Minor and later in Rome. In addition, these two regions could not agree on a common procedure to fix the date of Easter, giving rise to the so-called Easter Controversy.

It has already been demonstrated that the redactional concept of the Canonical Edition reflects an anti-Marcionite attitude.

A link between the canonical collection of Gospels and the Easter Controversy is just as easily established. Whereas Jesus was executed in the afternoon before the celebration of Passover, according to John's Gospel (Jn 18:28, 19:31), the synoptic Gospels report that Jesus celebrated the Passover meal with the disciples and died the following day. These two statements are placed next to each other within the Tetraeuangelion without being harmonized. They contradict each other.

Congregations in Asia Minor honored the tradition of the Gospel According to John. They celebrated the day of Jesus' death parallel to the Jewish Passover on the fourteenth day of the moon, no matter which day of the week this happened to be. Most other churches, however, insisted on the practice of celebrating the Resurrection of the Lord on no other day but Sunday (Eusebius, *h.e.* 5:23). Accordingly, the death of Jesus was always commemorated on a Friday. Although the two sides repeatedly tried to find a common solution, the church did not succeed in establishing a worldwide uniform date for Easter. Consequently, Christians were not able to observe a common fasting practice during the second century. Each party maintained its custom and tried to live in peace with the other. Irenaeus puts it this way: "The disagreement in the fast confirms our agreement in the faith" (Eusebius, *h.e.* 5:23:1). The literary solution in the canonical Tetraeuangelion perfectly represents this attitude. Instead of selecting one Gospel and declaring one tradition as authoritative, four Gospels are placed next to each other, forming the canonical Gospel collection. The unity of the gospel (*euangelion*) is based on the diversity of the four (*tetra*). The New Testament is spirit, not letter.

The atmosphere created by the conflict with the Marcionite movement and the Easter Controversy contains characteristic features of the implied readership of the Canonical Edition. The edition portrays Paul and the Jerusalem authorities in harmonious unity, presuming that the readers are conscious of the worldwide unity of the church. The success of this publication did not depend on an authoritative decision of the church; rather, readers found their convictions better expressed in the Canonical Edition than in competing literary works. During hard times of persecution, this book was capable of defining or reinforcing the identity and the unity of its readers. At the end of the second century and in the beginning of the third, Irenaeus was reading this edition in Lyons; Tertullian read it in Carthage and Asia Minor; Clement had it in Alexandria, and Origen in Palestine. This particular edition, in other words, was read worldwide.

The history of the Christian Bible is the history of a literary classic. Like every classic work, the Canonical Edition must be received, reconstituted, and published afresh by each generation. I hope that this study will be a contribution to this constant process of rereading and rewriting.

Notes

CHAPTER 1: INTRODUCTION

"Four-Gospel Book," "Letters of Paul," and "Praxapostolos" (combining Acts and General Letters) are capitalized when referring to the respective collection in the Canonical Edition.

1. B. F. Westcott, *A General Survey of the History of the Canon of the New Testament*, 6th ed. (Cambridge: Macmillan, 1889).

2. A. Loisy, *Histoire du canon du Nouveau Testament* (Paris, 1891; reprint, Frankfurt: Minerva, 1971).

3. Th. Zahn, *Geschichte des Neutestamentlichen Kanons*, vol. 1: *Das Neue Testament vor Origenes* (Erlangen: Deichert, 1888/1889); vol. 2: *Urkunden und Belege zum ersten und dritten Band* (Erlangen: Deichert, 1890/1892; reprint, New York: Olms 1975).

4. A. v. Harnack, *Die Entstehung des Neuen Testamentes und die wichtigsten Folgen der neuen Schöpfung* (Leipzig: Hinrichs, 1914). Of particular interest is Harnack's discussion of Th. Zahn's first volume: A. v. Harnack, *Das Neue Testament um das Jahr 200* (Freiburg: Mohr, 1889).

5. B. S. Childs, *The New Testament as Canon: An Introduction* (London: SCM Press, 1984; Philadelphia: Fortress, 1985).

6. Childs received much attention with his *Introduction to the Old Testament as Scripture* (Philadelphia: Fortress, 1979); see M. G. Brett, *Biblical Criticism in Crisis? The Impact of the Canonical Approach on Old Testament Studies* (Cambridge: Cambridge University Press, 1991); Ch. H. Scobie, "The Challenge of Biblical Theology," *Tyndale Bulletin* 42 (1991): 33–61. Childs summarized his theological conclusion in 1992: *Biblical Theology of the Old and New Testaments: Theological Reflection on the Christian Bible* (London: SCM Press, 1992).

7. Childs, *New Testament as Canon*, 18. K. Aland, "Das Problem der Anonymität und Pseudonymität in der christlichen Literatur der ersten beiden Jahrhun-

derte," in *Studien zur Überlieferung des Neuen Testaments und seines Textes*, ANTF 2 (Berlin: De Gruyter, 1967), 26, writes: The uniform canon of the New Testament "ist erst am Ausgang des 4.Jahrhunderts als Resultat eines langwierigen und komplizierten Prozesses in einer Reihe von Kirchenprovinzen erreicht worden, hat aber noch Jahrhunderte gebraucht, bis sie sich überall durchgesetzt hat." Other critical approaches may be placed within this extended frame as well, such as A. C. Sundberg, who challenged the dating of the Muratorian Canon as a second-century document; see A. C. Sundberg, "Towards a Revised History of the New Testament Canon," *Studia Evangelica* 4; *TU* 102 (1968): 452–61; *The Old Testament of the Early Church* (Cambridge: Harvard University Press, 1964); "Canon Muratori: A Fourth-Century List," *HThR* 66 (1973): 1–41; "Canon of the New Testament," supplementary volume, *Interpreter's Dictionary of the Bible* (Nashville: Abingdon, 1976); "The Bible Canon and the Christian Doctrine of Inspiration," *Interpretation* 29 (1975): 352–71. The late date of the Muratorian Canon has been supported by G. M. Hahneman's extensive study, *The Muratorian Fragment and the Development of the Canon*, Oxford Theological Monographs (Oxford: Clarendon, 1992).

8. Sundberg, "Revised History," 459–460.

9. See K. Aland, "Das Problem des neutestamentlichen Kanons," in *Studien zur Überlieferung des Neuen Testaments und seines Textes*, ANTF 2 (1967), 1–23; "Falsche Verfasserangaben? Zur Pseudonymität im frühchristlichen Schrifttum," *Th Rv* 75 (1979): 1–10; "Noch einmal: Das Problem der Anonymität und Pseudonymität in der christlichen Literatur der ersten beiden Jahrhunderte," *Pietas: Festschrift für Bernhard Kötting*, JAC.E 8 (1980), 121–39 (126). Aland contends that this epoch ended with Justin in the middle of the second century. The same view is held by K. M. Fischer, "Anmerkung zur Pseudepigraphie im Neuen Testament," *NTS* 23 (1977): 76–81; H. Kraft, "Das besondere Selbstbewußtsein der Verfasser der Neutestamentlichen Schriften," in *Moderne Exegese und historische Wissenschaft*, ed. J. M. Hollenbach and Hugo Staudinger (Trier: Spee, 1972), 77–93.

10. Research on this time period is extensive; see updated bibliographies in F. F. Bruce, *The Canon of Scripture* (Downers Grove, Il.: Inter Varsity Press, 1988); Childs, *New Testament as Canon*; A. F. J. Klijn, "Die Entstehungsgeschichte des Neuen Testaments," *ANRW* 2,26,1 (1992): 64–97; B. M. Metzger, *The Canon of the New Testament: Its Origin, Development, and Significance* (Oxford: Clarendon, 1987; reprint, 1997). The following presents a selection of pertinent individual treatments: B. Aland, "Die Rezeption des neutestamentlichen Textes in den ersten Jahrhunderten," in *The New Testament in Early Christianity*, BEThL 86 (Leuven: Leuven University Press, 1989), 1–38; Ch. P. Anderson, "The Epistle to the

Hebrews and the Pauline Letter Collection," *HThR* 59 (1966): 429–38 (interesting methodological approach); R. Beckwith, *The Old Testament Canon of the New Testament Church and Its Background in Early Judaism* (Grand Rapids, Mich.: Eerdmans, 1985); G. G. Blum, *Tradition und Sukzession: Studie zum Normbegriff des Apostolischen von Paulus bis Irenäus*, Arbeiten zur Geschichte und Theologie des Luthertums 9 (Berlin: Lutherisches Verlagshaus, 1963); F. F. Bruce, "Some Thoughts on the Beginning of the New Testament Canon," *Bulletin of the John Rylands University Library* 65 (Manchester, 1982–83): 37–60; Ch. H. Cosgrove, "Justin Martyr and the Emerging Christian Canon: Observations on the Purpose and Destination of the Dialogue with Trypho," *VigChr* 36 (1982): 209–32; I. Frank, *Der Sinn der Kanonbildung: Eine historisch-theologische Untersuchung der Zeit vom 1. Clemensbrief bis Irenäus von Lyon*, Freiburger Theologische Studien 90 (Freiburg: Herder, 1971); J. Hoh, *Die Lehre des Hl. Irenäus über das Neue Testament*, Neutestamentliche Abhandlungen 7 (Münster: Aschendorffsche Verlagsbuchhandlung, 1919); E. R. Kalin, "Re-examining New Testament Canon History: 1. The Canon of Origin," *Currents in Theology and Mission* (Chicago) 17 (1990): 274–82; J. Knox, *Marcion and the New Testament: An Essay in the Early History of the Canon* (Chicago: University of Chicago Press, 1942); H. Paulsen, "Die Bedeutung des Montanismus für die Herausbildung des Kanons," *VigChr* 32 (1978): 19–52; A. M. Ritter, "Die Entstehung des neutestamentlichen Kanons: Selbstdurchsetzung oder autoritative Entscheidung?" in *Kanon und Zensur: Beiträge zur Archäologie der literarischen Kommunikation*, 2, ed. Aleida Assman and Jan Assman (München: Fink, 1987); Ritter "Zur Kanonbildung in der alten Kirche," in *Charisma und Caritas: Patristische Aufsätze* (Göttingen: Vanderhoeck, 1993); A. Sand, *Kanon: Von den Anfängen bis zum Fragmentum Muratorianum*, Handbuch der Dogmengeschichte 1,3a,1 (Freiburg: Herder, 1974); F. Stuhlhofer, *Der Gebrauch der Bibel von Jesus bis Euseb: Eine statistische Untersuchung zur Kanonsgeschichte* (Wuppertal: R. Brockhaus, 1988).

11. H. v. Campenhausen, *Die Entstehung der christlichen Bibel*, BHTh 39 (1968), later published as *The Formation of the Christian Bible* (Philadelphia: Fortress, 1972), still represents a milestone in the history of research and serves as a reference work for all later studies. Here is a selection of more recent discussions on the history of the canon in general: K.-H. Ohlig, *Die theologische Begründung des neutestamentlichen Kanons in der alten Kirche* (Düsseldorf: Patmos, 1972); F. Hahn, "Die Heilige Schrift als älteste christliche Tradition und als Kanon," *Evangelische Theologie* 40 (1980): 456–66; D. Lührmann, "Gal 2,9 und die katholischen Briefe: Bemerkungen zum Kanon und zur regula fidei," *ZNW* 72 (1981): 65–87; W. R. Farmer and D. M. Farkasfalvy, *The Formation of the New Testament Canon* (New York: Paulist Press, 1983); H. Gamble, *The New Testament Canon: Its Making and Meaning* (Philadelphia: Fortress, 1985).

12. Frank, *Kanonbildung*, 9, organizes suggestions made during the twentieth century into four groups: "(a) die Autopistie der Schrift (Karl Barth); (b) die Apostolische Verfasserschaft (Oscar Cullmann); (c) die Tradition der Kirche (Nikolaus Appel); (d) die Entscheidung der Kirche (Hans von Campenhausen); (e) der Evangelische Inhalt (Werner Georg Kümmel et al.)." R. F. Collins, "The Matrix of the NT Canon," *BTB* 7 (1977): 51, regards the field in which the canon emerges as defined by four factors: "suitability for public reading, apostolicity, orthodoxy, and proper literary form."

13. See the anthology *Das Neue Testament als Kanon: Dokumentation und kritische Analyse zur gegenwärtigen Diskussion*, ed. E. Käsemann (Göttingen: Vandenhoeck, 1970).

14. The theological significance of the history of the canon for evangelical exegetes is nicely documented in the anthology *Der Kanon der Bibel,* ed., G. Maier (Wuppertal: R. Brockhaus, 1990). A thorough analysis and a description of the relevance for Catholic theologians are offered by J. Schumacher, *Der apostolische Abschluß der Offenbarung Gottes*, Freiburger Theologische Studien, 114 (Freiburg: Herder, 1979).

15. Ritter, "Die Entstehung des neutestamentlichen Kanons," 94.

16. Often the cryptic German formula of "der sich selbst durchsetzende Kanon" (the canon imposed itself) is used to describe this position; see G. Wanke, "Bibel, I. Die Entstehung des Alten Testaments als Kanon," *TRE* 6 (1980): 1–8. See also the criticism of this position by D. Georgi, "Die Aristoteles- und Theophrastausgabe des Andronikus von Rhodus: Ein Beitrag zur Kanonsproblematik," in *Konsequente Traditionsgeschichte: Festschrift für Klaus Baltzer*, ed. R. Bartelmus et al. OBO 126 (1993): 45–78. See also Campenhausen, *Formation*, 331 n. 13, who contends with considerable differentiation "that the Canon (thought of in terms of its content) imposed itself, and was in any case not a product of the Church on which it was binding."

17. 1 Timothy, 2 Timothy, Titus, and Hebrews were not included. A. v. Harnack, *Marcion: Das Evangelium vom fremden Gott: Eine Monographie zur Geschichte der Grundlegung der katholischen Kirche* (Leipzig: Hinrichs, 1921; reprint, Berlin: Akademie-Verlag, 1960). Campenhausen, *Formation*, has largely adapted Harnack's position in regard to Marcion. B. Aland convincingly argues that Harnack overemphasizes Marcion's influence: B. Aland, "Marcion: Versuch einer neuen Interpretation," *ZThK* 70 (1973): 420–47. See also U. Schmid, *Marcion und sein Apostolos: Rekonstruktion und historische Einordnung der marcionitischen Paulusbriefausgabe*, ANTF 25 (1995).

18. See R. J. Hoffmann, *Marcion: On the Restitution of Christianity: An Essay on the Development of Radical Paulinist Theology in the Second Century* (Chico, Calif: Scholars Press, 1984), 101–34.

19. B. Aland, "Marcion (ca. 85–160)/Marcioniten," *TRE* 22 (1992): 89–101.

20. Schmid, *Marcion*, 297–98.

CHAPTER 2: EVIDENCE FOR A FINAL REDACTION

1. *Merriam-Webster's Collegiate Dictionary*, 10th edition (Springfield, Mass.: Merriam-Webster Inc., 1993).

2. G. Krause et al., ed., *Theologische Realenzyklopädie* (Berlin: De Gruyter, 1977–).

3. L. Traube, *Nomina Sacra: Versuch einer Geschichte der christlichen Kürzungen* (München, 1907; reprint, Darmstadt: Wissenschaftliche Buchgesellschaft, 1967).

4. A. H. R. E. Paap, *Nomina Sacra in the Greek Papyri of the First Five Centuries A.D.* (Leiden: Brill, 1959).

5. C. H. Roberts, *Manuscript, Society, and Belief in Early Christian Egypt*, The Schweich Lectures of the British Academy 1977 (London: Oxford University Press, 1979), 27.

6. Among the *nomina sacra* the staurogram deserves special notice; it combines the Greek letters T and P to symbolize the cross in addition to the superscript line. Some of the oldest manuscripts contain the staurogram; see K. Aland, "Bemerkungen zum Alter und zur Entstehung des Christogrammes anhand von Beobachtungen bei P66 und P75," in *Studien zur Überlieferung des Neuen Testaments und seines Textes*, ANTF 2 (1967), 174–76. Lactantius, *De mortibus persecutorum* 44.5, reports that Constantine had this symbol painted onto the shields of his soldiers (see also ibid. 176). For a comprehensive study of the staurogram see Erika Dinkler von Schubert, "CTAYPOC: Vom 'Wort vom Kreuz' (1 Kor. 1,18) zum Kreuz-Symbol," in *Byzantine East, Latin West: Art-Historical Studies in Honor of Kurt Weitzmann*, ed. Christopher Moss and Katherine Kiefer (Princeton, N.J.: Princeton University Department of Art and Archeology, 1995), 29–38. See also Erich Dinkler, "Zur Geschichte des Kreuzsymbols," *ZThK* 48 (1951): 148–72.

7. Paap, *Nomina Sacra in the Greek Papyri*, 113–15. K. Aland, ed., *Repertorium der griechischen christlichen Papyri, 1: Biblische Papyri, Altes Testament, Neues Testament, Varia, Apokryphen* (Berlin: De Gruyter, 1976), 420–28, provides a comprehensive list of Greek Christian papyri that contains twenty-eight words noted as *nomina sacra*.

8. For a critique of Roberts, *Manuscript*, 27, see F. G. Kenyon, "Nomina Sacra in the Chester Beatty Papyri," *Aegyptus* 13 (1933): 5–10. Kenyon points out that the Chester Beatty Papyri have fewer *nomina sacra* than later witnesses (10): "The net result appears to be that in the third century several forms of abbreviation were occasionally used ($\overline{\text{αθν}}$, $\overline{\text{ιη}}$, $\overline{\text{πρ}}$, $\overline{\text{πς}}$, $\overline{\text{πτς}}$, $\overline{\text{υιν}}$, $\overline{\text{υιυ}}$) which failed to establish themselves in the general practice of the following centuries."

9. G. Rudberg, *Neutestamentlicher Text und Nomina Sacra*, Skrifter utgifna af K. Humanistiska Vetenskaps-Samfundet i Uppsala 17, no. 3 (Uppsala: Akademiska Bokhandeln; Leipzig: Harrassowitz, 1915), 49–50; Paap, *Nomina Sacra in the Greek Papyri*, 119–20.

10. The nonbiblical papyrus Egerton 2, dated around the middle of the second century, contains $\overline{\text{πρα}}$ = πατέρα, $\overline{\text{μω}}$ = Μωϋσῆς; $\overline{\text{η[σας}}$ = Ἠσαΐας; $\overline{\text{προφας}}$ = προφήτας; επρ$\overline{\text{οφσεν}}$ = επροφήτευσεν. H. Idris Bell and T. C. Skeat, eds., *Fragments of an Unknown Gospel and Other Early Christian Papyri*, 2nd ed. (London, 1935), 2–3; C. H. Dodd, "A New Gospel," in *The John Rylands Library*, 2nd ed. (Manchester: Manchester University Press, 1954), 56–92.

11. Kenyon, "Nomina Sacra," 6: The second-century Chester Beatty Codex with Numeri and Deuteronomy records the name Joshua in the same contracted form as the name Jesus in the New Testament. Cf. πνεῦμα, which is noted as a *nomen sacrum* in Nm 5:14; 27:16. 18, even though it does not designate the Holy Spirit.

12. Paap, *Nomina Sacra in the Greek Papyri*, 8–9. The dating is based entirely on paleographic considerations and therefore cannot be established with absolute certainty; for an earlier date, see Y. K. Kim, "Paleographical Dating of P46 to the Later First Century," *Bib.* 69 (1988): 248–57.

13. Paap, *Nomina Sacra in the Greek Papyri*, 110.

14. Latin manuscripts of the Christian Bible apparently used *nomina sacra* from the very beginning as well. In the oldest documents the ambiguity—created by the same beginning and ending letters of *dominus* and *deus*—was solved by writing $\overline{\text{deus}}$ and $\overline{\text{dms}}$ and later $\overline{\text{ds}}$ and $\overline{\text{dns}}$. In the case of $\overline{\text{deus}}$, the superscript line was more significant to the scribes than the contraction. Concerning Latin *nomina sacra* in addition to Traube, *Nomina Sacra*, 129–266 see C. P. H. Bammel, "Products of Fifth-Century Scriptoria Preserving Conventions Used by Rufinus of Aquileia," *JThS* 30 (1979): 430–62, which provides an extensive bibliography.

15. Not even these four terms are always contracted. Paap's tables document approximately 600 occurrences of θεός; ca. 500 times the word is contracted, and approximately 100 times it is written out in full. See also H. Gerstinger,

"Rezension: A. H. R. E. Paap: Nomina sacra in the Greek Papyri of the First Five Centuries A.D. (Leiden: Brill 1959)," *Gnomon* 32 (1960) 373.

16. See Paap, *Nomina sacra in the Greek Papyri*, 124. Manuscripts found at Qumran have confirmed this. After comparing the Masoretic text with 1QIsa[a], St. T. Byington, "יהוה and אדני," *JBL* 76 (1957): 58–59, draws the following conclusion: "Some passages indicate that יהוה was pronounced אדני at the time and place of the writing of 1QIsa[a]; no passage indicates the contrary." See also M. Delcor, "Des diverses manières d'écrire le tétragramme sacré dans les anciens documents hébraïques," *Revue de l'histoire des religions* 147 (1955): 145–73. See also the monumental work of W. W. Baudissin, Κυριος *als Gottesname im Judentum und seine Stelle in der Religionsgeschichte*, ed. Otto Eissfeldt 4 vols. (Giessen: Töpelmann, 1929).

17. Traube, *Nomina Ssacra*, 31–32.

18. The numerous corrections in 1QIsa[a] from יהוה to אדני and vice versa may result from dictation. If the text were dictated, only אדני would have been pronounced, leaving the scribe with the decision whether or not to write יהוה instead. The text would have to be corrected later. See G. Howard, "The Tetragram and the New Testament," *JBL* 96 (1977): 69.

19. See S. Brown, "Concerning the Origin of the Nomina Sacra," *Studia Papyrologica* 9 (1970): 8–12.

20. Howard, "Tetragram," 74.

21. K. Treu, "Die Bedeutung des Griechischen für die Juden im Römischen Reich," *Kairos* 15 (1973): 142–43, provides a list of the materials available.

22. Howard, "Tetragram," 65: "We can now say with almost absolute certainty that the divine name, יהוה, was not rendered by κύριος, in the pre-Christian Greek Bible, as so often has been thought." I am aware of only one example of the *nomen sacrum* in a Jewish edition. It is contained in the fragments of Aquila's translation found in the Cairo Geniza; see F. C. Burkitt, ed. *Fragments of the Books of Kings according to the Translation of Aquila* (Cambridge: Cambridge University Press, 1897); see also H. B. Swete, *An Introduction to the Old Testament in Greek*, with an appendix containing the Letter of Aristeas edited by H. St. J. Thackeray (Cambridge: Cambridge University Press, 1900; reprints rev. R. R. Ottley, New York: Ktav, 1968), 34–42. The palimpsest normally displays the tetragram in paleo-Hebrew script. In one instance, however, the scribe did not have enough room to fit the tetragram on the line. Instead of οἴκῳ *jhwh* he writes οἴκῳ $\overline{\text{κυ}}$; Fol. 2 verso, c. a, l. 15 in Burkitt, *Fragments of the Books of Kings*, 8, 16. It is difficult to make it out on the photograph, and the superscript line is unusually short. See also J. A. Fitzmyer, "Der semitische Hintergrund des

neutestamentlichen Kyriostitels," in *Jesus Christus in Historie und Theologie: Neutestamentliche Festschrift für Hans Conzelmann zum 60. Geburtstag*, ed. G. Strecker (Tübingen: Mohr, 1975), 288; F. Dunand, *Papyrus grecs bibliques (F. Inv. 266): Volumina de la Genèse et du Deutéronome*, Recherches d'archéologie, de philologie et d'histoire, 27 (Cairo 1966), 51.

23. For a survey of the various possibilities of notations, which are discussed in the following, and for an extensive bibliography, see Fitzmyer, "Kyriostitel," 282–85.

24. Jerome, *Prologus galeatus* (PL 28.594–95): "Nomen Domini tetragrammaton in quibusdam graecis voluminibus usque hodie antiquis expressum litteris invenimus" [In certain Greek manuscripts we find the name of God, the tetragram, noted in old script to this very day]."

25. For example: P.Fouad Inv. 266; edition including photographs, W. G. Waddell, "The Tetragrammaton in the LXX," *JThS* 45 (1944): 158–61; Zaki Aly, ed., *Three Rolls of the Early Septuagint: Genesis and Deuteronomy*, Papyrologische Texte und Untersuchungen 17 (Bonn: Rudolf Habelt, 1980). Cf. P.Oxy 50, 3522 Jb 42:11–12.

26. See the fragments of a leather scroll with an edition of the Greek minor prophets, end of first century C.E. (see figure 1). B. Lifshitz, "The Greek Documents from the Cave of Horror," *Israel Exploration Journal* 12 (1962): 201–7. D. Barthélemy, "Redécouverte d'un chaînon manquant de l'Histoire de la Septante," *RB* 60 (1953): 18–29. Emanuel Tov, ed., *The Greek Minor Prophets Scroll from Naḥal Ḥever (8ḤevXIIgr)* (The Seiyâl Collection, no. 1, Discoveries in the Judaean Desert, no. 8 (New York: Oxford University Press, 1990).

27. Jerome criticizes this practice. He understands it as a reading mistake (ΠΙΠΙ = יהוה): "Tetragrammum . . . quod quidam non intellegentes propter elementorum similitudinem, cum in graecis libris reppererint, πιπι legere consueuerunt. [The tetragram . . . is written using the following (Hebrew) characters: *Yod*, *He*, *Waw*, *He*. Some do not know that and finding it in Greek books they usually pronounce it as *PIPI* because of the similarity of the characters]." Jerome, *ep.* 25, *Ad Marcellam*; CSEL 54, 219. However, this is not the only reading mistake that might occur. See J. A. Montgomery, "A Survival of the Tetragrammaton in Daniel," *JBL* 40 (1921): 86. Since Π, T, and Γ are easily confused during the reading process, and since H and I sounded very much alike, the scribes probably working from dictation produced the following error in Dn 9:2: ΠΙΠΙ was copied as ΤΗΓΗ, which happens to make sense in the context. This is only one indication of the technical challenges publishers were facing when reproducing the Greek Jewish Scriptures and reproducing the tetragram in Hebrew characters.

28. Other examples from early Christian writers and from the pre-Christian era are listed in A. L. Williams, "The Tetragrammaton—Jahweh, Name or Surrogate?" *ZAW* 54 (1936): 266. Concerning Qumran's 4QLXXLev[b], see P. W. Skehan, "The Qumran Manuscripts and Textual Criticism," in *Volume du Congrès, Strasbourg 1956*, Supplements to Vetus Testamentum, no. 4 (Leiden: Brill, 1957), 157.

29. P. W. Skehan, "The Text of Isaias at Qumran," *CBQ* 17 (1955): 42–43.

30. For a description of MS B, see Y. Yadin, ed., *The Ben Sira Scroll from Masada* (Jerusalem: Israel Exploration Society, 1965), 5–11. Another variant is displayed by a Genesis fragment of the third century C.E., P.Oxy 7.1007: JHWH is noted as two *Z*s connected by a continuous line through the middle; Waddell, "Tetragrammaton," 158.

31. Howard, "Tetragram," 69–70.

32. The Samaritan edition that had already been canonized at the time is still extant.

33. J. P. Siegel, "The Employment of Palaeo-Hebrew Characters for the Divine Names at Qumran in the Light of Tannaitic Sources," *Hebrew Union College Annual* 42 (1971): 159–72. These regulations certainly also intended to establish a common practice in regard to the use of the tetragram and of אדוני.

34. See Jerome, *Praef. Sam. et Mal.* (Migne, PL, 28.549–50).

35. Howard, "Tetragram," 72–73.

36. M. Avi-Yonah, "Abbreviations in Greek Inscriptions," *Quarterly of the Department of Antiquities in Palestine* (Jerusalem) 9 (supplement) (1940): 9. See also K. McNamee, *Abbreviations in Greek Literary Papyri and Ostraca, Bulletin of the American Society of Papyrologists* 3 (supplements) (1981).

37. G. Rudberg, "Zur paläographischen Kontraktion auf griechischen Ostraka," *Eranos* 9 (1909): 71–100; *Neutestamentlicher Text und Nomina Sacra*; "Ad usum circumscribentem praepositionum Graecarum adnotationes," *Eranos* 19 (1919–20): 173–206.

38. E. Nachmanson, "Die schriftliche Kontraktion auf den griechischen Inschriften," *Eranos* 9 (1909): 101–41.

39. Paap, *Nomina Sacra in the Greek Papyri*, 3, 119–27. Avi-Yonah, "Abbreviations," 27.

40. McNamee, *Abbreviations*, xi. Pre-Christian contractions occur more frequently than assumed by Traube, who did not include material from inscriptions in his study. Avi-Yonah, "Abbreviations," 26, describes typical contractions in non-Christian sources as a combination of contracting and omitting the word ending. Avi-Yonah traces this practice back to a Roman convention of

writing down the first letters of compound words, e.g., *BF* for *bene-ficiarius* (ΒΦ = βενε-φικιάριος).

41. For example, $\overline{\chi\rho}$ for χριστου ($\mathfrak{P}^{45}$), $\overline{\iota\eta}$ for ἰησοῦς ($\mathfrak{P}^{45}$, P.Oxy 1079 = $\mathfrak{P}^{18}$; P.Oxy 1224 = Ap12 according to K. Aland, *Repertorium*, 12; F. G. Kenyon, ed, *The Chester Beatty Biblical Papyri: Descriptions and Texts of Twleve Manuscrips on Papyrus of the Greek Bible, Fasciculus II* (London: Walker, 1936/37), ix. In Codex D 05 these notations are combined to $\overline{\chi\rho\varsigma}$ and $\overline{\iota\eta\varsigma}$: Rudberg, *Nomina Sacra*, 49–50. The abbreviation, but not necessarily the *nomen sacrum* $\overline{\iota\eta}$ is implied by *Barn* 9:7–9 as well, where the number of Abraham's followers (318 is written as TIH) is interpreted as follows: T (300) symbolizes the cross, IH (18) represents Jesus; see C. H. Roberts and T. C. Skeat, *The Birth of the Codex* (London: Oxford University Press, 1983), 57; Roberts, *Manuscript*, 35–36. Although IH does not follow the later practice of noting the *nomen sacrum* for Jesus ($\overline{\iota\varsigma}$), there are at least seven Christian papyri preserving this unusual notation in 48 instances, opposing 159 occurrences of $\overline{\iota\eta\varsigma}$ and 823 of $\overline{\iota\varsigma}$; Paap, *Nomina Sacra in the Greek Papyri*, 102. See also Aland, "Bemerkungen," 177. Whether or not Barn 9:7 contains a *nomen sacrum* is uncertain. Assumptions about the superscript line are difficult to prove, and abbreviating a word by writing only the first letters conforms to ancient conventions. But even if there was a line, it would still not necessarily make it a *nomen sacrum*, because numbers are sometimes marked by a superscript line to distinguish them from characters (cf. the notation of *stichoi* in Codex Alexandrinus, fig. 5).

42. Avi-Yonah, "Abbreviations," 29–39.

43. The horizontal line on top of the last character of the word was frequently used to indicate that the word was abbreviated (ΑΓΙ$\overline{\Omega}$[Ν]), very much like the sign for a dropped 'ν' at the end of the line in literary texts. The line is occasionally placed on top of the next to the last (ΕΚ$\overline{\Lambda}$Η = ἐκ[κ]λη[σια]; *CIG* 8951) or the first character of the abbreviation ($\overline{\text{A}}$ΒΙ[διος]; *DAI* 1, 2 C.E.; 179, 224 C.E.), or it marks several letters ($\overline{\text{KAI}\Sigma}$[αρ]; *Baillet* 1206, 16 B.C.), and occasionally may even be drawn over the whole word ($\overline{\Gamma\text{A}}$[ϊος]; *IGRR* IV, 1101, before 103 C.E.). All these examples are quoted from Avi-Yonah, "Abbreviations."

44. Ibid., 26–27: The superscript line of the *nomina sacra* is sometimes omitted in inscriptions.

45. See H. J. M. Milne, *Greek Shorthand Manuals: Syllabary and Commentary* (London, 1936).

46. Examples are provided by G. Kloeters, "Buch und Schrift bei Hieronymus," (Ph.D. diss., Münster, 1957, 44–87.

47. See M. Hengel, *Die Evangelienüberschriften*, SHAW.PH 1984, no. 3 (Heidelberg: Winter, 1984), 41–42.

48. W. Schubart, *Das Buch bei den Griechen und Römern*, 2nd ed. (Berlin: De Gruyter, 1921), 80–81. Reading the *scriptio continua* out loud required specific skills and special training; R. J. Starr, "Reading Aloud: Lectores and Roman Reading," *Classical Journal* 86 (1991): 337–43.

49. Schubart, *Buch*, 3, fig. 4.

50. Paap, *Nomina Sacra in the Greek Papyri*, 2.

51. With one exception, all word boundaries are marked: ΜΟΝΩ $\overline{\text{ΘΩ}}$ $\overline{\text{ΣΗΡΙ}}$ ΗΜΩΝ ΔΙΑ $\overline{\text{ΙΥ}}$ $\overline{\text{ΧΥ}}$ ΤΟΥ $\overline{\text{ΚΥ}}$ ΗΜΩΝ.

52. See Roberts and Skeat, *Birth*, 57: "This . . . is strictly a Christian usage unknown to Jewish or pagan manuscripts."

53. From the lack of ancient parallels, U. Wilcken concluded that the notation system of the *nomina sacra* might very well be the invention of a single person. "Die Nomina sacra sind also nicht aus irgendwelchen gebräuchlichen profanen Schreibmoden organisch entwickelt, sondern sie sind die freie Erfindung eines Mannes, der gerade absichtlich das Gebräuchliche mied, um den Eindruck der Singularität dieser Worte zu sichern." L. Mitteis, Ulrich Wilcken, eds., *Grundzüge und Chrestomathie der Papyruskunde*, Erster Band: *Historischer Teil* (Leipzig, 1912; reprint, Hildesheim: Olms, 1963), xlv.

54. C. H. Roberts, "The Codex," *Proceedings of the British Academy* 40 (1954): 169–204.

55. Occasionally there are exceptions: only one side is used in the Homer Codex P.Lond 126 (British Museum). Concerning methodological problems evaluating codex fragments, see K. Aland, "Über die Möglichkeiten der Identifikation kleiner Fragmente neutestamentlicher Handschriften mit Hilfe des Computers," in *Studies in New Testament Language and Text: In Honour of George D. Kilpatrick*, ed. J. K. Elliott, *NT.S* 44 (1976): 14–38.

56. B. Aland and K. Aland, *The Text of the New Testament: An Introduction to the Critical Editions and to the Theory and Practice of Modern Textual Criticisms*, 2nd ed. (Grand Rapids, Mich.: Eerdmans; Leiden: Brill, 1989), 75–76, 102, mention four scroll fragments (but see n. 58 below): $\mathfrak{P}^{12}$ (three lines of the Letter to the Hebrews written on the margin of a private letter, formerly P.Amherst 3 b, presently New York, Pierpont Morgan Library, Pap G 3), $\mathfrak{P}^{13}$ (opisthograph, Latin Livius epitome on recto, fragments of Hebrews on verso; P.Oxy 657), $\mathfrak{P}^{18}$ (opisthograph, recto contains Exodus, verso Rv 1:4–7; P.Oxy 1079), and $\mathfrak{P}^{22}$ (opisthograph, verso contains two fragments of Jn 15 and 16, recto is blank, P.Oxy 1228). All of these scroll fragments were therefore privately produced copies. The originally unidentified Cairo Papyrus, whose text from Revelation was first recognized by D. Hagedorn (see Hagedorn, ed., "P.IFAO II 31:

Johannesapokalypse 1,13–20," *ZPE* 92 [1992]: 243–47), is a scroll fragment dating from the beginning of the third century. It displays text on both sides; the back side of what originally seems to have been a document was used for the Bible text (ibid., 243). In the case of small fragments with no text on verso, it cannot be determined whether they derive from a scroll or a codex (for example, 𝔓[31] P.Rylands 4, 𝔓[43]).

57. Roberts and Skeat, *Birth*, 38–44; based on the compilations of K. Aland, *Repertorium*; J. van Haelst, ed., *Catalogue des papyrus littéraires juifs et chrétiens* (Paris: Publications de la Sorbonne, 1976); and Kurt Treu, "Christliche Papyri VI," *APF* 26 (1978): 149–59; and "Christliche Papyri VII," *APF* 27 (1980): 251–58. Ninety-eight witnesses display text of the Old Testament and 74 of the New Testament.

58. For two of the four manuscripts mentioned (1) P.Oxy 10,1228 (𝔓[22]) and (2) P.Oxy 8,1075 (𝔓[18]), see n. 56 above (private copies). (3) The Vienna papyrus with Ps 9:12–22, listed in Roberts and Skeat, *Birth*, 39–40, is one of several fragments of the same manuscript, which originally had been registered separately with varying dates (P.Vindob. G 29525 + 30465 + 30893 + 39786 + 40405; Rahlfs 2053, 2086; K. Aland, *Repertorium*, AT 49, Var. 6; van Haelst, *Catalogue*, 104, 105). It is now evident that the fragment is part of a single page and does not derive from a scroll. Although the passage ends in the middle of a verse (Ps 9:25), the scribe added final lines to mark the conclusion and to indicate that no text is missing. See K. Treu, "24. LXX, Psalms 9,12–15 auf Einzelblatt," in *Papyrus Erzherzog Rainer (P.Rainer Cent.): Festschrift zum 100-jährigen Bestehen der Papyrussammlung der österreichischen Nationalbibliothek* (Wien: Hollinek, 1983), 268, Tafel 47. (4) Thus the scroll fragment P.Alex.Inv.203 (van Haelst, Nr. 300), which also contains a *nomen sacrum* (Is 48:6–8.11–14.17–18; third–fourth cent.), is the only one in the materials evaluated by Roberts and Skeat contradicting the monopoly of codices in published copies of the Christian Bible. However, this scroll fragment dates from a time when the use of codices for the Canonical Edition cannot be questioned anymore.

59. This does not exclude the possibility that one or more of the writings may originally have been distributed as codices.

60. Aland and Hengel nicely demonstrate that the methodology is undisputed. Both authors assume that the manuscripts convey much variation, a view that I am challenging in this present study, and therefore arrive at different conclusions. See Aland and Aland, *Text of the New Testament*, 79: "A glimpse of the developing New Testament canon may be caught in the varied and sometimes arbitrary sequences of the Gospels and the letters of Paul in the manuscripts. The Gospel circulated separately at first, and their association in a single

corpus developed under varied circumstances. The Pauline corpus represents a cumulative development from smaller collections, raising additional problems with its expansion to include the deutero-Pauline letters." See also Hengel, *Evangelienüberschriften*, 13: "Die wechselnde Reihenfolge erklärt sich gerade für die frühe Zeit daraus, daß zunächst in der Regel nur eine Evangelienschrift in einem Codex enthalten war und man die Evangelien entsprechend beliebig zueinander ordnen konnte."

61. Cotelier entitled the collection *SS. Patrum qui temporibus apostolicis floruerunt Barnabae, Clementis Rom., Hermae, Ignatii, Polycarpi opera . . .vera et suppositicia*. See J. B. Lightfoot and J. R. Harmer, eds., *The Apostolic Fathers*, 2nd ed. (London, 1891; reprint, Grand Rapids, Mich.: Baker, 1992), 3; J. A. Fischer, ed., *Die Apostolischen Väter: Griechisch und deutsch, Eingeleitet, herausgegeben, übertragen und erläutert* (Darmstadt: Wissenschaftliche Buchgesellschaft, 1956), ix.

62. See the edition of W. Bauer et al., eds., *Die Apostolischen Väter*, HNT.EB (Tübingen: Mohr, 1923); sequence: Didache 1 Clement 2 Clement, Ignatius Polycarp to the Philippians, Barnabas Hermas. The martyrdoms are omitted, and the Didache is included.

63. E. J. Goodspeed, *The Apostolic Fathers: An American Translation* (New York: Harper, 1950). This writing is closely related to Did. 1–6 and Barn. 18–20. See Goodspeed, *A History of Early Christian Literature*, rev. enl. Robert M. Grant (Chicago: University of Chicago Press, 1966), 11–13.

64. R. M. Grant, ed., *The Apostolic Fathers: A New Translation and Commentary* (New York: Nelson, 1964–68).

65. Lightfoot and Harmer, *The Apostolic Fathers.*

66. Fischer, *Die Apostolischen Väter* (1956). The second volume was published in 1984: K. Wengst, ed., *Schriften des Urchristentums: Zweiter Teil: Didache (Apostellehre), Barnabasbrief, Zweiter Klemensbrief, Schrift an Diognet, Eingeleitet, herausgegeben, übertragen und erläutert* (Darmstadt: Wissenschaftliche Buchgesellschaft, 1984).

67. At least, this is how B. Altaner, *Patrology* (New York: Herder, 1960), 97, interprets the selection.

68. The analysis is based on P. N. Harrison, *Polycarp's Two Epistles to the Philippians* (Cambridge: Cambridge University Press, 1936).

69. H. u. K. Lake, ed., *Codex Sinaiticus Petropolitanus: The New Testament, the Epistle of Barnabas, and the Shepherd of Hermas* (Oxford: Clarendon, 1911).

70. C. M. Martini, ed., *Novum Testamentum e Codice Vaticano Graeco 1209* (*Codex B*), 3rd ed. (Rome: Vatican, 1968).

71. F. G. Kenyon, ed., *British Museum: The Codex Alexandrinus: (Royal Ms 1 D V–VIII)* (Oxford: Oxford University Press, 1915). H. J. M. Milne and T. C. Skeat, *Scribes and Correctors of the Codex Sinaiticus* (Oxford: Oxford University Press, 1938), offers a detailed analysis of this manuscript and of the Codex Sinaiticus. A 02 included 1 Clement and 2 Clement at the end.

72. C. Tischendorf, ed., *Codex Ephraemi Syri Rescriptus: sive fragmenta utiusque testamenti e codice graeco parisiensi celeberrimo quinti ut videtur post christum saeculi*, 2 vols. (Leipzig: Taubnitz, 1843).

73. Of the original 248 pages of Codex Ephraemi Rescriptus, 145 survived. They preserve fragments from every writing of the New Testament except 2 Thessalonians and 2 John, but none of the writings is complete. Since the text of Acts, Romans, James, and Revelation starts out on a new page, it is not possible to discern the original sequence of the collection units. It is certain, however, that Hebrews followed the letters to the Thessalonians. See Tischendorf, *Codex Ephraemi*, 1:14–15.

74. Noteworthy in this context is Tischendorf's position that the scribe who copied the New Testament (hand B) in the Codex Vaticanus (B 03) is identical with the scribe D of the Codex Sinaiticus. Milne and Skeat do not share this assumption, "but the identity of the scribal tradition stands beyond dispute" (*Scribes*, 89–90).

75. B. Aland et al eds., *The Greek New Testament*, 4th rev. ed. (Stuttgart: Deutsche Bibelgesellschaft, 1993); Aland et al., eds., *Novum Testamentum Graece*, 27th ed. (Stuttgart: Deutsche Bibelgesellschaft, 1993); abbreviated in the following as *NTG*[27].

76. W. H. P. Hatch, "The Position of Hebrews in the Canon of the New Testament," *HThR* 29 (1936): 143, registers 329 miniscules in the sequence Romans, . . . Philemon, Hebrews, without identifying the manuscripts.

77. E.g., the Mischna derives from one archetype, which was strictly controlled from the very beginning. The manuscript tradition displays distinct collection units, which were copied in varying orders and created some diversity in the extant copies. See G. Stemberger, *Der Talmud: Einführung—Texte—Erläuterungen*, 2nd ed. (München: Beck, 1987), 38.

78. The Codex Sinaiticus adds Barnabas at the end; the Codex Alexandrinus adds 1 Clement and 2 Clement. The appendices demonstrate, on the one hand, that these writings were regarded very highly (K. Aland, "Noch einmal," 123). On the other hand, they document where the traditional collection unit ended: with Revelation. These additions form appendices. For a methodological reflection on how to discern appendices, see D. Trobisch, *Die Entstehung der*

Paulusbriefsammlung: Studien zu den Anfängen christlicher Publizistik, NTOA 10 (Freiburg: Universitätsverlag; Göttingen: Vandenhoeck, 1989), 49.

79. *NTG*[27], 40*.

80. Aland and Aland, *Text of the New Testament*, 78–79.

81. See M. Hengel, *Die johanneische Frage: Ein Lösungsversuch, mit einem Beitrag zur Apokalypse von Jörg Frey*, WUNT 67 (Tübingen: Mohr, 1993), 206, also published as *The Johannine Question* (London: SCM; Philadelphia: Trinity, 1989), 75. Although Hengel assumes that each Gospel originally was published and distributed separately, he agrees that the wording of the title of John is strongly influenced by the titles of the synoptic Gospels.

82. The data is based on the exhaustive manuscript list provided in the appendix of the *NTG*[27]. This list was then compared to Aland and Aland, *Text of the New Testament*. I did not attempt to be more comprehensive, and I added the dates provided by these publications. Dating manuscripts is difficult, and the results are often disputable.

83. P.Vindob G 29274 is a writing exercise (K. Aland, *Repertorium*, 332: Var 8; Rahlfs: 2090). P. Sanz, "Christliche Papyri aus der Papyrussammlung der Nationalbibliothek zu Wien" (Ph.D. diss., University of Vienna, 1936), 198–209. It is difficult to determine whether $\mathfrak{P}^{10}$ is a writing exercise, an amulet, or a page discarded because of evident errors; see E. M. Schofield, ed., *The Papyrus Fragments of the Greek New Testament* (Clinton, N.J., 1936), 137–39.

84. One fragment of the Paris Papyrus preserved the title of the Gospel of Matthew: ευαγγελιον κατα μαθθαιον; K. Aland, "Neue neutestamentliche Papyri II," *NTS* 12 (1966): 193–94.

85. C. Wessely, "Literarischer theologischer Text Nr.26," *Studien zur Paläographie und Papyruskunde* (Leipzig) 12 (1912): 246.

86. The three fragments, P.Mich 5562, were written by the same scribe, but it is not certain whether they originally were part of the same codex; K. Aland, *Repertorium*, 283.

87. Two separate fragments; oldest attestation of these verses of 2 Thessalonians; C. Gallazzi, "Frammenti di un codice con le Epistole di Paolo," *ZPE* 46 (1982): 117–22 (P.Narmuthis Inv.69.39a and 69.229a).

88. K. Aland, *Kurzgefaßte Liste der griechischen Handschriften des Neuen Testaments*, ANTF 1 (Berlin: De Gruyter, 1963), 39 n. 3: the transition from Luke to John is not preserved.

89. Sahidic-Greek diglot. Ibid., 39 n. 5: the transition from Luke to John is not preserved.

90. Ibid., 42 n. 11. Transitions between the Gospels are not preserved. Palimpsest. The upper writing is Georgian. K. Aland, "Die griechischen Handschriften des Neuen Testaments: Ergänzungen zur 'Kurzgefaßten Liste' (Fortsetzungsliste VII)," in *Materialien zur neutestamentlichen Handschriftenkunde*, ANTF 3 (1969), 7 n. 2: 067 and 078 could possibly be associated with other manuscripts, which at the time are still recorded by individual numbers.

91. These Greek-Coptic diglots include 0110, 0124, 0178, 0179, 0180, 0190, 0191, 0193, 0202; Aland and Aland, *Text of the New Testament*, 119.

92. The original sequence cannot be determined because the fragments of John and Mark do not belong to the same quire. Folio 3 preserved the *subscriptio*: Ευαγγε]λιον / κατα Μα]ρκον.

93. Since the transition between Matthew and Luke is not preserved, the sequence can only be presumed. One of the preserved fragments (Athos, Protatu 56; Mt 21:24–24:15) consists of a complete quire, which displays the quire number ζ (7) at the end. The preceding text of Matthew could be accommodated on exactly six quires, and six quires would provide precisely the space needed for the remainder of Matthew and the text of Mark up to the next preserved fragment (Athos, Vatopediu 1219; Lk 3:23–4:2). There is no good reason to conjecture an unusual sequence. R. Peppermüller, "Ein Unzialfragment auf dem Athos (Vatopediu und Protatu) und in Paris (0102 + [0138])," in *Materialien zur neutestamentlichen Handschriftenkunde*, ed. K. Aland, ANTF 3 (1969), 144–76.

94. Palimpsest, eight pages: "When 0104 was disassembled, its leaves were cut at the binding and folded into pages half the original size, so that the erased text is at right angles to the upper text." J. H. Greenlee, *Nine Uncial Palimpsests of the Greek New Testament*, Studies and Documents 39 (Salt Lake City: University of Utah Press, 1968), 22. The transition from Matthew to Luke is not preserved.

95. 0171: Fragments of two pages. Aland and Aland, *Text of the New Testament*, 104; plates, ibid., 63.

96. 0208: Two pages, Col 2:1–10, 13–14; 2 Thes 2:4–7, 12–17 (K. Wachtel and K. Witte, ed., *Das Neue Testament auf Papyrus: II. Die Paulinischen Briefe*, Teil 2 ANTF 22 [1994], xvii), München, Bayerische Staatsbibliothek Clm 29418.

97. Palimpsest. Greenlee, *Nine Uncial Palimpsests*, 91–115.

98. P.Oxy 13.1598; see Trobisch, *Entstehung*, 25; Wachtel and Witte, *Paulinischen Briefe*, xliv–xlv.

99. Only the sequence Rom, 1 Cor; Phil, Col, 1 Thes; Ti, Phlm can still be determined. Unfortunately, the position of Hebrews cannot be established any-

more. K. Aland, *Repertorium*, 290; Trobisch, *Entstehung*, 28; Wachtel and Witte, *Paulinischen Briefe*, lviii–lix.

100. R. Kasser and V. Martin, eds., *Papyrus Bodmer XVII, Actes des Apôtres, Epîtres de Jaques, Pierre, Jean et Jude* (Cologny-Genève: Bibliothèque Bodmer, 1961), 8.

101. This is a codex in one quire, originally containing Luke and John only. The sequence is therefore established. Just like the scribe of $\mathfrak{P}^{46}$, the scribe of this manuscript miscalculated the space needed and had to use smaller script for the second half of the codex to accommodate the text. R. Kasser and V. Martin, eds., *Papyrus Bodmer XIV, Evangile de Luc, Chap. 3–24* (Cologny-Genève: Bibliothèque Bodmer, 1961), 9–13, and *Papyrus Bodmer XV, Evangile de Jean, Chap. 1–15* (Cologny-Genève: Bibliothèque Bodmer, 1961).

102. H 015 and I 016 are very fragmentary; the sequence Phlm, Heb, 1 Tm is determinable. See Trobisch, *Entstehung*, 18, 20; Wachtel and Witte, *Paulinischen Briefe*, xiv–xv.

103. Palimpsest. The following transitions are preserved: 293v Col 1 Thes; 230r Eph Phil; 295r 1 Tm 2 Tm; 294r Ti Phlm; 222v Jas 1 Pt; 307r 2 Jn; 307v 3 Jn. The position of Hebrews remains unclear. D. E. Heath, *The Text of Manuscript Gregory 048* (*Vatican Greek 2061*) (Upland, Ind.: Taylor University, 1965).

104. The end of Matthew on fol. 5r and the beginning of Mark on fol. 6r are part of the same quire. J. R. Harris, ed., *Biblical Fragments from Mount Sinai* (London, 1890), xii.

105. Palimpsest. Manchester, J. Rylands Libr. P. Copt. 20. Aland and Aland, *Text of the New Testament*, 126: 1 Pt 5:13–14, 2 Pt 1:5–8, 14–16.

106. Single page. Aland and Aland, *Text of the New Testament*, 124: 3 John 12–15; Jude 3–5.

107. Wachtel and Witte, *Paulinischen Briefe*, xix. The manuscript also contains fragments of Ephesians.

108. Editions: H. A. Sanders, ed., *A Third-Century Papyrus Codex of the Epistles of Paul*, University of Michigan Studies, Humanistic Series, 38 (Ann Arbor: University of Michigan Press, 1935); F. G. Kenyon, ed., *The Chester Beatty Biblical Papyri: Descriptions and Texts of Twelve Manuscripts on Papyrus of the Greek Bible, Fasciculus III Supplement: Pauline Epistles* (London: Emery Walker, 1936–37). For the date of the manuscript, see U. Wilcken, "The Chester Beatty Biblical Papyri," *APF* 11 (1935): 112–14. Kim, "Paleographical Dating of $\mathfrak{P}^{46}$," dates it into the first century.

109. For a detailed discussion on the sequence of the Pauline Letters in the manuscripts, see Trobisch, *Entstehung*, 14–61; for $\mathfrak{P}^{46}$, see ibid., 26–28, 60. An

older collection containing only letters with a general address (Romans, Hebrews, 1 Corinthians, Ephesians) may have influenced the sequence (ibid., 60). Even in this case, 𝔓[46] would still attest the Canonical Edition, showing that it conflated with an older and smaller collection of letters by Paul.

110. M. Testuz, ed., *Papyrus Bodmer VII–IX, VII: L'Epître de Jude, VIII: Les deux Epîtres de Pierre, IX: Les Psaumes 33 et 34* (Cologny-Genève: Bibliothèque Bodmer, 1959).

111. Washington, D.C.; Smithsonian Institute, Freer Gallery of Art, 06.274. H. A. Sanders, ed., *Facsimile of the Washington Manuscript of the Four Gospels in the Freer Collection: With an Introduction*, University of Michigan Studies, Humanistic Series 9, no. 1 (Ann Arbor: University of Michigan Press, 1912).

112. Further proof for the so-called Western arrangement are D 05 (see the following), X 033 (tenth century, München, Universitätsbibliothek, fol. 30); the commentary manuscript 055 (Paris, bibl. nat Gr. 202); according to C. Tischendorf, ed., *Novum Testamentum Graece ad antiquissimos testes denuo recensuit, apparatum criticum apposuit*, editio octava critica maior (Leipzig: Hinrichs, 1894), 3:516, the manuscript Mosqu. registered as number 256 syn 138, ninth century; according to Sanders, *Facsimile*, 27, the miniscule 594; of the translations the Latin manuscripts a, b, e, f, ff_2, q, and the Gothic translation. For the unusual arrangement of the gospels in other manuscripts than the Greek, see Zahn, *Kanons*, 2:364–75; Metzger, *Canon*, 296–97.

113. Sanders, *Facsimile*, 6, 40.

114. Ibid., 134. There are only three more little spots in the manuscript, on page 326.

115. Ibid., 135.

116. Ch. R. Morey in ibid., ix.

117. For a description of the codex, see D. C. Parker, *Codex Bezae: An Early Christian Manuscript and Its Text* (Cambridge: Cambridge University Press, 1992).

118. J. Chapman, "The Order of the Gospels in the Parent of Codex Bezae," *ZNW* 6 (1905): 339–46, 341. According to the calculations of H.-W. Bartsch, *Codex Bezae versus Codex Sinaiticus im Lukasevangelium* (Hildesheim: Georg Olms, 1984), 2, there is not enough room left.

119. The Chester Beatty collection has thirty pages. One page is located in the papyrus collection in Vienna: Österreichische Nationalbibliothek, Pap. G. 31974. F. G. Kenyon, ed., *Gospels and Acts.*

120. Following 11–12 and 13–14. T. C. Skeat, "Irenaeus and the Four-Gospel Canon," *NT* 34 (1992): 198, argues that 𝔓[45] displayed the Western arrangement: Matthew, John, Luke, Mark.

121. Kenyon, *Gospels and Acts*, vi. The pagination is preserved only one more time. It was read as 193 but the reading is not certain. The page contains text from Acts 14:15–23.

122. Ibid., vii–viii.

123. See B. M. Metzger, *The Text of the New Testament: Its Transmission, Corruption, and Restoration*, 3rd ed. (New York: Oxford University Press, 1992), 37: "Originally the codex consisted of about 220 leaves . . . and contained all four Gospels and the Acts."

124. See the tables in E. G. Turner, *The Typology of the Early Codex* (Philadelphia: University of Pennsylvania Press, 1977), 58–64. Whether the binding in *uniones* allows for an assertion about the maximum length cannot be determined due to the scarcity of evidence; see ibid., 61.

125. Trobisch, *Entstehung*, 22–23.

126. Farmer and Farkasfalvy (*Formation*, 87), did not recognize this traditional unit. They understand the different sequences only as variations concerning the place of Acts. The fact that Acts is associated with the General Letters might have been very valuable for their interpretation. See Childs, *New Testament as Canon*, 495; Childs follows Zahn.

127. Aland and Aland, *Text of the New Testament*, 91–92.

128. Ritter, "Entstehung," 94: "Daß sich keines der großen Konzile der Alten Kirche je mit dem Kanon befaßt hat."

129. Eusebius, *h.e.* 6.16.3.

130. Tertullian, *Adversus Hermogenem* 22.

131. Rv 22:18–19: "I warn everyone who hears the words of the prophecy of this book: if anyone adds to them, God will add to that person the plagues described in this book; if anyone takes away from the words of the book of this prophecy, God will take away that person's share in the tree of life and in the holy city, which are described in this book." Zahn, *Kanons*, 1:113: "[Man kann doch] kaum zweifeln, daß der Antimontanist wie der Montanist das drohende Schlußwort der Apokalypse im Sinn haben und dieses als den Grenzstein der biblischen Literatur betrachten."

132. Zahn, *Kanons*, 1:113: "Man meint in der Hand dieser Männer ein vom Evangelium des Matthäus bis zur Apokalypse des Johannes sich erstreckendes Exemplar des NT's zu sehen, wie solche heute in Leipzig und Cambridge gedruckt werden; nur die letzte Ziffer der Jahreszahl des jüngsten Drucks müßte gestrichen werden. Man verzeihe diese Zuspitzung des Irrthums, welcher hier zu beseitigen ist. "

133. Ibid.

134. Eusebius, *h.e.* 6.25.11–14.

135. "For not without reason have the men of old time handed it down as Paul's" (Eusebius, *h.e.* 6.25.13).

136. For text and commentary see Zahn, *Kanons*, 2:203–12.

137. H. Lietzmann, *Wie wurden die Bücher des Neuen Testaments heilige Schrift? Fünf Vorträge* (Tübingen: Mohr, 1907), 53.

138. Hahneman, *The Muratorian Fragment*.

139. See the index for a list of the evidence evaluated in this study.

140. The first edition of the Codex Sinaiticus (א 01) was published by Tischendorf in 1862. The first photographic reproduction of the Codex Vaticanus (B 03), which replaced the few and faulty earlier editions, was published in 1889–90, one year after the first volume of Zahn's *Geschichte des Neutestamentlichen Kanons* had appeared.

141. The following observations are based on the critical apparatus of the *NTG*[27]. Therefore orthographic variations, marginal notes, and other additions in the manuscripts are not evaluated. Observations based on microfilm or the original manuscript are noted as such.

142. The *inscriptiones* in B 03 and א 01 are written by a second hand (*NTG*[27], 719ff). B 03 contains the short form κατὰ Μαθθαῖον, κατὰ Μάρκον, etc., in *inscriptio* and *subscriptio*, while all the other relevant witnesses add εὐαγγέλιον. א 01 displays the abbreviated form in the *inscriptiones* and the long form in the *subscriptiones*. The *subscriptio* of the Gospel of Matthew is missing. Three older papyri preserve titles, each displaying the long form, $\mathfrak{P}^{66}$, dated at around 200 for John; $\mathfrak{P}^{75}$ of the third century for Luke and John; and $\mathfrak{P}^{64}$, which is part of the same manuscript as $\mathfrak{P}^{67}$ and is dated ca. 200, for the Gospel of Matthew. The short form is not representative for the tradition; in my opinion, it should be interpreted as an editorial characteristic of the Codex Vaticanus and not of the original form. See Hengel, *Evangelienüberschriften*, 10–12. Other early witnesses for the long form: D 05 (fifth century), W 032 (fifth century), 083 (sixth–seventh centuries).

143. G. Strecker, "εὐαγγέλιον, ου, τό; euaggelion; Evangelium," *EWNT* 2 (1992): 176–86; Strecker, *Literaturgeschichte des Neuen Testaments* (Göttingen: Vandenhoeck, 1992), 122–48. For a discussion of the form-critical classification of the genre, see K. Berger, *Formgeschichte des Neuen Testaments* (Heidelberg: Quelle & Meyer, 1984), 367–71; D. Dormeyer, *Evangelium als literarische und theologische Gattung*, Erträge der Forschung 263 (Darmstadt: Wissenschaftliche Buchgesellschaft, 1989); H. Frankemölle, *Evangelium: Begriff und Gattung: Ein*

Forschungsbericht, Stuttgarter Biblische Beiträge 15 (Stuttgart: Katholisches Bibelwerk, 1988). The question of where the name of the genre originated and who first used it has recently led to numerous scholarly propositions: H. Koester, *Ancient Christian Gospels: Their History and Development* (London: SCM; Philadelphia: Trinity Press International, 1990), 1–48, and Strecker, *Literaturgeschichte*, 128, associate it with Marcion; Hengel, *Evangelienüberschriften*, 49, links it to the Gospel of Mark; in opposition to Koester and Hengel, G. N. Stanton, *A Gospel for a New People: Studies in Matthew* (Edinburgh: Clark, 1992), 14–16, suggests that the author of Matthew first used the term. See also n. 146.

144. Some late examples are listed in Hengel, *Evangelienüberschriften*, 9. Authors are usually referred to in the genitive case; examples are the titles of the General Letters and of the Revelation of John.

145. F. Blaß and A. Debrunner, *Grammatik des neutestamentlichen Griechisch*, 17th ed., ed. Friedrich Rehkopf (Göttingen: Vandenhoeck, 1990), §224,2 n. 4; Wettstein, *Novum Testamentum Graecum* (Amsterdam: Dommerian, 1752; reprint Graz: Akademische Verlagsanstalt, 1962), 223; see also Josephus, *ContraApionem* 1.3.18 τὴν καθ΄ αὑτὸν ἱστορίαν: "his history." According to Hengel, *Evangelienüberschriften*, 10, κατά does not simply replace a *genetivus auctoris*, as is suggested by W. Bauer, K. Aland, and B. Aland, *Griechisch-deutsches Wörterbuch zu den Schriften des Neuen Testaments und der übrigen urchristlichen Literatur*, 6th ed. (Berlin: De Gruyter, 1988), 828.7c.

146. Personally, I think that the editors combined various older traditions that were in use for the Gospel titles. The term *euangelion* could be taken from Mk 1:1: "Beginning of the *euangelion* of Jesus Christ." In this case ἀρχὴ would mark the beginning of a new book like, e.g., Hos 1:2 does ('Αρχὴ λόγου κυρίου πρὸς Ωσηε) or like many manuscripts do (Latin: *incipit*); cf. figure 2, which indicates scripture lessons. If this interpretation is correct, the word *euangelion* in Mk 1:1 was understood as the heading of the following book; consequently, it could be used by the editors for other similar writings, and it was eventually employed for the canonical Gospels. Papias's note regarding the Gospel of Matthew claims that this Gospel is a translation from the Hebrew (Eusebius, *h.e.* 3.39.16). Papias may simply have drawn this conclusion from the title κατὰ Μαθθαῖον, which reminded him of the title of the Greek Jewish Scriptures, the Septuagint, clearly a translation from the Hebrew. In this case the editors of the Canonical Edition may simply have combined elements of the traditional titles of Matthew and Mark and applied them to the Gospels of Luke and John. This is, of course, only a hypothesis. Concerning Mk 1:1, see B. D. Ehrman, "The Text of Mark in the Hands of the Orthodox," *Lutheran Quarterly* (Milwaukee) 5 (1991): 149–52; M. E. Boring, "Mark 1:1–15 and the Beginning of the Gos-

pel," *Semeia* 52 (1991): 43–81, which provides a comprehensive bibliography; D. E. Smith, "Narrative Beginnings in Ancient Literature and Theory," *Semeia* 52 (1991): 4 (referring to Mt 1:1 as well). For a treatment of the *inscriptiones* to the prophets in the Old Testament, which clearly constitute a formal parallel, see G. M. Tucker, "Prophetic Superscriptions and the Growth of a Canon," in *Canon and Authority: Essays in Old Testament Religion and Theology* (Philadelphia: Fortress, 1977): 56–70. For a textual-critical discussion see P. M. Head, "A Text-Critical Study of Mark 1.1: 'The Beginning of the Gospel of Jesus Christ,'" *NTS* 37 (1991): 621–29.

147. Codex Sinaiticus (ℵ 01) has πράξεις by a second hand in the *inscriptio* (*NTG*[27], 735), while other manuscripts usually add (τῶν) ἀποστόλων; see G. Schneider, *Die Apostelgeschichte*, HThK 5 (1980–82): 74.

148. The author of Acts presents himself as the author of the Gospel According to Luke: "In the first book, Theophilus, I wrote about all that Jesus did and taught from the beginning" (Acts 1:1).

149. U. v. Wilamowitz-Moellendorf, *Die griechische und lateinische Literatur und Sprache*, 3rd ed. (Leipzig: Teubner, 1912), 262, sees an analogy between the "Acts of the Apostles" and the "Acts of Augustus" or the "Acts of Herakles," all of which share the notion of a godly mission of their heroes. W. v. Christ, *Geschichte der Griechischen Literatur*, 7th ed., ed. Wilhelm Schmid, HAW 7 (1913), 2:967, compares Acts to πράξεις Ἀλεξάνδρου of Kallisthenes, to περὶ Ἀννίβου πράξεων of Sosylos, and to the life of Apollonius by Philostratos. Ph. Vielhauer, *Geschichte der urchristlichen Literatur: Einleitung in das Neue Testament, die Apokryphen und die Apostolischen Väter*, 2nd ed. (Berlin: De Gruyter, 1978), 399, indicates that typically the deeds of only one hero are told, not those of several heroes. See also E. Haenchen, *Die Apostelgeschichte*, 7th ed., KEK 3 (1977), 143; Schneider, *Apostelgeschichte*, 73–76. For recent studies on the genre see L. M. Wills, "The Depiction of the Jews in Acts," *JBL* 110 (1991): 648–50; Strecker, *Literaturgeschichte*, 236–43.

150. Schneider, *Apostelgeschichte*, 152.

151. Outside of the manuscript evidence, Apollonius uses this title to refer to the letter collection ca. 197/198 (Altaner, *Patrology*, 108). Apollonius accuses Themison, who bought himself free from prison with a large sum of money instead of dying for his faith: "Themiso dared, in imitation of the apostle, to compose an epistle general [μιμούμενος τὸν ἀπόστολον, καθολικήν τινα συνταξάμενος]" (Eusebius, *h.e.* 5.18.1, 5). See also the contents sheet of the Codex Alexandrinus (figure 5), which was added to the manuscript in the seventh or eighth century; K. P. Donfried, *The Setting of Second Clement in Early Christianity*, NT.S 38 (1974), 20. Zahn, *Kanons*, 2:289.

152. For example, the title of the Letter of James in P 025 is Ιακοβου αποστολου επιστολη καθολικη; the *subscriptio* runs Ιακωβου απο(στολου) επιστολη καθολικη (microfilm).

153. Cf. R. Schnackenburg, *Die Johannesbriefe*, 2nd ed., HThK 13 (1963), 1–3.

154. For example, the title of the Letter to the Romans in P 025 is επιστολη του παναγιου Παυλου του αποστολ(ου) προς Ρωμαιους (microfilm).

155. The address "Ephesus" is given in the title; it is not repeated in the text of codices ℵ 01 and B 03 by the first hand but was added at a later time. See Trobisch, *Entstehung*, 80–81; E. Best, "Ephesians i,1," in *Text and Interpretation: Studies in the New Testament presented to Matthew Black*, ed. E. Best and R. McL. Wilson (Cambridge: Cambridge University Press, 1979), 29–41; D. A. Black, "The Peculiarities of Ephesians and the Ephesian Address," *Grace Theological Journal* 2 (1981): 59–73. The Letter to the Ephesians seems to be the only writing of the New Testament where an alternative title is documented. In the edition of Marcion this letter was entitled "To the Laodiceans" (Tertullian, *AdvMarc* 5.11.17). The view that the title of 1 John may at some time have been "To the Parthians" is not based on extant titles in the manuscripts. Some *subscriptiones* to this letter, however, discuss possible addresses of this letter, and it is in this context that the Parthians are mentioned. For the documentation of the Parthian address, see H.-J. Klauck, *Die Johannesbriefe*, Erträge der Forschung 276 (Darmstadt: Wissenschaftliche Buchgesellschaft, 1991), 37–40.

156. By referring to the addressee in the title, the Letter to the Hebrews clearly presents itself as part of the collection of Pauline letters. Hengel, *Evangelienüberschriften*, 26, points out that the uniformity of the title indicates an early date.

157. Metzger, *Canon*, 303, adds the Letter to the Colossians "where the oldest manuscript evidence (𝔓[46], A, B*, K, al.) spells the name in the title [Kolassaeis], whereas in Col. 1.2 almost all witnesses spell the name [Kolossais]. . . . The evidence proves that the title was added at a different time (and place) from the writing of the Epistle." In the spurious correspondence between Paul and Seneca, the Second Letter to the Corinthians is identified for the reader as "the letter to the Achaians" (*ep*. 7; cf. 2 Cor 1:1).

158. For example, in manuscripts that do not contain 2 Clement, 1 Clement does not carry a number in the title. See R. Warns, "Untersuchungen zum 2.Clemens-Brief" (Ph.D. diss., University of Marburg, 1985).

159. See R. Gregson, "A Solution of the Problems of the Thessalonian Epistles," *Evangelical Quarterly* 38 (1966): 76–80.

160. Paul uses the term *Hebrew*, referring to himself, in 2 Cor 11:22, Ἑβραῖοί εἰσιν κἀγώ; and Phil 3:5, περιτομῇ ὀκταήμερος, ἐκ γένους Ἰσραήλ, φυλῆς

Βενιαμίν Ἑβραῖος ἐξ Ἑβραίων, κατὰ νόμον Φαρισαῖος. Referring to a group within the Jerusalem congregation, it is used in Acts 6:1.

161. In ℵ* 01 and A 02: ΙΩΑΝΟΥ. Later additions are του θεολογου [majority text] (+ και ευαγγελιστου [046 *pc*]).

162. The inclusion of a genre description in the title corresponds to the observation that very often titles would briefly refer to the contents of the book. See Schubart, *Buch*, 98: Schubart points out that a number of scrolls found in Herkulaneum have brief titles like "Epicurus about nature 11." The name of the author is usually given in the genitive, and the reader would add the word *books*. This way the titles give all the important information: name of the author, contents, and number of scrolls.

163. Hengel, "Daß die Einheitlichkeit der Evangelientitel gegen Ende des 2.Jh.s wenige Jahrzehnte zuvor irgendwo durch eine zentrale Evangelienredaktion, d.h. durch ein innerkirchliches Machtwort, zustande kam, ist sehr unwahrscheinlich" ("Evangelienüberschriften", 48); "The form of the title, εὐαγγέλιον κατὰ Ἰωάννην, imitated the titles of the earlier Gospels according to Mark, Luke and Matthew which were already quite widespread around 100 CE" (*Johannine Question*, 75).

164. Concerning the use of the term *New Testament*, see Zahn, *Kanons*, 1:103–5; critically reviewed by Harnack, *Jahr 200*, 42–43. W. C. van Unnik, "Ἡ καινὴ διαθήκη—A Problem in the Early History of the Canon," *Studia Patristica* (Berlin) 4, TU 79 (1961): 212–227; reprinted in *Sparsa Collecta* (Leiden) 2 (1980): 216: "It is a matter of course that various other designations like 'the Scriptures,' 'the Word' etc. remained in use, as is the case up till the present time, but as a title ἡ καινὴ διαθήκη was and is dominant." For the use within the New Testament see J. Behm, *Der Begriff ΔΙΑΘΗΚΗ im Neuen Testament* (Leipzig: Deichert, 1912); E. Lohmeyer, *Diatheke: Ein Beitrag zur Erklärung des neutestamentlichen Begriffs* (Leipzig: Hinrichs, 1913); E. Kutsch, *Neues Testament—Neuer Bund? Eine Fehlübersetzung wird korrigiert* (Neukirchen-Vluyn: Neukirchner Verlag, 1978). A compilation of the oldest evidence is offered by W. Kinzig, "Ἡ καινὴ διαθήκη: The Title of the New Testament in the Second and Third Centuries," *JThS* 45 (1994): 519–44; Kinzig traces the title back to Marcion.

165. Verbatim: τὴν τῶν παλαιῶν βιβλίων . . . ἀκρίβειαν πόσα τὸν ἀριθμὸν καὶ ὁποῖα τὴν τάξιν εἶεν τὰ τῆς παλαιᾶς διαθήκης βιβλία. Melito's Eklogai are preserved only in Eusebius of Caesarea's quotes from the introduction (Eusebius, *h.e.* 4.26.13–14). See van Unnik, "A Problem in the Early History," 215, 218–19.

166. Eusebius, *h.e.* 5.16.3. For a detailed analysis of the concept of a closed number of writings, see W. C. van Unnik, "De la regle Μήτε προσθεῖναι μήτε ἀφελεῖν dans l'histoire du canon," *VigChr* 3 (1949): 1–36, reprinted in *Sparsa Collecta* (Leiden) 2 (1980): 157–71.

167. Clemens Alexandrinus, *stromata* 2.29.2–3 (GCS 15,128). See J. Fischer, "Die Einheit der beiden Testamente bei Laktanz, Viktorin von Pettau und deren Quellen," *Münchener Theologische Zeitschrift* 1 (1950): 100; van Unnik, "A Problem in the Early History," 215.

168. Irenaeus uses the term repeatedly, but he does not use it in reference to the book; see van Unnik, "A Problem in the Early History," 219–20; Harnack, *Jahr 200*, 42; H. J. Vogt, "Die Geltung des Alten Testaments bei Irenäus von Lyon," Theologische Quartalschrift 160 (München: Erich Wewel, 1980), 17–28; Hoh, *Irenäus*.

169. Tertullian, *DePud* 1, *ContraPrax* 15. Origen, *InJoannem* 5.8: "συμφωνίας δογμάτων κοινῶν τῇ καλουμένῃ παλαιᾷ πρὸς τὴν ὀνομαζομένην καινὴν διαθήκην."

CHAPTER 3: THE EDITORIAL CONCEPT

1. The redactional-critical approach chosen in this study to describe the final redaction of anthologies parallels a methodological principle of the Reformation, *scriptura sui ipsius interpres*. The interpreter does not concentrate on the immediate context of a specific passage only but tries to place the passage within the central message of the Christian Bible as a whole. See G. T. Sheppard, "Canonization: Hearing the Voice of the Same God through Historically Dissimilar Traditions," *Interpretation: A Journal of Bible and Theology* 36 (1982): 21–33; D. A. Oss, "Canon as Context: The Function of Sensus Plenior in Evangelical Hermeneutics," *Grace Theological Journal* 9 (1988): 105–27.

2. The following description does not pursue the question of whether or not the editors were able to identify the name of the author. That this is possible is demonstrated for the Gospels in R. Pesch, "Die Zuschreibung der Evangelien an apostolische Verfasser," *ZKTh* 97 (1975): 56–71. Instead I ask whether the editors wanted the readers to identify the alleged authors.

3. R. Pesch, "Levi-Matthäus (Mc 2,14/Mt 9,9 10,3): Ein Beitrag zur Lösung eines alten Problems," *ZNW* 59 (1968): 40–56, explains the change from Levi to Matthew differently. Only one of the twelve is a likely candidate to be called to be a disciple. The first four disciples called may safely be eliminated, just like those disciples with a second name (Judas Iscariot, James, and Simon). This leaves Matthew, Bartholomew, Philip, Thaddaeus, and Thomas (ibid., 55). Pesch does not answer why Matthew in particular was chosen; he suspects that it was an old tradition, which suggested the title (ibid., 56).

4. See H. A. Kent, "The Gospel According to Matthew," in *The Wycliffe Bible Commentary: The New Testament*, 4th ed., ed, Everett F. Harrison (New York:

Iversen-Norman Associates, 1973), 1: "As a former taxgatherer Matthew was well qualified to produce such a Gospel. His business knowledge of shorthand enabled him to record fully the discourses of Jesus. His acquaintance with figures is reflected in his frequent mention of money, his interest in large sums (Matth 18:24; 25:15), and his general interest in statistics (e.g., 1:17)." See also ibid., 32, referring to Mt 10:3: "Matthew the publican. A self-effacing epithet employed only in the author's Gospel."

5. For a detailed discussion see U. H. J. Körtner, "Markus der Mitarbeiter des Petrus," *ZNW* 71 (1980): 160–73.

6. John Mark's departure from Pamphylia is mentioned briefly (Acts 13:13) and without further explanation.

7. The *Stuttgarter Jubiläumsbibel mit erklärenden Anmerkungen* (Stuttgart: Privilegiente. Württembergische Bibelanstalt, 1912), which was published to commemorate the hundredth anniversary of this institution, nicely demonstrates how these cross-references function, commenting on Acts 15:35–41: "Barnabas als Verwandter war nicht ganz unparteiisch. So kam's zu einem peinlichen Auftritt, bei dem wohl beide etwas zu weit gingen. . . . Ebenso ist dem Markus die erfahrene Demütigung gewiß gesund gewesen; hernach ist doch etwas Tüchtiges aus ihm geworden und Paulus hat weder ihm noch seinem Oheim die Sache nachgetragen (1.Kor.9,6 und Kol. 4,10; Philem.24; 2.Tim.4,11)."

8. Ἀσπάζεται ὑμᾶς . . καί Μᾶρκος ὁ ἀνεψιὸς Βαρναβᾶ, περὶ οὗ ἐλάβετε ἐντολάς, ἐὰν ἔλθῃ πρὸς ὑμᾶς δέξασθε αὐτόν.

9. Εὔχρηστος εἰς διακονίαν.

10. However, see *Stuttgarter Jubiläumsbibel*, 54, concerning the authorship of Mark: "Wer sich über die persönlichen Verhältnisse des Evangelisten Johannes Markus, insonderheit über seine Beziehungen zu den Aposteln Paulus und Petrus, unterrichten will, der lese Apg. 12,12; 13,13; 15,37–39; Kol. 4,10.11; Philem. 24; 2. Tim. 4,11; 1. Petr. 5,13 (Mark. 14,51.52)."

11. The identification of the evangelist Matthew depends on the notion that the name Matthew in Mt 9:9 was added by Matthew, the author, himself. At the same time it is necessary to assume that the author wanted to stay in the background; see *Stuttgarter Jubiläumsbibel* for Mt 9:9–10: "Daß Matthäus das Zeug zu einem Apostel hatte, das beweist er damit, daß er . . . Leute von schlechtem Ruf zu einem Abschiedsessen einladet, um sie mit dem Sünderfreund bekannt zu machen. Und demütig verschweigt er in seinem Evangelium, daß solches seine Veranstaltung und daß es sein Haus war." The reading technique—to interpret specific information that is unparalleled in the other Gospels as an autobiographical comment of the author—has often been applied to the short account of the

young man who, at Jesus' arrest, escapes from the grip of the soldiers by dropping his clothes and running away naked. The missing name of the young man indicates that this was the author, Mark. See *Stuttgarter Jubiläumsbibel,* Mk 14:50–51: "Da nur Markus diesen Zug berichtet, so liegt der Schluß nahe, daß er selbst dieser Jüngling gewesen. Er war ja auch wirklich in Jerusalem zu Hause (Acts 12:24f.; 15:37f.)." It is possible that Secret Mark, which may be seen as an edition of Mark competing with the canonical version, contained additional references to this young man in analogy to the portrayal of the "beloved disciple" in John. These references identified the Gospel author with the rich young man who does not want to give up his wealth to become a follower of Jesus (Mk 10:17–22; cf. Mt 19:20). He was allegedly raised from the dead and lived in Jericho and is identical with the messenger in the empty tomb (Mk 16:5). See the discussion in *Semeia* 49 (1990) between J. D. Crossan, "Thoughts on Two Extracanonical Gospels," 161–66, and M. W. Meyer, "The Youth in the Secret Gospel of Mark," 129–154.

12. . . . καθὼς παρέδοσαν ἡμῖν οἱ ἀπ΄ ἀρχῆς αὐτόπται καὶ ὑπηρέται γενόμενοι τοῦ λόγου . . .

13. In 1 Cor 4:1 Paul writes, "Think of us in this way, as servants [ὡς ὑπηρέτας Χριστοῦ] of Christ and stewards of God's mysteries." The designation is repeated in Acts 26:16: "I have appeared to you for this purpose, to appoint you to serve [ὑπηρέτης] and testify to the things in which you have seen me and to those in which I will appear to you." From a reader's perspective the text endorses Paul's testimony and, indirectly, the writings of Paul's biographer, Luke. In Acts 13:5, too, Mark John is expressly called a servant, ὑπηρέτης.

14. For an attempt to place the we-passages within the literary conventions of the time, see J. Wehnert, *Die Wir-Passagen der Apostelgeschichten: Ein lukanisches Stilmittel aus jüdischer Tradition*, GTA 40 (1989). A very different interpretation, one that does not understand these passages as references to the author, is provided by W. Bindemann in "Verkündigter Verkündiger: Das Paulusbild der Wir-Stücke in der Apostelgeschichte: Seine Aufnahme und Bearbeitung durch Lukas," *ThLZ* 114 (1989): 706–19.

15. The Codex Bezae (D 05) has an additional we-passage in Acts 11:28. See C.-J. Thornton, *Der Zeuge des Zeugen: Lukas als Historiker der Paulusreisen*, WUNT 56 (Tübingen: Mohr, 1991), 268–69.

16. Thornton, *Zeuge*, has collected the relevant evidence and builds a strong case for Luke as the author of the Gospel and Acts.

17. Origenes, *In Lucam Homiliae* 1:6 (PG 13,1804), identified the nameless brother and travel companion of Titus, who is mentioned in 2 Cor 8:18, as Luke.

This connection is based on the characterization as "the brother who is famous among all the churches for the gospel [τὸν ἀδελφὸν οὗ ὁ ἔπαινος ἐν τῷ εὐαγγελίῳ διὰ πασῶν τῶν ἐκκλησιῶν]; the term *gospel* here is understood as a reference to the Gospel According to Luke. See R. Riesner, "Ansätze zur Kanonbildung innerhalb des Neuen Testaments," in *Der Kanon der Bibel*, ed. G. Maier (Basel: Brunnen; Wuppertal: Brockhaus, 1990), 155; J. Wenham, "The Identification of Luke," *Evangelical Quarterly* (London) 63 (1991): 4.

18. Clement of Alexandria, *stromata* 7.106.4, reports that Basilides used the traditions of Glaukias, who was Peter's translator, whereas Valentinus's source of information was Theodas, a student of Paul. These designations sound surprisingly similar to the constructions that led to the identification of Mark and Luke in the Canonical Edition.

19. John the Baptist: Jn 1:6; 1:15, 19, 26, 28, 32, 35, 40; 3:23, 27; 4:1; 5:33; 5:36; 10:40, 41; John, father of Peter: John 1:42; 21:15, 16, 17.

20. From the readers' perspective, Jn 21 confirms Jesus' announcement in Mk 10:39 that John will die as a martyr.

21. M. Franzmann and M. Klinger, "The Call Stories of John 1 and John 21," *St. Vladimir's Theological Quarterly* 36 (1992): 7–15, draws attention to the first (Jn 1:37–39, one of the disciples remains anonymous) and last call stories (Jn 21:19b-23). They complement each other so well that it may be assumed that "the unknown disciple of chapter 1, the beloved disciple, and the author of the Fourth Gospel are one and the same person" (15).

22. R. A. Culpepper, *Anatomy of the Fourth Gospel: A Study in Literary Design* (Philadelphia: Fortress Press, 1983), 215: "The Beloved Disciple, somewhat surprisingly, is introduced as a character unknown to the reader (13,23; 21,24)." When first mentioned, he is introduced to the readers as one of many disciples of Jesus (13:23: εἷς ἐκ τῶν μαθητῶν αὐτοῦ ἐν τῷ κόλπῳ τοῦ Ἰησοῦ, ὃν ηγάπα ὁ Ἰησοῦς); later he is referred to as "the" beloved disciple (19:26; 20:2; 21:7. 20).

23. In analogy to Matthew, who corrects the name Levi to Matthew, Eusebius of Caesarea reads John's Gospel as correcting the synoptic account. For example, Eusebius points out that Jn 3:24 insists that some of the events, which are placed following the arrest of John the Baptist in the synoptic version, actually occurred before his imprisonment (Eusebius, *h.e.* 3.24.7–13). Because John, the author of the Gospel, was a follower of John the Baptist before becoming a disciple of Jesus, he was an eyewitness to the event and therefore wanted to set the record straight.

24. While to preserve the anonymity of the author seems to have been an objective of the traditional material, the title of the book in the Canonical Edi-

tion allows the readers to identify the author. A similar process may have occurred during the final redaction of the canonical Book of Psalms. By ascribing psalms to Moses, Salomo, David, Korah, or Asaph, the editors created cross-references to other texts of the collection, thus enabling the readers to identify the "anonymous" opponents, e.g., Absalom in Ps 3; Saul in Psalms 18 and 57; Abimelech in Psalm 34; the Philistines in Psalm 56. See G. T. Sheppard, "'Enemies' and the Politics of Prayer in the Book of Psalms," in *The Bible and the Politics of Exegesis*, ed. D. Jobling, P. L. Day, and G. T. Sheppard (Cleveland: Pilgrim Press, 1991), 78–79.

25. Apart from the book titles (John, 1 John, 2 John, 3 John, and Revelation), the name John is mentioned 131 times in the following contexts: (1) John, son of Zebedee and one of Jesus' twelve disciples; (2) John the Baptist; (3) the author of Revelation (Rv 1:1, 4, 9; 22:8); (4) John, the father of Peter (Jn 1:42; 21:15–17); (5) John Mark (Acts 12:12, 25; 15:37); (6) John, the high priest (Acts 4:6).

26. See Ed. L. Miller, "The Johannine Origins of the Johannine Logos," *JBL* 112 (1993): 453; Schnackenburg, *Johannesbriefe*, 51.

27. E.g., Hengel, *Johannine Question*, 107 (or *Johanneische Frage*, 272), regarding 1 John: "The reason why the letter contains more stylistic difficulties and obscurities than the Gospel is connected with the fact that the author, an old man, dictated it quickly and in understandable agitation."

28. The name John is repeated several times in the text of Revelation (Rv 1:1, 4, 9; 22:8).

29. See Mk 6:3: "Is not this the carpenter, the son of Mary and brother of James and Joses and Judas and Simon, and are not his sisters here with us?"

30. John is called to be a disciple in Mt 4:21 and parallels.

31. Mt 4:21; 10:2–4; 17:1; 20:20–23; 26:37; Mk 1:19–20; 3:16–19; 5:37; 9:2; 10:35–40; 14:33; Lk 5:10–11; 6:14–16; 8:51; 9:28; Acts 1:13; 12:2.

32. Mt 10:3; Mk 3:18; Lk 6:15; Acts 1:13.

33. 1 Cor 9:5; cf. Mt 13:55; Mk 6:3; Acts 1:14; Gal 1:19.

34. Mk 15:40.

35. Lk 6:16.

36. See Ch. Burchard, "Zu Jakobus 2,14–26," *ZNW* 71 (1980): 27–45; 44, (quote): "Jak 2,14–26 liest sich wohl nicht nur zufällig wie gegen Paulus gerichtet."

37. Lührmann called attention to the link between the authors of the General Letters and Gal 2:9 (Lührmann, "Gal 2, 9," 71). Unlike the Pauline Letters the Catholic Epistles are not arranged according to their length. My own computer-

assisted count arrived at the following results (spaces are not counted, reflecting *scriptio continua*, and *nomina sacra* are not abbreviated): 1 John, 9,832 Greek characters; 1 Peter 9,412, James, 9,174.

38. Concerning Paul's Roman citizenship, see W. Stegemann, "War der Apostel Paulus ein römischer Bürger?" *ZNW* 78 (1987): 200–229.

39. D. Trobisch, *Paul's Letter Collection: Tracing the Origins* (Minneapolis: Fortress Press, 1994).

40. Hebrews is identified as a letter of Paul by editorial elements only. For a thorough discussion of the early history see Anderson, "Hebrews." In my opinion Hebrews does not want to mislead the readers as far as the identity of the author is concerned and therefore should not be treated as a literary forgery. D. Trobisch, "Das Rätsel um die Verfasserschaft des Hebräerbriefes und die Entdeckung eines echten Paulustextes," in *In Dubio pro Deo*, D. Trobisch ed. (Heidelberg: Wissenschaftlich theologisches Seminar, 1993), 320–23.

41. 2 Pt 3:14–16 expresses complete agreement between Peter and Paul.

42. The authority of apostolic tradition is promoted in the Letter of Jude as well: μνήσθητε τῶν ῥημάτων τῶν προειρημένων ὑπὸ τῶν ἀποστόλων τοῦ κυρίου ἡμῶν Ἰησοῦ Χριστοῦ (Jude 17; cf. 2 Pt 3:2).

43. Early readers of the Canonical Edition assume that the writings of the New Testament were written by the authors mentioned in the titles (Tertullian, *AdvMarc* 4.2; Irenaeus, *AdvHaer* 1.1.19, 3.1.2; *CanMur* 9). E. Flesseman-van Leer, "Prinzipien der Sammlung und Ausscheidung bei der Bildung des Kanons," *ZThK* 61 (1964): 411.

44. Trobisch, *Entstehung* and *Paul's Letter Collection*.

45. Rom 15:31: ἵνα ῥυσθῶ ἀπὸ τῶν ἀπειθούντων ἐν τῇ Ἰουδαίᾳ καὶ ἡ διακονία μου ἡ εἰς Ἰερουσαλὴμ εὐπρόσδεκτος τοῖς ἁγίοις γένηται ...

46. 1 Cor 9:5: οἱ λοιποὶ ἀπόστολοι καὶ οἱ ἀδελφοὶ τοῦ κυρίου καὶ Κηφᾶς.

47. The controversy concerning Paul's gospel is illustrated but not resolved in Galatians. 1 Cor 1–4 deals with parties in Corinth and expressly mentions the Peter party (1:12). See D. Trobisch, "The Council of Jerusalem in Acts and Paul's Letter to the Galatians," in *Theological Exegesis: Essays in Honor of Brevard S. Childs*, ed. Chr. Seitz and K. Greene-McCreight (Grand Rapids, Mich.: Eerdmans, 1999), 331–38.

48. The Jewish tradition of the term *New Testament* is prominent in Jer 31:31–34 and referred to in 2 Cor 3:14 and Heb 8:8 and 9:15–17, which quotes Jer 31:31– (Heb 12:24, however, has διαθήκη νέα); the institution of the Lord's Supper is found in Lk 22:20 (in D 05 19b–20 is missing) and 1 Cor 11:25. See van Unnik, "A Problem in the Early History." Combinations of *testament* and

book are mentioned Sir 24:23; 1 Mc 1:57 (βιβλίον διαθήκης); and Ex 24:7 (τὸ βιβλίον τῆς διαθήκης).

49. The New Testament texts seem to use καινός and νέος as synonyms. R. A. Harrisville, "The Concept of Newness in the New Testament," *JBL* 74 (1955): 79: "Four distinctive features are found to be inherent in the concept of newness: the elements of contrast, continuity, dynamic, and finality."

50. Main text witnesses for the Greek Old Testament are Codices Vaticanus (B 03), Sinaiticus (א 01), Alexandrinus (A 02), and Ephraemi Rescriptus (C 04). The arguably oldest fragment of the Greek Old Testament preserving *nomina sacra* is the Heidelberg Papyrus VBP IV 56, with the notation of κύριος and θεός, dated toward the end of the second century C.E. K. Aland, *Repertorium*, designates it as 03, AT 15, and AT 30 (18, 84, 97); Turner, *Typology*, as OT 24 (166); van Haelst, *Catalogue*, as Nr. 33 (35); the Göttingen edition of Deuteronomy, ed. J. W. Wevers; as Sigle 970. Editions: F. Bilabel, ed., "56: Septuagintapapyrus," *Veröffentlichungen der badischen Papyrus-Sammlungen* 4 (1923): 24–27; H.-J. Dorn, V. Rosenberger, and D. Trobisch eds., "Zu dem Septuagintapapyrus VBP IV 56," *ZPE* 61 (1985): 115–21, tables V–VI; "Nachtrag zu dem Septuagintapapyrus VBP IV 56," *ZPE* 65 (1986): 106; tables IIIa–b.

51. For a good introduction to the Jewish Bible in Greek, see E. Tov, "Die griechischen Bibelübersetzungen," part 2: "Principat," *ANRW* 20, no. 1 (1987): 121–89; I. L. Seeligmann, "Problems and Perspectives in Modern Septuagint Research," in *Textus: Studies of the Hebrew University Bible Project*, no. 15, ed. E. Tov (Jerusalem: Magnes Press, 1990), 169–232.

52. Origen uses these designations (Eusebius, *h.e.* 6.25), as well as Melito (Eusebius, *h.e.* 4.26.14). Philo mentions Γένεσις, Ἔξοδος, Λευιτικὸν (Λενιτικὴ βίβλος) Δευτερονόμιον, Βασιλεῖ, Παροιμίαι. Occasionally he refers to Exodus as ἡ ἐξαγωγή, to Deuteronomy as ἡ ἐπινομίς, and to Judges as τῶν κριμάτων βίβλος. Similar titles are found in the Mishnah for Genesis, Numeri, Proverbs, and Lamentations (Swete, *Introduction*, 214–15). Of interest in this context are the contributions of P. Kahle, "Der gegenwärtige Stand der Erforschung der in Palästina neu gefundenen hebräischen Handschriften: 27. Die im August 1952 entdeckte Lederrolle mit dem griechischen Text der kleinen Propheten und das Problem der Seputaginta," *ThLZ* 79 (1954): 82–94; "Problems of the Septuagint," *Studia Patristica* 1; *TU* 63 (1957): 328–38; "The Greek Bible and the Gospels: Fragments from the Judaean Desert," in *Studia Evangelica: Papers Presented to the International Congress on "The Four Gospels" in 1957*, ed. K. Aland et al. (Berlin: Akademie-Verlag, 1959), 613–21; "The Greek Bible Manuscripts Used by Origen," *JBL* 79 (1960): 111–18.

53. Whether the Hebrew canon consisted of two parts or three is a matter of debate. See R. Beckwith, "A Modern Theory of the Old Testament Canon," *Vetus Testamentum* 41 (1991): 385–95, criticizing J. Barton, *Oracles of God: Perceptions of Ancient Prophecy in Israel after the Exile* (London: Darton, Longman & Todd, 1986).

54. See Swete, *Introduction*, 217.

55. "This distribution is clearly due to the characteristically Alexandrian desire to arrange the books according to their literary character or contents, or their supposed authorship" (ibid., 218).

56. Codex Sinaiticus (א 01) has the sequence Gospels, Paul, Praxapostolos, while Codex Vaticanus (B 03) has Gospels, Praxapostolos, Paul.

57. Maybe the arrangement of Codex Vaticanus (B 03) prevailed in the manuscript tradition because it represents the events in chronological order. David and Salomo did live before Hosea and Isaiah. Perhaps it was more appropriate from the Christian point of view to place those prophets whose promises are fulfilled in the New Testament directly before the New Testament.

58. Swete, *Introduction*, 129: "As to the order of the books nothing can be ascertained, the scribe who converted the MS. into a palimpsest having used the leaves for his new text without regard to their original arrangement."

59. Revelation is full of allusions to the Septuagint without formally quoting it. See St. Thompson, *The Apocalypse and Semitic Syntax* (Cambridge: Cambridge University Press, 1985); according to D. D. Schmidt, "Semitisms and Septuagintalisms in the Book of Revelation," *NTS* 37 (1991): 602, these allusions create a "biblical effect."

60. That the editors wanted to refer to 2 Corinthians 3 by choosing the title *Old Testament* is supported by the observation that 2 Corinthians 3 is the only passage in the Christian Bible where the expression παλαιὰ διαθήκη is used.

61. In my opinion the editors and publishers try to suggest an early date for the formation of the New Testament, during Paul's days. This is supported by the construction of Acts, which seems to suggest that Luke published this book when Paul was still alive (see the next chapter).

62. Irenaeus, e.g., *AdvHaer* 3.17, uses the contraposition of *letter* (Old Testament) and *spirit* (New Testament) to argue for divine inspiration of the Christian Bible. See van Unnik, "A Problem in the Early History," 224–26.

63. Howard, "Tetragram," draws attention to the ambiguity and provides several examples: "The first century saw: εἶπεν יהוה τῷ κυρίῳ μου (Matt 22:44; Mark 12:36; Luke 20:42), while that of the second century saw: εἶπεν κύριος τῷ κυρίῳ μου. To the second-century church ἑτοιμάσατε τὴν ὁδὸν κυρίου

(Mark 1:3) must have meant one thing, since it immediately followed the words: ἀρχὴ τοῦ εὐαγγελίου Ἰησοῦ Χριστοῦ, but quite something else to the first-century church which saw ἑτοιμάσατε τὴν ὁδὸν יהוה" (78).

64. This is how Howard, "Tetragram," 78, explains the large number of variants in passages with *nomina sacra*. Of interest in this context, see P. Winter, "Some Observations on the Language in the Birth and Infancy Stories of the Third Gospel," *NTS* 1 (1954–55): 113. Winter observes that κύριος in Luke 1–2 represents the tetragram, whereas in the rest of the Gospel it refers to the person Jesus. He raises the question of whether this constitutes a good criterion for reconstructing an older written source, possibly in Hebrew.

65. H.-D. Wendland, *Die Briefe an die Korinther*, NTD 3 (1965): 158.

66. Ex 34:34 LXX: ἡνίκα δ' ἂν εἰσεπορεύετο Μωυσῆς ἔναντι יהוה λαλεῖν αὐτῷ, περιῃρεῖτο τὸ κάλυμμα ἕως τοῦ ἐκπορέυεσθαι.

67. It is not very likely that Paul would have avoided the tetragram to please his Gentile audience. He assumes that his readers are familiar with the Jewish Bible in Greek. As I have demonstrated, the extant exemplars preserve the tetragram in one form or another.

68. See *Stuttgarter Jubiläumsbibel*, 243, for 2 Cor 3:12–16: "Für die jüdischen Leser des Alten Testaments liegt eine Hülle über der Schrift oder vielmehr auf ihrem Herzen: so bleibt ihnen verborgen, daß der Gesetzesbund in Christus abgetan ist (Röm.11,25 ff.)."

69. Howard, "Tetragram," 78–82, gives additional examples for the confusion of Christ and JHWH in the New Testament: Rom 10:16–17, 14:10–11; 1 Cor 2:16, 10:9; 1 Pt 3:14–15; Jude 5.

70. Sometimes θεός represents the tetragram; see Howard, "Tetragram," 65, and Lifshitz, "Cave of Horror," 203–5: Zec 4:9; Jl 1:14. J. A. Fitzmyer, "The Contribution of Qumran Aramaic to the Study of the New Testament," *NTS* 20 (1973–74): 382–407, suggests that Aramaic may supply the missing link. 11QtgJob renders אלהא as מרא, which is Aramaic for "Lord." "Thus in this Palestinian Jewish document we have an instance of the missing link in the development from the construct and suffixal forms of מרא to the absolute usage of κύριος in the New Testament as a title for both Yahweh and Jesus" (388). See also Howard, "Tetragram," 69–70. Brown, "Nomina Sacra," 13, points to an Alexandrian convention of writing the tetragram in golden characters; see also Traube, *Nomina Sacra*, 21–23; Paap, *Nomina Sacra*, 1n. As mentioned before, אל, צבאות, אדוני, and אלוהים are sometimes written in paleo-Hebrew letters. This could be a close parallel to the fact that the *nomina sacra* spread to other *nomina divina*, a suggestion made by Brown in "Nomina Sacra," 18–19.

71. To represent the tetragram with Greek characters (πιπι), which show some resemblance to the Hebrew letters, nicely demonstrates how some scribes struggled with the technical problem of using different alphabets.

72. A suggestion made by Brown in "Nomina Sacra," 19.

73. For early Jewish evidence, see R. T. Herford, *Christianity in Talmud and Midrash* (reprint, Clifton, N.J.: Reference Book, 1966), 146–71. Readers were able to immediately recognize a non-Jewish edition because of the missing tetragram.

74. Roberts and Skeat, *Birth*, 41, cite five Christian manuscripts of the second century that are not biblical manuscripts: (1) British Library Egerton Papyrus 2 (van Haelst 586), two fragmentary codex pages with *nomina sacra*; see Bell and Skeat *Unknown Gospel*. (2) P.Mich. 129, Shepherd of Hermas (incorrectly recorded by van Haelst 657 and consequently also in Roberts and Skeat, *Birth*), is a one-layered codex with seventeen sheets (C. Bonner, ed., *A Papyrus Codex of the Shepherd of Hermas* (*Similitudes 2–9*) *with a Fragment of the Mandates*, Humanistic Series 22 [Ann Arbor: University of Michigan Press, 1934], 8), and it contains *nomina sacra*. (3) The fragment of Hermas, P.Mich. 130, is written on the verso of a used scroll; *nomina sacra* are not preserved but are very probable in the lacunae (Bonner, *Shepherd*, 130). (4) P.Oxy. 1:1, Gospel of Thomas (van Haelst 594), codex page with *nomina sacra*. (5) P.Oxy. 3:405 (supplement P.Oxy. 4, 264–65), Irenaeus, *AdvHaer* (van Haelst 671), scroll with *nomina sacra*. During the first four centuries Christians clearly favored the codex as they published their literature. In contrast to editions of the Christian Bible, however, the codex does not completely replace the scroll; for statistical data see Roberts and Skeat, *Birth*, 43–44.

75. The arguably oldest Latin fragment of a leather codex according to Roberts, "Codex," 180, is dated 100 C.E. It contains the text of an otherwise unknown writing, *De Bellis Macedonicis* (P.Oxy. 1:30 = P.Lit.Lond. 121), possibly from the *Historiae Philippicae* of Trogus Pompeius. The first editors, Grenfell and Hunt, 59, dated it no earlier than the third century. This late dating was challenged by J. Mallon in "Quel est le plus ancien exemple connu d'un manuscrit Latin en forme de codex?" *Emerita* (Madrid) 17 (1949): 1–8. The next oldest fragment of a Latin codex is P.Ryl 3:472 (third–fourth centuries), a liturgical text written on papyrus.

76. Seneca, philosopher, writer, and teacher of emperor Nero, died in 65 C.E.

77. Seneca, *De Brevitate Vitae* 13.4: "quia plurium tabularum contextus caudex apud antiquos vocatur unde publicae tabulae codices dicuntur." See Seneca, *controversiae 1*, praef. 18; Varro *ap.* non. p. 535 M: "quod antiqui plures tabulas

codices dicebant." For evidence from Cicero's writings see Th. Birt, *Kritik und Hermeneutik nebst Abriss des antiken Buchwesens*, HKAW 1, no. 3 (München: Beck, 1913), 284.

78. *Der Kleine Pauly: Lexikon der Antike*, ed. Konrat Ziegler and Walther Sontheimer (München: Deutscher Taschenbuch Verlag, 1979), 1052–1054.

79. Martial advertises the bookstore of Atrectus and even quotes the price of the book, five denars (*Epigrams* 1:117). In *Epigrams* 13:3, Martial makes fun of the bookseller Tryphon and his price calculations. See Schubart, *Buch*, 153; H. L. M. van der Valk, "On the Edition of Books in Antiquity," *VigChr* 11 (1957): 1–3. At the end of his first book of letters (*ep* 1:20), Horatius refers to the brothers Sosius as the publishers of the volume.

80. D. R. Shackleton Bailey, ed., *Martial: Epigrams* (Cambridge: Harvard University Press, 1993).

81. Roberts, "Codex," 179–80: "But whether this innovation, marketed jointly by a struggling author and an enterprising publisher, was a success is another question; there are reasons for thinking that it was not." Roberts admits that the fact that only very few Latin codices are preserved cannot carry a strong argument. Due to the dry climate, Egypt is almost the only place where ancient papyri survived. Latin texts were not as widely distributed in Egypt as they were in Rome, therefore the low number of extant Latin papyri is not a surprise. Roberts interprets Martial's lack of later comments on the codex form and the bookseller, Secundus, in his succeeding literary endeavors as an indication that the entire project had failed economically (ibid., 180). Valk, "Edition of Books," 3, disagrees, "Martial's social position may have improved, so that he no longer wished to resort openly to this device. Further, in his first book he had introduced himself to the public and, as we know, had become famous."

82. Sueton, *Divus Iulius* 56:6: "Epistulae quoque eius ad senatum extant, quas primum videtur ad paginas et formam memorialis libelli convertisse, cum antea consules et duces non nisi transversa charta scriptas mitterent."

83. Schubart, *Buch*, 115.

84. For the oldest legal definition of the term *codex*, see Roberts, "Codex," 180–81; Schubart, *Buch*, 114–16.

85. Galen, Περὶ Συνθέσεως Φαρμάκων; *Opera*, Karl Gottlob Kühn, ed., *Claudii Galeni opera omnia* (Leipzig: Knobloch, 1821), 12:423.

86. Augustinus, *Contra Cresconium* 3.27.30.

87. Roberts, "Codex," 195–96. For other cases when Christians deceived their persecutors in an attempt to protect their Holy Scriptures, see C. Wendel, "Bibliothek," *RAC* 2 (1954): 248–49, reprinted in *Kleine Schriften*, 180.

88. Augustinus, *ep* 171. For Jerome see H. I. Marrou, "La technique de l'édition à l'époque patristique," *VigChr* 3 (1949): 208–24, and Kloeters, "Buch."

89. E.g., the miniscules 1241, 2127 (see Trobisch, *Entstehung*, 16) or 𝔓[72].

90. So that a scroll could be rolled up after it had been read, it usually was wrapped around a stick that protruded at both sides and was called *cornua* (horns). The stick was tucked under the chin as the scroll was rolled up. Martial refers to this in *Epigrams* 1:66. See also Schubart, *Buch*, 104–7, 111.

91. Martial makes fun of the young poet Picens: "Picens writes his epigrams on the back of the papyrus and complains: the muse shows me her ass [*scribit in aversa Picens epigrammata charta / et dolet averso quod facit illa deo*]" see Martial, *Epigrams* 8:62. A scroll with writing on both sides, an opisthograph, is mentioned in Rv 5:1: βιβλίον γεγραμμένον ἔσωθεν καὶ ὄπισθεν.

92. Plinius remarks in *Naturalis historiae* 13:23 that a scroll was made up of no more than twenty sheets pasted together (*numquam plures scapo quam vicenae*). This description may refer to the size that was shipped to the customers. The papyri themselves contain references to scrolls, which were made up from as many as fifty or seventy sheets. See T. C. Skeat, "The Length of the Standard Papyrus Roll and the Cost-advantage of the Codex," *ZPE* 45 (1982): 169–75, esp. 169. This would allow for a standard size of 320–60 centimeters or 10–12 feet.

93. A scroll would have a strip of leather attached and hanging out from the top. This was referred to as the *Syllybos* in Greek and as *index* or *titulus* in Latin and usually gave the name of the author and the title of the book; see Schubart, *Buch*, 104, referring to Ovid, *Tristia* 1:105–110. The same information was repeated at the end of the text as a *subscriptio* in scrolls, whereas codices usually provide *superscriptiones* at the beginning of the text. F. Zucker, "Rezension: K. Ohly, Stychometrische Untersuchungen," *Gnomon* 8 (1932): 388; concerning the change from *subscriptio* to *superscriptio* in the Jewish Bible, see H. M. I. Gevaryahu, "Biblical Colophons: A Source for the 'Biography' of Authors, Texts and Books," in *Supplements to Vetus Testamentum*, vol. 28 (Leiden: Brill, 1975), 42–59.

94. T. Kleberg, *Buchhandel und Verlagswesen in der Antike* (Darmstadt: Wissenschaftliche Buchgesellschaft, 1967) 78: "Sehr starke Gründe sprechen dafür, daß die Kodexform römischen oder wenigstens italischen Ursprungs ist." See also Roberts, "Codex," 172; Schubart, *Buch*, 113; H. A. Sanders, "The Beginning of the Modern Book: The Codex of the Classical Era," *Michigan Alumnus* 44, no. 15 (1938): 101. The basic meaning of *liber* is "bark."

95. Roberts, "Codex," 176.

96. Even Martial, who clearly refers to the codex form, never uses the term *codex*.

97. Roberts, "Codex," 176. The Romans adapted the Greek *charta* (χάρτης) to refer to papyrus (Kleberg, *Buchhandel*, 70). In Greek τεῦχος may indicate a book but not necessarily a codex; see F. W. Hall, *Companion to Classical Texts* (Oxford: Clarendon, 1913; reprint, Hildesheim: Georg Olms, 1968), 15. A nice example for this use is the title πεντάτευχος.

98. The amount and quality of training of Christian scribes is a matter of debate. Roberts, "Codex," 198: "Some of the . . . earliest [codices] are written in hands which in varying degrees are blends of the literary and documentary styles such as might be written by men who, while not trained calligraphers, were practiced writers aware that they were not just copying a document or a private letter. In this category I should place the Rylands St. John, the Unknown Gospel in the British Museum, the Baden Deuteronomy, and the Chester Beatty Pauline Epistles." Aland and Aland, *Text of the New Testament*, 70, assume that the early codices were copied privately by professional scribes. The production probably asked for more professional know-how (see Dinkler v. Schubert, "CTAΥPOC," 8–9) than Hengel, *Evangelienüberschriften*, 42, would suggest.

99. Martial, *Epigrams*, 1:66, attacks plagiarists. He lists as two major factors in the price calculation of books the costs for copying and the price of the book cover.

100. The famous orator and writer Marcus Fabius Quintilianus (ca. 30 to 96), who lived in Rome since 69, describes (in *Institutio Oratoria* 10.3.31) sheets bound together to be used as notebooks in school. Roberts, "Codex," 175, gives P.Lit.Lond. 4 and 182 from the third and fourth century as examples. I have seen P.Vindob G 29274 (K. Aland, *Repertorium*, 332: Var 8; Rahlfs: 2090), which is a notebook with writing exercises. First only the right side of each page was used. And when they reached the middle page the notebook was turned around and upside down so that the final page of the booklet became the first page. This way the pupils kept writing on the nicer recto, the verso was left blank.

101. See Jerome, *ep* 112. When a brother visited who planned to travel to Africa in three days, Jerome wrote this lengthy letter in a hurry, in order to respond to Augustine. See Kloeters, "Buch," 139.

102. The Chester Beatty Codex $\mathfrak{P}^{46}$, which was produced toward the end of the second century in Egypt, documents typical problems. The scribe of this codex, which consists of a single layer, did not calculate correctly the number of papyrus sheets needed. In the second half of the book he had to add more lines per page and more letters per line to accommodate the text, but he had little success. See Trobisch, *Entstehung*, 26–28.

103. Augustine had a wider public in mind when he wrote letters to Jerome. *Ep* 40, which sums up the points where both disagreed, never arrived in Bethlehem.

Copies of this letter were distributed in Rome, and it was one of these copies that Jerome finally received. See R. Hennings, *Der Briefwechsel zwischen Augustinus und Hieronymus und ihr Streit um den Kanon des Alten Testaments und die Auslegung von Gal. 2,11–14*, Supplements to Vigiliae Christianae 21 (Leiden: Brill, 1994), 35–36; J. Scheele, "Buch und Bibliothek bei Augustinus," *Bibliothek und Wissenschaft* 12 (1978): 18.

104. According to Martial, *Epigrams* 1:118, the bookstores had several copies of his works in stock. See H. Göll, "Der Buchhandel in Griechenland und Rom," *Kulturbilder aus Hellas und Rom*, 2nd ed. (Leipzig: Hartknoch, 1869), 3:114.

105. T. C. Skeat, "The Use of Dictation in Ancient Book-Production," *Proceedings of the British Academy* 42 (1956): 179–208.

106. Van der Valk, "Edition of Books," 1–2: "In the opening poem, he recommends the edition in membrana, which is the popular and less costly one. In I 117 he has in view the deluxe edition which, apparently, was sold in a different bookshop." The difference in price may in part be caused by the fact that one edition is in codex form, while the other uses scrolls. Skeat, "Length," 169–75, calculates a 26 percent saving when books are produced as codices (175). However, he considers the costs only for the scribes and the material, not the binding.

107. See Hengel, *Johannine Question*, 26, concerning 2 John and 3 John: "It is a miracle that despite the enigmatic sender *ho presbyteros* and their insignificant contents these two letters were preserved at all."

108. Martial, in *Apophoreta* 184–92, insists that the *Metamorphosis* of Ovid and the writings of Homer, Virgil, and Cicero each can be held in one codex. See van der Valk, "Editions of Books," 2, n. 4; Roberts, "Codex," 179; Kleberg, *Buchhandel*, 76; Hall, *Companion to Classical Texts*, 16–17. Roberts, "Codex," 202, concludes that a codex could hold about six times as much text as a scroll. Gregor the Great (*ep* 5.53a) states that a literary work that originally occupied thirty-five scrolls filled only six codices. The thirteen Nag Hammadi codices, which were discovered in 1947, together comprise 794 pages; see J. Doresse and T. Mina, "Nouveaux textes gnostiques coptes découverts en Haute-Egypte: La bibliotheque de Chenoboskion," *VigChr* 3 (1949): 129–41; Roberts, "Codex," 193–94.

109. The Greek word σωμάτιον refers to a closed literary corpus, not necessarily to a codex.

110. The number of *stichoi* of a specific writing often varies from manuscript to manuscript and was probably added after the copy was made. See E. Kuhnert, "Geschichte des Buchhandels vom Altertum bis zur Gegenwart: Die Entwicklung in Umrissen," in *Handbuch der Bibliothekswissenschaft*, vol. 1: *Schrift und Buch*,

ed. Fritz Milkau (Leipzig: Harrassowitz, 1931), 724–25; Zucker, "Rezension: K. Ohly," 383–88. The Masoretes noted the number of verses (*pesukim*: פְּסוּקִים) at the end of a writing or at the end of a collection unit (Deuteronomy 955, Torah 5,888 *pesukim*; Swete, *Introduction*, 342). Another measurement for the length of the text, which is older than the Talmud, are the open *paraschot*, which mark the beginning of a new paragraph, and the closed ones, which mark a section within the paragraph. The former is marked in the *Biblia Hebraica Stuttgartensia* as פ, the latter as ס. When Augustine sends the finished manuscript of *De Civitate* to his publisher Firmus, he adds a contents sheet and suggests that the publisher publish it in two or in five volumes; see C. Lambot, "Lettre inédite de S. Augustin relative au 'De Civitate Dei,'" *Revue Bénédictine* 51 (1939): 109–21.

111. Text edited by Zahn, *Kanons*, 2:143–45. Other examples of canon lists with *stichoi* are Catalogus Claromontanus (ibid., 158–59) and the canon of Nicephorus (ibid., 297–301). See Swete, *Introduction*, 345.

112. Migne, *PG* 17, 628 C, 692 A. A certain Fidentinus managed to get a page of his own poetry into one of Martial's books. Martial is very upset about this; in *Epigrams* 1:53, he makes a nice play on the words *index* and *iudex*; Schubart, *Buch*, 104.

113. As Egypt had an international monopoly on the production of papyrus, Schubart, *Buch*, 164, suggests that the deteriorating political relations between Rome and Egypt promoted the use of leather. Because leather is much more expensive than papyrus, book manufacturers may have been attracted to the book form by the fact that codices need less material than scrolls. Also, leather sheets do not allow the scribes to write over the edges, where they were sewn together. Some of the Dead Sea Scrolls offer a good demonstration of the technical difficulties. The skins had to be cut to sheets of the same height and to a width that would accommodate a multiple of the standard column size. A considerable amount of leather probably had to be discarded to allow for these sizes.

114. R. J. Starr, "The Used-Book Trade in the Roman World," *Phoenix* 44 (1990): 156.

115. Describing the extraordinary library of Federigo da Montefeltro, the Italian bookseller Vespasiano da Bisticci (1421–98) remarks that Vespasiano would have been ashamed to collect printed books: "In dieser Bibliothek sind alle Bücher ausnehmend schön, alle mit der Feder geschrieben, alle mit feinsten Miniaturen geschmückt, und es sind keine gedruckten darunter, denn der Herzog hätte sich deren geschämt"; H. Widmann, "Herstellung und Vertrieb des Buches in der griechisch-römischen Welt," *Archiv für die Geschichte des Buchwesens* 8 (1967): 602.

116. Skeat revokes his earlier skepticism (Roberts and Skeat, *Birth*, 62–66) and after revisiting the evidence insists ("Irenaeus," 199): "I would now go so far as to suggest that the Four-Gospel Canon and the Four-Gospel codex are inextricably linked, and that each presupposes the other."

117. Granted that the effect of an edition does not necessarily reflect the intention of the editors, the polemic bias should not be underestimated. See B.-J. Diebner, "Zur Funktion der kanonischen Textsammlung im Judentum der vor-christlichen Zeit: Gedanken zu einer Kanon-Hermeneutik," *DBAT* 22 (1985–86): 58–73. Diebner points out that Paul uses the Greek term κανών relating to Ἰσραήλ τοῦ θεοῦ (Gal 6:16), which can be paralleled in writings found in Qumran (ibid., 63). The search for the "canon" is one result of the quest for the "true Israel." "Canon" defines a specific group and contains a distinct polemical element (ibid., 62).

118. Roberts and Skeat, *Birth*, 57.

119. B. Aland, "Marcion," 89–101; Hoffmann, *Marcion*. For a valuable analysis of text supporting a connection between the pseudepigrapha of the Canonical Edition and Marcion, see M. Rist, "Pseudepigraphic Refutations of Marcionism," *Journal of Religion* 22 (1942): 39–62.

120. Supported by Schmid, *Marcion*.

CHAPTER 4: A NOTE TO THE READERS OF THE CANONICAL EDITION

1. The noun *editorial* is defined as "a newspaper or magazine article that gives the opinions of the editors or publishers; *also*: an expression of opinion that resembles such an article"; *Merriam-Webster's Collegiate Dictionary*, 10th ed., s.v. "editorial" (Springfield, Mass.: Merriam-Webster, 1993).

2. Another example of an editorial note to the reader is Rv 1:1–3. The introductory passage to Luke's Gospel, Lk 1:1–4, is not an editorial, because its author addresses the readers rather than an editor.

3. The readers are informed about Paul's impending martyrdom in his farewell speech in Milet (Acts 20:24–25) and just before he leaves Judea for Jerusalem (Acts 21:13).

4. Within the framework of the whole New Testament, the ending of Acts provides the readers with important clues for establishing a relative chronology of the writings. However, when Acts is interpreted on its own merits and not as an integral part of the New Testament, the ending is often experienced as unsatisfactory. This has occasionally led to text changes in Christian editions.

For example, an Ethiopic edition published in the seventeenth or eighteenth century adds a passage at the end. The editors even continued the numbering of verses to indicate the canonical character. The addition reports that Paul's legal battle under Nero was successful at first and that he stayed in Rome for two full years. After a long journey, which is not disclosed in detail (see Rom 15:24; Phil 2:24; Phlm 22), Paul returned to the capital, baptized several members of the emperor's family (see Phil 4:22), and as a consequence was beheaded under Nero. See S. Uhlig, "Ein pseudepigraphischer Actaschluß in der äthiopischen Version," *Oriens Christianus* 73 (1989): 130.

5. Jn 21:19: "He said this to indicate the kind of death by which he would glorify God."

6. Jn 21:23: "So the rumor spread in the community that this disciple would not die. Yet Jesus did not say to him that he would not die, but, 'If it is my will that he remain until I come, what is that to you?'"

7. Irenaeus, *AdvHaer* 3.1.1, interprets the arrangement of the Gospels as reflecting the chronological order.

8. A study attempting to identify the historical publishers will certainly have to discuss questions of authorship within the framework of authenticity, pseudonymity, and forgery. From a methodological point of view a comparison to other ancient anthologies seems a promising approach. Under the supposition that 2 Peter and 2 Timothy are not authentic, the striking similarities between these writings and the redactional concept of the Canonical Edition may serve as a valuable guide. To keep the project focused, I decided not to deal with these questions in this study.

9. B. H. McLean, "Galatians 2.7–9 and the Recognition of Paul's Apostolic Status at the Jerusalem Conference: A Critique of G. Luedemann's Solution," *NTS* 37 (1991): 67–76, makes a strong argument that Paul's apostleship was at the center of the conflict reported in Gal 2:7–9.

10. Acts 21:20: πόσαι μυριάδες εἰσὶν ἐν τοῖς Ἰουδαίοις τῶν πεπιστευκότων καὶ πάντες ζηλωταὶ τοῦ νόμου ὑπάρχουσιν.

11. Gal 2:12: Paul insists that certain people who came from James had caused the Antiochian incident.

12. M. Karrer, "Petrus im paulinischen Gemeindekreis," *ZNW* 80 (1989): 210–31. In regard to the critical portrayal of Peter in John, see A. J. Droge, "The Status of Peter in the Fourth Gospel: A Note on John 18:10–11," *JBL* 109 (1990): 307–11.

13. For a discussion of Gal 2:11–14 and its connection to the circumcision of Timothy in the writings of the early church, see Hennings, *Briefwechsel*, 218–64.

14. See Gal 5:11–12: "But my friends, why am I still being persecuted if I am still preaching circumcision? In that case the offense of the cross has been removed. I wish those who unsettle you would castrate themselves!"

15. The commentators of the *Stuttgarter Jubiläumsbibel*, 179, make the point that the Bible differs from profane depictions of heroes. Even saints make mistakes, and the Bible records them.

16. Stegemann, "War der Apostel Paulus ein römischer Bürger?" 200–229.

17. Links between the pastoral Letters and Acts are compiled by J. D. Quinn in "The Last Volume of Luke: The Relation of Luke-Acts to the Pastoral Epistles," in *Perspectives on Luke-Acts*, ed. Charles H. Talbert (Danville, Va.: Association of Baptist Professors of Religion, 1978), 62–75.

18. H. Paulsen, *Der Zweite Petrusbrief und der Judasbrief*, KEK 12, no. 2 (Göttingen: Vandenhoeck, 1992), 115. The text points not to a saying of Jesus but to the redactional interpretation of a saying of Jesus. The theme of "reminding and understanding" runs through 2 Peter as a whole. See Ch. H. Talbert, "II Peter and the Delay of the Parousia," *VigChr* 20 (1966): 138: "The recurrence of these catchwords 'remind' and 'understand' divides the document into two parts, 1:3–2:22 and 3:1–18." J. Zmijewski demonstrated that this motif is very characteristic for pseudepigraphic publications; see "Apostolische Paradosis und Pseudepigraphie im Neuen Testament. 'Durch Erinnerung wachhalten' (2 Peter 1,13; 3,1)," *BZ* 23 (1979): 161–71. D. G. Meade's analysis seems to support this view: *Pseudonymity and Canon: An Investigation into the Relationship of Authorship and Authority in Jewish and Earliest Christian Tradition*, WUNT 39 (Tübingen: Mohr, 1986). Meade discerns actualization as the main function of pseudepigraphy.

19. See 2 Pt 1:13: δίκαιον δὲ ἡγοῦμαι, ἐφ᾽ ὅσον εἰμὶ ἐν τούτῳ τῷ σκηνώματι, διεγείρειν ὑμᾶς ἐν ὑπομνήσει. "Refreshing your memory" may refer to 2 Peter.

20. Acts 12:12; 1 Pt 5:13. Concerning the identification of the writer of Mark's Gospel, see the previous chapter.

21. Another signal that second-century readers may have picked up and that points to the Gospel According to Mark is the repeated reference to Peter's writings as "memories" (ὑπομιμνῄσκειν, 2 Pt 1:12; ἐν ὑπομνήσει, 1:13; μνήμην ποιεῖσθαι, 1:15; ἐν ὑπομνήσει . . . μνησθῆναι, 3:1–2). Justin, *DialTryph* 106.9–10, introduces a quote from Mark with the phrase "it is written in his [Peter's] memoirs [γεγράφθαι ἐν τοῖς ἀπομνημονεύμασιν αὐτοῦ]." Papias's comment in Eusebius is very similar: "Mark became Peter's translator and recorded accurately what he remembered [ὅσα ἐμνημόνευσεν]. . . . Mark did nothing wrong when he recorded details the way he remembered them [ὡς ἀπεμνημόνευσεν]"

(Eusebius, *h.e.* 3.39.14–15). See B. Orchard and H. Riley, *The Order of the Synoptics: Why Three Synoptic Gospels?* (Macon, Ga.: Mercer University Press, 1987), 188–94.

22. Irenaeus, *AdvHaer* 3.1.1, and Eusebius, *h.e.* 2.15.2 and 3.39.15, interpret 2 Pt 1:12–15 as a reference to Mark's Gospel. Most modern interpreters appear to identify the promised writing as an allusion to 2 Peter; see Paulsen, *Zweite Petrusbrief*, 115; A. Vögtle, "Die Schriftwerdung der apostolischen Paradosis nach 2 Peter 1,12–15," in *Offenbarungsgeschehen und Wirkungsgeschichte* (Freiburg: Herder, 1985), 297–304. However, this solution is not without serious problems; see J. N. D. Kelly, *A Commentary on the Epistles of Peter and of Jude*, Black's New Testament Commentaries (London: Black, 1969; reprint, London: Black, 1977), 312, 315. One of the difficulties is that the writing is promised in future tense (σπουδάσω) and not in present tense or aorist, which is normally used to refer to the letter just being written. Examples are Rom 15:15, Phlm 21, 1 Pt 5:12, Heb 13:22, Rom 16:22; Ignatius, IgnRom 8:3, 10:3, IgnMagn 14, IgnTral 12:3; and 2 Peter 3:1 (δευτέραν ὑμῖν γράφω ἐπιστολήν). C. Spicq, *Les Epîtres de Saint Pierre*, Sources Bibliques (Paris: Gabalda, 1966), 218, and Ch. Bigg, *A Critical Exegetical Commentary on the Epistles of St. Peter and St. Jude*, 2nd ed., ICC (1902; reprint, Edinburgh: Clark, 1956), 264–65, expressly oppose the reference to 2 Peter.

23. See J. H. Neyrey, "The Apologetic Use of the Transfiguration in 2 Peter 1:16–21," *CBQ* 42 (1980): 504–19; and, dealing with the historical background of 2 Peter and its relationship to the Letter of Jude, Neyrey, "The Form and Background of the Polemic in 2 Peter" (Ph.D. diss., Yale University, 1977).

24. A comparison with Mk 9:7b: (Οὗτός ἐστιν ὁ υἱός μου ὁ ἀγαπητός), Mt 17:5 (Οὗτός ἐστιν ὁ υἱός μου ὁ ἀγαπητός, ἐν ᾧ εὐδόκησα), and Lk 9:35 (Οὗτός ἐστιν ὁ υἱός μου ὁ ἐκλελεγμένος) demonstrates that 2 Peter does not provide a direct quote from either Gospel. There may be a distinctive attempt to harmonize Matthew with Mark. However, the sequence of words is altered, and the syntactical link through ἐν ᾧ is without parallel. 2 Peter may appear as an independent witness and not cause great difficulty for the readers of the Canonical Edition, who were introduced to four Gospels, not one. Presenting differing accounts from witnesses to the same tradition conforms to the editorial concept of the New Testament.

25. Regarding the expression προφητεία γραφῆς see Spicq, *Les Epîtres de Saint Pierre*, 226, and Kelly, *Commentary*, 325. The expression clearly does not refer to prophecies of Jesus or the apostles; see A. Vögtle, "'Keine Prophetie ist Sache eigenwilliger Auslegung' (2Petr 1,20f)," in *Offenbarungsgeschehen und Wirkungsgeschichte* (Freiburg: Herder, 1985), 309–10.

26. The references to apocryphal literature in the Letter of Jude, like the dispute between the archangel Michael and the devil over the body of Moses (Jude 9) and the quote from Henoch (Jude 14–15), are not included in 2 Peter. "Plainly he [author of 2 Peter] has stricter views on the OT and is reluctant to employ apocryphal books" (Kelly, *Commentary*, 227). Most commentators seem to agree that 2 Peter uses Jude. Under this assumption, the missing references to extracanonical material may be interpreted as an intentional redactional decision displaying canonical awareness.

27. M. Luther, *Sermons on the Epistle of St. Jude*, vol. 30 of *Luther's Works*, ed. Jaroslav Pelikan and Walter Hansen (Saint Louis: Concordia, 1967), 205. For an extensive summary of recent research on Jude see R. Heiligenthal, "Der Judasbrief: Aspekte der Forschung in den letzten Jahrhunderten," *ThR* 51 (1986): 117–29; see also Heiligenthal, *Zwischen Henoch und Paulus: Studien zum theologiegeschichtlichen Ort des Judasbriefes*, TANZ 6 (1992).

28. See O. Knoch, *Der Erste und Zweite Petrusbrief. Der Judasbrief, übersetzt und erklärt*, RNT (Regensburg: Pustet, 1990), 200–208; Paulsen, *Zweite Petrusbrief*, 97–100; H. Windisch, *Die Katholischen Briefe*, 3rd ed., HNT 15 (1951), 91–92; Bigg, *Epistles of St. Peter and St. Jude*, 216–23. For a thorough redactional-critical analysis see Neyrey, "Form and Background," 119–67.

29. A. Vögtle, "Petrus und Paulus nach dem Zweiten Petrusbrief," in *Kontinuität und Einheit*, ed. P.-G. Müller and W. Stenger (Freiburg et al.: Herder, 1981), 223–39.

30. *Jubiläumsbibel* refers to the Old Testament only.

31. See Mt 24:43: ἐκεῖνο δὲ γινώσκετε ὅτι εἰ ᾔδει ὁ οἰκοδεσπότης ποίᾳ φυλακῇ ὁ κλέπτης ἔρχεται, ἐγρηγόρησεν ἂν καὶ οὐκ ἂν εἴασεν διορυχθῆναι τὴν οἰκίαν αὐτοῦ.

32. I do not think that Jn 21 is simply an appendix to a book ending with Jn 20. This was suggested, for example, by J. N. Sanders and B. A. Mastin, *A Commentary on the Gospel According to St John*, BNTC (1968), 458; J. H. Bernard, *A Critical Exegetical Commentary on the Gospel According to St. John*, ICC (Edinburgh: Clark, 1928), 687. The links between this chapter and the preceding text seem too elaborate to warrant the solution. Jn 21 may be better understood as the product of the final editors of this Gospel, who not only added a chapter but also revised the manuscript produced by the "beloved disciple." For an investigation of these links, see, for example, P. S. Minear, "The Original Functions of John 21," *JBL* 102 (1983): 85–98; L. Hartman, "An Attempt at a Text-Centered Exegesis of John 21," *Studia Theologica* 38 (1984): 29–45; F. F. Segovia, "The Final Farewell of Jesus: A Reading of John 20:30–21:25," *The*

Fourth Gospel from a Literary Perspective, Semeia 53 (1991), 167–90; J. Breck, "John 21: Appendix, Epilogue or Conclusion?" *St. Vladimir's Theological Quarterly* 36 (1992): 27–49; Franzmann and Klinger, "Call Stories"; Ellis, "The Authenticity of John 21," *St. Vladimir's Theological Quarterly* 36 (1992): 17–25. Breck, Klinger (not Franzmann), and Ellis insist that Jn 21 was written by the "beloved disciple"; for other representatives of this thesis see Hengel, *Johanneische Frage*, 225. However, the close links between Jn 1–20 and Jn 21 do not answer questions of authorship. They simply demonstrate how carefully crafted the final chapter is, which could be the work of author or publisher alike. See the note to the readers in Rv 1:1–3 and its numerous links to the text of Revelation. Of special interest in this context are the cross-references of Mk 1:16–18, Lk 5, and Jn 21. See Droge, "Peter," 308: "The Beloved Disciple has displaced Peter from his privileged position in the Johannine version of the first call story. Indeed, Peter is not even called by Jesus, but by his brother, Andrew (John 1:41)." H. Thyen, "Johannes und die Synoptiker," in *John and the Synoptics*, ed. A. Denaux, BEThL 51 (Leuven: Peeteus, 1992), 84, insists that the texts about Peter reach their culmination point only in the last chapter. Thyen strongly supports the notion that the author of Jn 21 is the editor of the Gospel in its final form.

33. Most commentators do not see this break. See J. Schneider, *Das Evangelium nach Johannes*, ThHK (1976), 334–35; W. Bauer, *Das Johannesevangelium*, 2nd ed., HNT 6 (1925), 234; B. Weiss, *Kritisch exegetisches Handbuch über das Evangelium des Johannes*, 7th ed., KEK (1886), 714–16; R. Bultmann, *Das Evangelium des Johannes*, 12th ed., KEK (1952), 555–56; Bernard, *Gospel According to St. John*, 713–14; Sanders and Mastin, *Gospel According to St. John*, 47–48. Hengel, however, agrees that there is a break (*Johannine Question*, 83): "The only clear indication of any activity in editing is the *oidamen* in 21,24 or the *oimai* in 21,25."

34. Milne and Skeat, *Scribes*, 12. The photograph was made under ultraviolet light (Milne and Skeat, *Scribes*, fig. 3). I scanned the photo and traced the reconstruction of the first hand by computer.

35. K. Lake, "Rezension: H. J. M. Milne, T. C. Skeat, *Scribes and Correctors of the Codex Sinaiticus* (London: British Museum, 1938)," *Classical Philology* 37 (1942): 91, interprets the evidence as a clerical error: "The omission of the verse has now no critical importance. It was merely a scribal error, corrected immediately." See also Hengel, *Johanneische Frage*, 272 n. 195.

36. Milne and Skeat, *Scribes*, 12–13, refer to Dublin Trin. Coll A.1.8 and miniscule 700 (non vidi).

37. Jn 21 contains numerous links to the synoptic Gospels. The most evident one is probably the reference to the miraculous catch of fish, Lk 5:1–11. See F. Neirynck, "John 21," *NTS* 36 (1990): 321–29. Apprehensive readers may

find a reference from the story of Peter denying Jesus three times to Jesus repeating three times to Peter: "Tend my sheep" (see, for example, Bernard, *Gospel According to St. John*, 691).

38. Clement of Alexandria interpreted the chronological information given in the Canonical Edition to mean that Paul, who Clement thought was executed under Nero, was the last of the New Testament authors to die. Arguing against Basilides, Valentinus, and Marcion, he writes: "The teaching of the apostles, including the ministry of Paul, ends with Nero. Only later, in the times of Hadrian the king, those who invented the heresies arose." Clement concludes, "Such being the case, it is evident, from the high antiquity and perfect truth of the Church, that these later heresies, and those yet subsequent to them in time, were new inventions" (*stromata* 7:106:4, 7:107:2).

CHAPTER 5: OUTLOOK

1. See S. Lieberman, *Hellenism in Jewish Palestine: Studies in the Literary Transmission, Beliefs, and Manners of Palestine in the I Century* B.C.E.*–IV Century* C.E., Texts and Studies of the Jewish Theological Seminary of America 18 (New York: Jewish Theological Seminary, 1950).

2. R. Rendtorff, "Zur Bedeutung des Kanons für eine Theologie des Alten Testaments," in "*Wenn nicht jetzt, wann dann?*": *Festschrift Hans-Joachim Kraus* (Neukirchen-Vluyn: Neukirchner, 1983), 11.

Bibliography

Aland, Barbara. "Die Rezeption des neutestamentlichen Textes in den ersten Jahrhunderten." In *The New Testament in Early Christianity*, BEThL 86 (Leuven: Leuven University Press, 1989), 1–38.

———. "Marcion: Versuch einer neuen Interpretation." *ZThK* 70 (1973): 420–47.

———. "Marcion (ca. 85–160)/Marcioniten." *TRE* 22 (1992): 89–101.

Aland, Barbara, and Kurt Aland. *Der Text des Neuen Testaments: Einführung in die wissenschaftlichen Ausgaben sowie in Theorie und Praxis der modernen Textkritik*. 2nd ed. (Stuttgart: Deutsche Bibelgesellschaft, 1989); also published as *The Text of the New Testament: An Introduction to the Critical Editions and to the Theory and Practice of Modern Textual Criticisms*, 2nd ed. (Grand Rapids, Mich.: Eerdmans; Leiden: Brill, 1989).

Aland, Barbara, Kurt Aland, Johannes Karavidopoulos, Carlo M. Martini, and Bruce M. Metzger, eds. *The Greek New Testament*. 4th ed. (Stuttgart: Deutsche Bibelgesellschaft, 1993).

———. *Novum Testamentum Graece*. 27th ed. (Stuttgart: Deutsche Bibelgesellschaft, 1993).

Aland, Kurt. "Bemerkungen zum Alter und zur Entstehung des Christogrammes anhand von Beobachtungen bei P66 und P75." In *Studien zur Überlieferung des Neuen Testaments und seines Textes*, ANTF 2 (1967), 173–79.

———. "Das Problem der Anonymität und Pseudonymität in der christlichen Literatur der ersten beiden Jahrhunderte." In *Studien zur Überlieferung des Neuen Testaments und seines Textes*, ANTF 2 (1967), 24–34.

———. "Das Problem des neutestamentlichen Kanons." In *Studien zur Überlieferung des Neuen Testaments und seines Textes*, ANTF 2 (1967), 1–23.

———. "Die griechischen Handschriften des Neuen Testaments: Ergänzungen zur 'Kurzgefaßten Liste' (Fortsetzungsliste VII)." In *Materialien zur neutestamentlichen Handschriftenkunde*, ANTF 3 (1969), 1–53.

———. "Falsche Verfasserangaben? Zur Pseudonymität im frühchristlichen Schrifttum." *Th Rv* 75 (1979): 1–10.

———. *Kurzgefaßte Liste der griechischen Handschriften des Neuen Testaments.* ANTF 1 (Berlin: De Gruyter, 1963).

———. "Neue neutestamentliche Papyri." *NTS* 3 (1957): 261–286.

———. "Neue neutestamentliche Papyri II." *NTS* 12 (1966): 193–210.

———. "Noch einmal: Das Problem der Anonymität und Pseudonymität in der christlichen Literatur der ersten beiden Jahrhunderte." In *Pietas: Festschrift Bernhard Kötting*, JAC.E 8 (1980), 121–39.

———. "Über die Möglichkeiten der Identifikation kleiner Fragmente neutestamentlicher Handschriften mit Hilfe des Computers." In *Studies in New Testament Language and Text in Honour of George D. Kilpatrick*, ed. J. K. Elliott, NT.S 44 (1976), 14–38.

———. *Materialien zur neutestamentlichen Handschriftenkunde.* ANTF 3 (1969).

———. *Repertorium der griechischen christlichen Papyri, 1: Biblische Papyri, Altes Testament, Neues Testament, Varia, Apokryphen*, im Namen der patristischen Arbeitsstelle Münster herausgegeben (Berlin: De Gruyter, 1976).

Aland, Kurt, Matthew Black, Carlo M. Martini, Bruce M. Metzger, and Allen Wikgren, eds. *Novum Testamentum Graece.* 26th ed. (Stuttgart: Deutsche Bibelgesellschaft, 1979).

Altaner, Berthold. *Patrology.* Trans. Hilda C. Graef (New York: Herder, 1960).

Altaner, Berthold, and Alfred Stuiber., *Patrologie: Leben, Schriften und Lehre der Kirchenväter.* 9th ed. (Freiburg: Herder, 1980).

Aly, Zaki (ed.), *Three Rolls of the Early Septuagint: Genesis and Deuteronomy.* Papyrologische Texte und Untersuchungen 17 (Bonn: Rudolf Habelt, 1980).

American Bible Society, ed. *The American Bible Society Reference Bible on CD-ROM.* Release 1.02 (New York: American Bible Society, 1993).

Anderson, Ch. P. "The Epistle to the Hebrews and the Pauline Letter Collection." *HThR* 59 (1966): 429–38.

Avi-Yonah, M. "Abbreviations in Greek Inscriptions." *Quarterly of the Department of Antiquities in Palestine* (Jerusalem), supplement to vol. 9 (1940): 1–125.

Bammel, C. P. Hammond. "Products of Fifth-Century Scriptoria Preserving Conventions Used by Rufinus of Aquileia." *JThS* 30 (1979): 430–62.

Barthélemy, D. "Redécouverte d'un chaînon manquant de l'Histoire de la Septante." *RB* 60 (1953): 18–29.

Barton, John. *Oracles of God: Perceptions of Ancient Prophecy in Israel after the Exile* (London: Darton, Longman & Todd, 1986).

Bartsch, Hans-Werner. *Codex Bezae versus Codex Sinaiticus im Lukasevangelium* (Hildesheim: Georg Olms, 1984).

Baudissin, Wolf Wilhelm. Κυριος *als Gottesname im Judentum und seine Stelle in der Religionsgeschichte*. Ed. Otto Eissfeldt. 4 vols. (Giessen: Töpelmann, 1929).

Bauer, Walter. *Das Johannesevangelium*. 2nd ed., HNT 6 (1925).

Bauer, Walter, Kurt Aland, and Barbara Aland. *Griechisch-deutsches Wörterbuch zu den Schriften des Neuen Testaments und der übrigen urchristlichen Literatur*. 6th ed. (Berlin: De Gruyter, 1988).

Bauer, Walter, Martin Dibelius, Rudolf Knopf, and Hans Windisch, eds. *Die Apostolischen Väter*. HNT.EB (Tübingen: Mohr, 1923).

Beckwith, Roger T. "A Modern Theory of the Old Testament Canon." *Vetus Testamentum* 41 (1991): 385–95.

———. *The Old Testament Canon of the New Testament Church and Its Background in Early Judaism* (Grand Rapids, Mich.: Eerdmans, 1985).

Behm, Johannes. *Der Begriff ΔΙΑΘΗΚΗ im Neuen Testament* (Leipzig: Deichert, 1912).

Bell, H. Idris, and T. C. Skeat eds., *Fragments of an Unknown Gospel and Other Early Christian Papyri*. 2nd ed. (London, 1935).

Berger, Klaus. *Formgeschichte des Neuen Testaments* (Heidelberg: Quelle & Meyer, 1984).

Bernard, J. H. *A Critical Exegetical Commentary on the Gospel according to St. John*. ICC (Edinburgh: Clark, 1928).

Best, Ernest. "Ephesians i, 1." In *Text and Interpretation: Studies in the New Testament Presented to Matthew Black*, ed. Ernest Best and R. McL. Wilson (Cambridge: Cambridge University Press, 1979), 29–41.

Bigg, Charles. *A Critical Exegetical Commentary on the Epistles of St. Peter and St. Jude*. 2nd ed., ICC (1902; reprint, Edinburgh: Clark, 1956).

Bihlmeyer, Karl, ed. *Die Apostolischen Väter*. Neubearbeitung der Funkschen Ausgabe. 2 vols. 2nd ed. (Tübingen: Mohr, 1956).

Bilabel, Friedrich, ed. "56: Septuagintapapyrus." *Veröffentlichungen aus den badischen Papyrus-Sammlungen: Griechische Papyri* (*Urkunden, Briefe, Schreibtafeln, Ostraka etc.*) *mit 2 Tafeln* 4 (1923): 24–27.

Bindemann, Walther. "Verkündigter Verkündiger: Das Paulusbild der Wir-Stücke in der Apostelgeschichte: Seine Aufnahme und Bearbeitung durch Lukas." *ThLZ* 114 (1989): 706–19.

Birt, Theodor. *Kritik und Hermeneutik nebst Abriss des antiken Buchwesens*. HKAW 1, no. 3 (München: Beck, 1913).

Black, David Allen. "The Peculiarities of Ephesians and the Ephesian Address." *Grace Theological Journal* 2 (1981): 59–73.

Blaß, F., and A. Debrunner. *Grammatik des neutestamentlichen Griechisch*. 17th ed. Ed. Friedrich Rehkopf (Göttingen: Vandenhoeck, 1990).

Blum, Georg Günter. *Tradition und Sukzession: Studie zum Normbegriff des Apostolischen von Paulus bis Irenäus*. Arbeiten zur Geschichte und Theologie des Luthertums 9 (Berlin: Lutherisches. Verlagshaus, 1963).

Bonner, Campbell, ed. *A Papyrus Codex of the Sheperd of Hermas* (*Similitudes 2–9*) *with a Fragment of the Mandates*. Humanistic Series 22 (Ann Arbor: University of Michigan Press, 1934).

Boring, M. Eugene. "Mark 1:1–15 and the Beginning of the Gospel." *Semeia* 52 (1991): 43–81.

Breck, John. "John 21: Appendix, Epilogue, or Conclusion?" *St. Vladimir's Theological Quarterly* 36 (1992): 27–49.

Brett, Mark G. *Biblical Criticism in Crisis? The Impact of the Canonical Approach on Old Testament Studies* (Cambridge: Cambridge University Press, 1991).

Brown, Schuyler. "Concerning the Origin of the Nomina Sacra." *Studia Papyrologica* 9 (1970): 7–19.

Bruce, F. F. "Some Thoughts on the Beginning of the New Testament Canon." *Bulletin of the John Rylands University Library* (Manchester) 65 (1982–83): 37–60.

———. *The Canon of Scripture* (Downers Grove, Ill: Inter Varsity Press, 1988).

Bultmann, Rudolf. *Das Evangelium des Johannes*. 12th ed., KEK (1952).

Burchard, Christoph. "Zu Jakobus 2, 14–26." *ZNW* 71 (1980): 27–45.

Burkitt, F. C., ed. *Fragments of the Books of Kings according to the Translation of Aquila* (Cambridge: Cambridge University Press, 1897).

Byington, Steven T. "יהוה and אדני." *JBL* 76 (1957): 58–59.

Campenhausen, Hans von. *Die Entstehung der christlichen Bibel*. BHTh 39 (1968). Reprinted as *The Formation of the Christian Bible* (Philadelphia: Fortress, 1972).

Chapman, J. "The Order of the Gospels in the Parent of Codex Bezae." *ZNW* 6 (1905): 339–46.

Childs, Brevard S. *Biblical Theology of the Old and New Testaments: Theological Reflection on the Christian Bible* (London: SCM Press, 1992).

———. *Introduction to the Old Testament as Scripture* (Philadelphia: Fortress, 1979).

———. *The New Testament as Canon: An Introduction* (London: SCM Press, 1984; Philadelphia: Fortress, 1985).

Christ, Wilhelm von. *Geschichte der Griechischen Literatur*. 7th ed. Ed. Wilhelm Schmid. HAW 7 (1913).

Collins, Raymond F. "The Matrix of the New Testament Canon." *BTB* 7 (1977): 51–59.

Cosgrove, Charles H. "Justin Martyr and the Emerging Christian Canon: Observations on the Purpose and Destination of the Dialogue with Trypho." *VigChr* 36 (1982): 209–32.

Crossan, John Dominic. "Thoughts on Two Extracanonical Gospels." *Semeia* 49 (1990): 161–66.

Culpepper, R. Alan. *Anatomy of the Fourth Gospel: A Study in Literary Design* (Philadelphia: Fortress, 1983).

Dallas Theological Seminary, ed. *CDWORD: The Interactive Bible Library* (Dallas: Dallas Theological Seminary, 1990).

Deissmann, Adolf. *Die Septuaginta-Papyri und andere altchristliche Texte der Heidelberger Papyrus-Sammlung*. Veröffentlichungen aus den Heidelberger Papyrus-Sammlung 1 (Heidelberg: Winter, 1905).

Delcor, M. "Des diverses manières d'écrire le tétragramme sacré dans les anciens documents hébraïques." *Revue de l'histoire des religions* 147 (1955): 145–73.

Deutsche Bibelstiftung, Stuttgart; Katholische Bibelanstalt, Stuttgart; and Österreichisches Katholisches Bibelwerk, Klosterneuburg, eds. *Einheitsübersetzung der Heiligen Schrift: Die Bibel.* Gesamtausgabe. (Stuttgart: Katholische Bibelanstalt, 1980).

Diebner, Bernd Jørg., "Zur Funktion der kanonischen Textsammlung im Judentum der vor-christlichen Zeit: Gedanken zu einer Kanon-Hermeneutik." *DBAT* 22 (1985–86): 58–73.

Dinkler, Erich. "Zur Geschichte des Kreuzsymbols." *ZThK* 48 (1951): 148–72.

Dinkler von Schubert, Erika. "CTAYPOC: Vom 'Wort vom Kreuz' (1 Kor. 1, 18) zum Kreuz-Symbol." *Byzantine East, Latin West: Art-Historical Studies in Honor of Kurt Weitzmann*, ed. Christopher Moss and Katherine Kiefer (Princeton, N.J.: Princeton University Department of Art and Archeology, 1995), 29–38.

Dodd, C. H. "A New Gospel." In *The John Rylands Library*, 2nd ed. (Manchester: Manchester University Press, 1954), 56–92.

Dodrowski, Günther, ed. *Duden: Das große Wörterbuch der deutschen Sprache.* Durchgesehener Nachdruck. (Mannheim: Bibliographische Institut, 1977).

Donfried, Karl P. *The Setting of Second Clement in Early Christianity.* NT.S 38 (1974).

Doresse, Jean, and Togo Mina. "Nouveaux textes gnostiques coptes découverts en Haute-Egypte: La bibliotheque de Chenoboskion." *VigChr* 3 (1949): 129–41.

Dormeyer, Detlev. *Evangelium als literarische und theologische Gattung.* Erträge der Forschung 263 (Darmstadt: Wissenschaftliche Buchgesellschaft, 1989).

Dorn, H.-J., V. Rosenberger, and D. Trobisch, eds. "Nachtrag zu dem Septuagintapapyrus VBP IV 56." *ZPE* 65 (1986): 106, table IIIa–b.

———. "Zu dem Septuagintapapyrus VBP IV 56." *ZPE* 61 (1985): 115–21, table V–VI.

Droge, Arthur J. "The Status of Peter in the Fourth Gospel: A Note on John 18:10–11." *JBL* 109 (1990): 307–11.

Dunand, F. *Papyrus grecs bibliques (F. Inv. 266): Volumina de la Genèse et du Deutéronome*. Recherches d'archéologie, de philologie et d'histoire 27 (Cairo: Institut français d'archéologie orientale, 1966).

Ehrman, Bart D. "The Text of Mark in the Hands of the Orthodox." *Lutheran Quarterly* (Milwaukee) 5 (1991): 143–56.

Ellis, Peter F. "The Authenticity of John 21." *St. Vladimir's Theological Quarterly* 36 (1992): 17–25.

Färber, Hans, and Wilhelm Schöne, eds. *Horaz: Sämtliche Werke lateinisch und deutsch*. 9th ed. (Darmstadt: Wissenschaftliche Buchgesellschaft, 1982).

Farmer, William R., and Denis M. Farkasfalvy. *The Formation of the New Testament Canon* (New York et al.: Paulist Press, 1983).

Fischer, Joseph. "Die Einheit der beiden Testamente bei Laktanz, Viktorin von Pettau und deren Quellen." *Münchener Theologische Zeitschrift* 1 (1950): 96–101.

Fischer, Joseph A., ed. *Die Apostolischen Väter: Griechisch und deutsch, Eingeleitet, herausgegeben, übertragen und erläutert* (Darmstadt: Wissenschaftliche Buchgesellschaft, 1956).

Fischer, Karl Martin. "Anmerkung zur Pseudepigraphie im Neuen Testament." *NTS* 23 (1977): 76–81.

Fitzmyer, Joseph A. "Der semitische Hintergrund des neutestamentlichen Kyriostitels." In *Jesus Christus in Historie und Theologie: Neutestamentliche Festschrift für Hans Conzelmann zum 60. Geburtstag*, ed. G. Strecker (Tübingen: Mohr, 1975), 267–98.

———. "The Contribution of Qumran Aramaic to the Study of the New Testament." *NTS* 20 (1973–74): 382–407.

Flesseman-van Leer, Ellen, "Prinzipien der Sammlung und Ausscheidung bei der Bildung des Kanons." *ZThK* 61 (1964): 404–20.

Frank, Isidor. *Der Sinn der Kanonbildung: Eine historisch-theologische Untersuchung der Zeit vom 1. Clemensbrief bis Irenäus von Lyon*. Freiburger Theologische Studien 90 (Freiburg: Herder, 1971).

Frankemölle, Hubert. *Evangelium—Begriff und Gattung: Ein Forschungsbericht*. Stuttgarter Biblische Beiträge, 15 (Stuttgart: Katholisches Bibelwerk, 1988).

Franzmann, M., and M. Klinger, "The Call Stories of John 1 and John 21." *St. Vladimir's Theological Quarterly* 36 (1992): 7–15.

Gallazzi, C. "Frammenti di un codice con le Epistole di Paolo." *ZPE* 46 (1982): 117–22.

Gamble, Harry. *The New Testament Canon: Its Making and Meaning* (Philadelphia: Fortress, 1985).

Georgi, Dieter. "Die Aristoteles- und Theophrastausgabe des Andronikus von Rhodus: Ein Beitrag zur Kanonsproblematik." In *Konsequente Traditionsgeschichte: Festschrift für Klaus Baltzer*, ed. Rüdiger Bartelmus et al., OBO 126 (1993).

Gerstinger, Hans. "Rezension: A. H. R. E. Paap: Nomina sacra in the Greek Papyri of the First Five Centuries A.D. (Leiden: Brill, 1959)." *Gnomon* 32 (1960): 371–74.

Gevaryahu, H. M. I. "Biblical Colophons: A Source for the 'Biography' of Authors, Texts, and Books." In *Supplements to Vetus Testamentum*, vol. 28 (Leiden: Brill, 1975), 42–59.

Göll, Hermann. "Der Buchhandel in Griechenland und Rom." In *Kulturbilder aus Hellas und Rom*, 2nd ed. (Leipzig: Hartknoch, 1869), 3:98–124.

Goodspeed, Edgar J. *A History of Early Christian Literature*. Rev./enl. Robert M. Grant (Chicago: University of Chicago Press, 1966).

———. *The Apostolic Fathers: An American Translation* (New York: Harper, 1950).

Grant, Robert M., ed., *The Apostolic Fathers: A New Translation and Commentary* (New York: Nelson, 1964–68).

Greenlee, J. Harold. *Nine Uncial Palimpsests of the Greek New Testament*. Studies and Documents 39 (Salt Lake City: University of Utah Press, 1968).

Gregson, R. "A Solution of the Problems of the Thessalonian Epistles." *Evangelical Quarterly* 38 (1966): 76–80.

Haenchen, Ernst. *Die Apostelgeschichte*. 7th ed., KEK 3 (1977).

Hagedorn, Dieter, ed. "P.IFAO II 31: Johannesapokalypse 1, 13–20." *ZPE* 92 (1992): 243–47.

Hahn, Ferdinand. "Die Heilige Schrift als älteste christliche Tradition und als Kanon." *Evangelische Theologie* 40 (1980): 456–66.

Hahneman, Geoffrey Mark. *The Muratorian Fragment and the Development of the Canon*. Oxford Theological Monographs (Oxford: Clarendon, 1992).

Hall, F. W. *Companion to Classical Texts* (Oxford: Clarendon, 1913; reprint, Hildesheim: Georg Olms, 1968).

Harnack, Adolf von. *Das Neue Testament um das Jahr 200* (Freiburg: Mohr, 1889).

———. *Die Entstehung des Neuen Testamentes und die wichtigsten Folgen der neuen Schöpfung* (Leipzig: Hinrichs, 1914).

———. *Marcion: Das Evangelium vom fremden Gott: Eine Monographie zur Geschichte der Grundlegung der katholischen Kirche* (Leipzig: Hinrichs, 1921; reprint, Berlin: Akademie-Verlag, 1960).

Harris, J. Rendell, ed. *Biblical Fragments from Mount Sinai* (London, 1890).

Harrison, P. N. *Polycarp's Two Epistles to the Philippians* (Cambridge: Cambridge University Press, 1936).

Harrisville, R. A. "The Concept of Newness in the New Testament." *JBL* 74 (1955): 69–79.

Hartman, Lars. "An Attempt at a Text-Centered Exegesis of John 21." *Studia Theologica* 38 (1984): 29–45.

Hatch, William H. P. "The Position of Hebrews in the Canon of the New Testament." *HThR* 29 (1936): 133–51.

Head, Peter M. "A Text-Critical Study of Mark 1.1: 'The Beginning of the Gospel of Jesus Christ.'" *NTS* 37 (1991): 621–29.

Heath, Dale Eldon. *The Text of Manuscript Gregory 048* (*Vatican Greek 2061*) (Upland, Ind.: Taylor University, 1965).

Heiligenthal, Roman. "Der Judasbrief: Aspekte der Forschung in den letzten Jahrhunderten." *ThR* 51 (1986): 117–29.

———. *Zwischen Henoch und Paulus: Studien zum theologiegeschichtlichen Ort des Judasbriefes.* TANZ 6 (1992).

Helm, Rudolf, ed. *Martial: Epigramme, Eingeleitet und im antiken Versmaß übertragen.* Bibliothek der Alten Welt (Zürich: Artemis, 1957).

Hengel, Martin, *Die Evangelienüberschriften.* SHAW.PH 1984, no. 3 (Heidelberg: Winter, 1984).

———. *Die johanneische Frage: Ein Lösungsversuch, mit einem Beitrag zur Apokalypse von Jörg Frey.* WUNT 67 (Tübingen: Mohr, 1993).

———. *The Johannine Question* (London: SCM; Philadelphia: Trinity, 1989).

Hennings, Ralph. *Der Briefwechsel zwischen Augustinus und Hieronymus und ihr Streit um den Kanon des Alten Testaments und die Auslegung von Gal. 2, 11–14.* Supplements to Vigiliae Christianae 21 (Leiden: Brill, 1994).

Herford, R. Travers. *Christianity in Talmud and Midrash.* (1905; reprint, Clifton, N.J.: Reference Book, 1966).

Hoffmann, R. Joseph. *Marcion: On the Restitution of Christianity: An Essay on the Development of Radical Paulinist Theology in the Second Century* (Chico, Calif.: Scholars Press, 1984).

Hoh, J. *Die Lehre des Hl. Irenäus über das Neue Testament.* Neutestamentliche Abhandlungen 7 (Münster: Aschendorffsche Verlagsbuchhandlung, 1919).

Howard, George. "The Tetragram and the New Testament." *JBL* 96 (1977): 63–83.

Kahle, P. "Der gegenwärtige Stand der Erforschung der in Palästina neu gefundenen hebräischen Handschriften: 27. Die im August 1952 entdeckte Lederrolle mit dem griechischen Text der kleinen Propheten und das Problem der Seputaginta." *ThLZ* 79 (1954): 82–94.

———. "Problems of the Septuagint." *Studia Patristica* 1; *TU* 63 (1957): 328–38.

———. "The Greek Bible and the Gospels: Fragments from the Judaean Desert." In *Studia Evangelica: Papers Presented to the International Congress on "The Four Gospels" in 1957*, ed. K. Aland et al. (Berlin: Akademie-Verlag, 1959), 613–21.

———. "The Greek Bible Manuscripts Used by Origen." *JBL* 79 (1960): 111–18.

Kalin, Everett R. "Re-examining New Testament Canon History: 1. The Canon of Origin." *Currents in Theology and Mission* (Chicago) 17 (1990): 274–82.

Karrer, Martin. "Petrus im paulinischen Gemeindekreis." *ZNW* 80 (1989): 210–31.

Käsemann, Ernst, ed. *Das Neue Testament als Kanon: Dokumentation und kritische Analyse zur gegenwärtigen Diskussion* (Göttingen: Vandenhoeck, 1970).

Kasser, Rudolphe, and Victor Martin, eds. *Papyrus Bodmer XIV, Evangile de Luc, Chap. 3–24* (Cologny-Genève: Bibliothèque Bodmer, 1961).

———. *Papyrus Bodmer XV, Evangile de Jean, Chap. 1–15* (Cologny-Genève: Bibliothèque Bodmer, 1961).

———. *Papyrus Bodmer XVII, Actes des Apôtres, Epîtres de Jaques, Pierre, Jean et Jude* (Cologny-Genève: Bibliothèque Bodmer, 1961).

Kelly, J. N. D. *A Commentary on the Epistles of Peter and of Jude*. Black's New Testament Commentaries (London: Black, 1969; reprint, London: Black, 1977).

Kent, Homer A. "The Gospel According to Matthew." In *The Wycliffe Bible Commentary: The New Testament*, 4th ed. Ed. Everett F. Harrison (New York: Iversen-Norman Associates, 1973), 1–112.

Kenyon, F. G. "Nomina Sacra in the Chester Beatty Papyri." *Aegyptus* 13 (1933): 5–10.

———, ed. *British Museum: The Codex Alexandrinus* (*Royal Ms 1 D V-VIII*) (London: Oxford University Press, 1915). In Reduced Photographic Facsimile: Old Testament.

———, ed. *The Chester Beatty Biblical Papyri, Descriptions and Texts of Twelve Manuscripts on Papyrus of the Greek Bible, Fasciculus II: The Gospels and Acts* (*Plates*) (London: Emery Walker, 1934).

———, ed. *The Chester Beatty Biblical Papyri: Descriptions and Texts of Twelve Manuscripts on Papyrus of the Greek Bible, Fasciculus III: Pauline Epistles* (London: Emery Walker, 1936–37).

Kim, Young Kyu. "Paleographical Dating of P46 to the Later First Century." *Bib.* 69 (1988): 248–57.

Kinzig, Wolfram. "Ἡ καινὴ διαθήκη: The Title of the New Testament in the Second and Third Centuries." *JThS* 45 (1994): 519–44.

Klauck, Hans-Josef. *Die Johannesbriefe*. Erträge der Forschung 276 (Darmstadt: Wissenschaftliche Buchgesellschaft, 1991).

Kleberg, Tönnes. *Buchhandel und Verlagswesen in der Antike* (Darmstadt: Wissenschaftliche Buchgesellschaft, 1967).

Der Kleine Pauly: Lexikon der Antike. Ed. Konrat Ziegler and Walther Sontheimer (München: Deutscher Taschenbuch Verlag, 1979).

Klijn, A. F. J. "Die Entstehungsgeschichte des Neuen Testaments." *ANRW* 2, 26, 1 (1992): 64–97.

Kloeters, Gert. "Buch und Schrift bei Hieronymus." (Ph.D. diss., University of Münster, 1957).

Knoch, Otto. *Der Erste und Zweite Petrusbrief. Der Judasbrief, übersetzt und erklärt.* RNT (Regensburg: Pustet, 1990).

Knox, John. *Marcion and the New Testament: An Essay in the Early History of the Canon* (Chicago: University of Chicago Press, 1942).

Koester, Helmut. *Ancient Christian Gospels: Their History and Development* (London: SCM; Philadelphia: Trinity Press International, 1990).

Körtner, Ulrich H. J. "Markus der Mitarbeiter des Petrus." *ZNW* 71 (1980): 160–173.

Kraft, Heinrich, "Das besondere Selbstbewußtsein der Verfasser der Neutestamentlichen Schriften." In *Moderne Exegese und historische Wissenschaft*, ed. J. M. Hollenbach and Hugo Staudinger (Trier: Spee-Verlag, 1972), 77–93.

Krause, Gerhard et al., eds. *Theologische Realenzyklopädie* (Berlin: De Gruyter, 1977–).

Kühn, Karl Gottlob, ed. *Claudii Galeni opera omnia* (Leipzig: Knobloch, 1821).

Kuhnert, Ernst. "Geschichte des Buchhandels vom Altertum bis zur Gegenwart: Die Entwicklung in Umrissen." In *Handbuch der Bibliothekswissenschaft*, ed. Fritz Milkau. Vol. 1: *Schrift und Buch* (Leipzig: Harrassowitz, 1931), 717–827.

Kutsch, Ernst. *Neues Testament—Neuer Bund? Eine Fehlübersetzung wird korrigiert* (Neukirchen-Vluyn: Neukirchner Verlag, 1978).

Lake, Helen, and Kirsopp Lake, eds. *Codex Sinaiticus Petropolitanus: The New Testament, the Epistle of Barnabas and the Shepherd of Hermas* (Oxford: Clarendon, 1911). Reproduced in facsimile from photographs, with a description and introduction to the history of the codex.

———. *Codex Sinaticus Petropolitanus et Frederico-Augustanus Lipsiensis: The Old Testament: Preserved in the Public Library of Petrograd, in the Library of the Society of Ancient Literature in Petrograd, and in the Library of the University of Leipzig* (Oxford: Clarendon, 1922). Reproduced in facsimile from photographs, with a description and introduction to the history of the codex by Kirsopp Lake.

Lake, Kirsopp. "Rezension: H. J. M. Milne, T. C. Skeat, *Scribes and Correctors of the Codex Sinaiticus* (London: British Museum, 1938)." *Classical Philology* 37 (1942): 91–96.

Lambot, C. "Lettre inédite de S. Augustin relative au 'De Civitate Dei.'" *RevBen* 51 (1939): 109–21.

Lieberman, Saul. *Hellenism in Jewish Palestine: Studies in the Literary Transmission, Beliefs, and Manners of Palestine in the I Century B.C.E.–IV Century C.E.* Texts and Studies of the Jewish Theological Seminary of America 18 (New York: Jewish Theological Seminary, 1950).

Lietzmann, Hans. *Wie wurden die Bücher des Neuen Testaments heilige Schrift? Fünf Vorträge* (Tübingen: Mohr, 1907).

Lifshitz, B. "The Greek Documents from the Cave of Horror." *Israel Exploration Journal* 12 (1962): 201–7.

Lightfoot, J. B., and J. R. Harmer, eds. *The Apostolic Fathers*. 2nd ed. Ed./rev. by Michael W. Holmes (London, 1891, reprint, Grand Rapids, Mich.: Baker Book House, 1992).

Lohmeyer, Ernst. *Diatheke: Ein Beitrag zur Erklärung des neutestamentlichen Begriffs* (Leipzig: Hinrichs, 1913).

Loisy, A. *Histoire du canon du Nouveau Testament* (Paris, 1891; reprint, Frankfurt: Minerva, 1971).

Lührmann, Dieter. "Gal 2, 9 und die katholischen Briefe: Bemerkungen zum Kanon und zur regula fidei." *ZNW* 72 (1981): 65–87.

Luther, Martin. *Sermons on the Epistle of St. Jude*. Vol. 30 of *Luther's Works*. Ed. Jaroslav Pelikan and Walter Hansen (Saint Louis: Concordia, 1967).

Maier, Gerhard, ed. *Der Kanon der Bibel* (Wuppertal: R. Brockhaus, 1990).

Mallon, Jean. "Quel est le plus ancien exemple connu d'un manuscrit Latin en forme de codex?" *Emerita* (Madrid) 17 (1949): 1–8.

Marrou, H. I. "La technique de l'édition à l'époque patristique." *VigChr* 3 (1949): 208–24.

Martini, Carolus M., ed. *Novum Testamentum e Codice Vaticano Graeco 1209 (Codex B): Tertia vice phototypice expressum* (Rome: Vatican, 1968).

McLean, Bradley H. "Galatians 2.7–9 and the Recognition of Paul's Apostolic Status at the Jerusalem Conference: A Critique of G. Luedemann's Solution." *NTS* 37 (1991): 67–76.

McNamee, Kathleen. *Abbreviations in Greek Literary Papyri and Ostraca*. Bulletin of the American Society of Papyrologists, Supplement 3 (1981).

Meade, David G. *Pseudonymity and Canon: An Investigation into the Relationship of Authorship and Authority in Jewish and Earliest Christian Tradition*. WUNT 39 (Tübingen: Mohr, 1986).

Merriam-Webster's Collegiate Dictionary. 10th ed. (Springfield, Mass.: Merriam-Webster, 1993).

Metzger, Bruce M., *Manuscripts of the Greek Bible: An Introduction to Greek Palaeography* (New York: Oxford University Press, 1981).

———. *The Canon of the New Testament: Its Origin, Development, and Significance* (Oxford: Clarendon, 1987; reprint, Oxford: Clarendon, 1997). Originally published as *Der Kanon des Neuen Testaments: Entstehung, Entwicklung, Bedeutung* (Düsseldorf: Patmos, 1987).

———. *The Text of the New Testament: Its Transmission, Corruption, and Restoration*. 3rd ed. (New York: Oxford University Press, 1992).

Meyer, Marvin W. "The Youth in the Secret Gospel of Mark." *Semeia* 49 (1990): 129–54.

Miller, Ed. L. "The Johannine Origins of the Johannine Logos," *JBL* 112 (1993): 445–57.

Milne, H. J. M., *Greek Shorthand Manuals: Syllabary and Commentary* (London, 1936).

Milne, H. J. M., and T. C. Skeat. *Scribes and Correctors of the Codex Sinaiticus* (Oxford: Oxford University Press, 1938).

Minear, Paul S. "The Original Functions of John 21." *JBL* 102 (1983): 85–98.

Minor, Mark. *Literary-Critical Approaches to the Bible: An Annotated Bibliography* (West Cornwall, Conn.: Locust Hill Press, 1992).

Mitteis, L., and Ulrich Wilcken, eds., *Grundzüge und Chrestomathie der Papyruskunde*. Erster Band: *Historischer Teil* (Leipzig 1912; reprint, Hildesheim: Olms, 1963).

Montgomery, J. A. "A Survival of the Tetragrammaton in Daniel." *JBL* 40 (1921): 86.

Nachmanson, Ernst. "Die schriftliche Kontraktion auf den griechischen Inschriften." *Eranos* 9 (1909): 101–41.

Neirynck, Frans. "John 21." *NTS* 36 (1990): 321–36.

Neyrey, Jerome H. "The Apologetic Use of the Transfiguration in 2 Peter 1:16–21." *CBQ* 42 (1980): 504–19.

———. "The Form and Background of the Polemic in 2 Peter" (Ph.D. diss., Yale University, 1977).

Ohlig, Karl-Heinz. *Die theologische Begründung des neutestamentlichen Kanons in der alten Kirche* (Düsseldorf: Patmos, 1972).

Orchard, Bernhard, and Harold Riley. *The Order of the Synoptics: Why Three Synoptic Gospels?* (Macon, Ga.: Mercer University Press, 1987).

Oss, Douglas A. "Canon as Context: The Function of Sensus Plenior in Evangelical Hermeneutics." *Grace Theological Journal* 9 (1988): 105–27.

Paap, A. H. R. E. *Nomina Sacra in the Greek Papyri of the First Five Centuries A.D.* (Leiden: Brill, 1959).

Pack, Roger A. *Greek and Latin Literary Texts from Greco-Roman Egypt*. 2nd ed. (Ann Arbor: University of Michigan Press, 1965).

Parker, David C. *Codex Bezae: An Early Christian Manuscript and Its Text* (Cambridge: Cambridge University Press, 1992).

Paulsen, Henning. *Der Zweite Petrusbrief und der Judasbrief.* KEK 12, no. 2 (Göttingen: Vandenhoeck, 1992).

———. "Die Bedeutung des Montanismus für die Herausbildung des Kanons." *VigChr* 32 (1978): 19–52.

Peppermüller, Rolf. "Ein Unzialfragment auf dem Athos (Vatopediu und Protatu) und in Paris (0102 + [0138])." In *Materialien zur neutestamentlichen Handschriftenkunde*, ed. K. Aland, ANTF 3 (1969), 144–76.

Pesch, Rudolf. "Die Zuschreibung der Evangelien an apostolische Verfasser." *ZKTh* 97 (1975): 56–71.

———. "Levi-Matthäus (Mc 2, 14/Mt 9, 9 10, 3): Ein Beitrag zur Lösung eines alten Problems." *ZNW* 59 (1968): 40–56.

Quinn, Jerome D. "The Last Volume of Luke: The Relation of Luke-Acts to the Pastoral Epistles." In *Perspectives on Luke-Acts*, ed. Charles H. Talbert (Danville, Va.: Association of Baptist Professors of Religion, 1978), 62–75.

Rendtorff, Rolf. "Zur Bedeutung des Kanons für eine Theologie des Alten Testaments." In *"Wenn nicht jetzt, wann dann?": Festschrift für Hans-Joachim Kraus zum 65. Geburtstag* (Neukirchen-Vluyn: Neukirchner, 1983), 2–11.

Riesner, Rainer. "Ansätze zur Kanonbildung innerhalb des Neuen Testaments." In *Der Kanon der Bibel*, ed. G. Maier (Basel: Brunnen; Wuppertal: Brockhaus, 1990), 153–64.

Rist, Martin. "Pseudepigraphic Refutations of Marcionism." *Journal of Religion* 22 (1942): 39–62.

Ritter, Adolf Martin. "Die Entstehung des neutestamentlichen Kanons: Selbstdurchsetzung oder autoritative Entscheidung?" In *Kanon und Zensur: Beiträge zur Archäologie der literarischen Kommunikation*, vol. 2. Ed. Aleida Assman und Jan Assman (München: Fink, 1987).

———. "Zur Kanonbildung in der alten Kirche." In *Charisma und Caritas: Patristische Aufsätze* (Göttingen: Vandenhoeck, 1993).

Roberts, Colin Henderson. *Manuscript, Society and Belief in Early Christian Egypt.* The Schweich Lectures of the British Academy 1977 (London: Oxford University Press, 1979).

———. "P. Yale 1 and the Early Christian Book." In *Essays in Honor of C. Bradford Welles*, American Studies in Papyrology 1 (New Haven: American Society of Papyrologists, 1966), 25–28.

———. "The Codex." *Proceedings of the British Academy* 40 (1954): 169–204.

Roberts, Colin Henderson, and T. C. Skeat. *The Birth of the Codex* (London: Oxford University Press, 1983).

Rudberg, Gunnar. "Ad usum circumscribentem praepositionum Graecarum adnotationes." *Eranos* 19 (1919–20): 173–206.

———. *Neutestamentlicher Text und Nomina sacra*. Skrifter utgifna af K. Humanistiska Vetenskaps-Samfundet i Uppsala 17, no. 3 (Uppsala: Akademiska Bokhandeln, 1915; Leipzig: Harrassowitz, 1915).

———. "Zur paläographischen Kontraktion auf griechischen Ostraka." *Eranos* 9 (1909): 71–100.

Sand, A. *Kanon: Von den Anfängen bis zum Fragmentum Muratorianum*. Handbuch der Dogmengeschichte 1, 3a, 1 (Freiburg: Herder, 1974).

Sanders, Henry A. "The Beginning of the Modern Book: The Codex of the Classical Era." *Michigan Alumnus* 44, no. 15 (1938): 95–111.

———. ed. *A Third-Century Papyrus Codex of the Epistles of Paul*. University of Michigan Studies, Humanistic Series 38 (Ann Arbor: University of Michigan Press, 1935).

———. *Facsimile of the Washington Manuscript of the Four Gospels in the Freer Collection, with an Introduction*. University of Michigan Studies, Humanistic Series 9, no. 1 (Ann Arbor: University of Michigan Press, 1912).

Sanders, J. N., and B. A. Mastin. *A Commentary on the Gospel According to St John*. BNTC (1968).

Sanz, P. "Christliche Papyri aus der Papyrussammlung der Nationalbibliothek zu Wien" (Ph.D. diss., University of Vienna, 1936).

Scheele, Jürgen. "Buch und Bibliothek bei Augustinus." *Bibliothek und Wissenschaft* 12 (1978): 14–114.

Schmid, Ulrich. *Marcion und sein Apostolos: Rekonstruktion und historische Einordnung der marcionitischen Paulusbriefausgabe*. ANTF 25 (1995).

Schmidt, Daryl D. "Semitisms and Septuagintalisms in the Book of Revelation." *NTS* 37 (1991): 592–603.

Schnackenburg, Rudolf. *Die Johannesbriefe*. 2nd ed., HThK 13 (1963).

Schneider, Gerhard. *Die Apostelgeschichte*. HThK 5 (1980–82).

Schneider, Johannes. *Das Evangelium nach Johannes*. Ed. Erich Fascher. ThHK (1976).

Schofield, E. M., ed. *The Papyrus Fragments of the Greek New Testament* (Clinton, N.J., 1936).

Schön, Franz, ed. *C. Suetonius Tranquillus: Sämtliche erhaltene Werke*. Unter Zugrundelegung der Übertragung von Adolf Stahr neu bearbeitet von Franz Schön und Gerhard Waldherr; mit einer Einführung von Franz Schön (Essen: Phaidon, 1987).

Schubart, Wilhelm. *Das Buch bei den Griechen und Römern*. 2nd rev. ed. (Berlin: De Gruyter, 1921); 3rd abbrev. ed., ed. E. Paul (Heidelberg: Schneider, 1962). (Page numbers refer to the comprehensive 2nd edition.)

Schumacher, Joseph. *Der apostolische Abschluß der Offenbarung Gottes*. Freiburger Theologische Studien 114 (Freiburg: Herder, 1979).

Scobie, Charles H. "The Challenge of Biblical Theology." *Tyndale Bulletin* 42 (1991): 33–61.

Seeligmann, Isaac L. "Problems and Perspectives in Modern Septuagint Research." In *Textus: Studies of the Hebrew University Bible Project*, ed. Emanuel Tov, vol. 15 (Jerusalem: Magnes Press, 1990), 169–232.

Segovia, Fernando F. "The Final Farewell of Jesus: A Reading of John 20:30–21:25." *Semeia* 53 (1991), 167–90.

Shackleton Bailey, D. R., ed. *Martial: Epigrams* (Cambridge: Harvard University Press, 1993).

Sheppard, Gerald T. "Canonization: Hearing the Voice of the Same God through Historically Dissimilar Traditions." *Interpretation: A Journal of Bible and Theology* 36 (1982): 21–33.

———. "'Enemies' and the Politics of Prayer in the Book of Psalms." In *The Bible and the Politics of Exegesis*, ed. David Jobling, Peggy L. Day, and Gerald T. Sheppard (Cleveland: Pilgrim Press, 1991), 61–82, 308–11.

Siegel, Jonathan P. "The Employment of Palaeo-Hebrew Characters for the Divine Names at Qumran in the Light of Tannaitic Sources." *Hebrew Union College Annual* 42 (1971): 159–72.

Skeat, T. C. "Irenaeus and the Four-Gospel Canon." *NT* 34 (1992): 194–99.

———. "The Length of the Standard Papyrus Roll and the Cost-advantage of the Codex." *ZPE* 45 (1982): 169–75.

———. "The Use of Dictation in Ancient Book-Production." *Proceedings of the British Academy* 42 (1956): 179–208.

Skehan, P. W. "The Qumran Manuscripts and Textual Criticism." In *Volume du Congrès, Strasbourg 1956*, Supplements to Vetus Testamentum 4 (Leiden: Brill, 1957), 148–60.

———. "The Text of Isaias at Qumran." *CBQ* 17 (1955): 158–63.

Smith, Dennis E. "Narrative Beginnings in Ancient Literature and Theory." *Semeia* 52 (1991): 1–9.

Spicq, C. *Les Epîtres de Saint Pierre*. Sources Bibliques (Paris: Gabalda, 1966).

Stanton, Graham N. *A Gospel for a New People: Studies in Matthew* (Edinburgh: Clark, 1992).

Starr, Raymond J. "Reading Aloud: Lectores and Roman Reading." *Classical Journal* 86 (1991): 337–43.

———. "The Used-Book Trade in the Roman World." *Phoenix* 44 (1990): 148–57.

Stegemann, Wolfgang. "War der Apostel Paulus ein römischer Bürger?" *ZNW* 78 (1987): 200–229.

Stemberger, Günter. *Der Talmud: Einführung—Texte—Erläuterungen*. 2nd ed. (München: Beck, 1987).

Strecker, Georg. "εὐαγγέλιον, ου, τό; euaggelion; Evangelium." *EWNT* 2 (1992): 176–86.

———. *Literaturgeschichte des Neuen Testaments* (Göttingen: Vandenhoeck, 1992).

Stuhlhofer, Franz. *Der Gebrauch der Bibel von Jesus bis Euseb: Eine statistische Untersuchung zur Kanonsgeschichte* (Wuppertal: R. Brockhaus, 1988).

Stuttgarter Jubiläumsbibel mit erklärenden Anmerkungen: Die Bibel oder die ganze Heilige Schrift des Alten u. Neuen Testaments nach der deutschen Übersetzung D. Martin Luthers. Neu durchgesehen nach dem vom Deutschen Evangelischen Kirchenausschuß genehmigten Text, mit erklärenden Anmerkungen (Stuttgart: Privilegierte Württembergische Bibelanstalt, 1912).

Sundberg, Albert C. "Canon Muratori: A Fourth-Century List." *HThR* 66 (1973): 1–41.

———. "Canon of the New Testament." Supplementary vol. to *Interpreters Dictionary of the Bible* (Nashville: Abingdon, 1976).

———. "The Bible Canon and the Christian Doctrine of Inspiration." *Interpretation* 29 (1975): 352–71.

———. *The Old Testament of the Early Church* (Cambridge: Harvard University Press, 1964).

———. "Towards a Revised History of the New Testament Canon." *Studia Evangelica* 4; *TU* 102 (1968): 452–61.

Swete, Henry Barclay. *An Introduction to the Old Testament in Greek*, appendix containing the Letter of Aristeas, ed. H. St. J. Thackeray (Cambridge: Cambridge University Press, 1900; rev. R. R. Ottley, reprint, New York: Ktav, 1968).

Talbert, Charles H. "II Peter and the Delay of the Parousia." *VigChr* 20 (1966): 137–45.

Testuz, Michel, ed. *Papyrus Bodmer VII–IX. VII: L'Epître de Jude; VIII: Les deux Epîtres de Pierre; IX: Les Psaumes 33 et 34* (Cologny-Genève: Bibliothèque Bodmer, 1959).

Thompson, Steven. *The Apocalypse and Semitic Syntax* (Cambridge: Cambridge University Press, 1985).

Thornton, Claus-Jürgen. *Der Zeuge des Zeugen: Lukas als Historiker der Paulusreisen.* WUNT 56 (Tübingen: Mohr, 1991).

Thyen, Hartwig. "Johannes und die Synoptiker." In *John and the Synoptics*, ed. A. Denaux, BEThL 51 (Leuven: Leuven University Press, 1992), 81–107.

Tischendorf, Constantin, ed. *Codex Ephraemi Syri Rescriptus: Sive fragmenta utriusque testamenti e codice graeco parisiensi celeberrimo quinti ut videtur post christum saeculi.* 2 vols. (Leipzig: Taubnitz, 1843).

———. *Novum Testamentum Graece ad antiquissimos testes denuo recensuit, apparatum criticum apposuit Constantinus Tischendorf.* Editio octava critica maior volumen III, Prolegomena scripsit Caspar Renatus Gregory (Leipzig: Hinrichs, 1894).

Tov, Emanuel. "Die griechischen Bibelübersetzungen." part 2: "Principat." *ANRW* 20, no. 1 (1987): 121–89.

Tov, Emanuel ed. *The Greek Minor Prophets Scroll from Naḥal Ḥever (8ḤevXIIgr)*. (The Seiyâl Collection, no. 1. Discoveries in the Judaean Desert, no. 8 (New York: Oxford University Press, 1990).

Traube, Ludwig. *Nomina Sacra: Versuch einer Geschichte der christlichen Kürzungen* (München, 1907; reprint, Darmstadt: Wissenschaftliche Buchgesellschaft, 1967).

Treu, Kurt. "24. LXX, Psalm 9, 12–15 auf Einzelblatt." *Papyrus Erzherzog Rainer (P. Rainer Cent.); Festschrift zum 100-jährigen Bestehen der Papyrussammlung der österreichischen Nationalbibliothek* (Wien: Hollinek, 1983).

———. "Christliche Papyri VI." *APF* 26 (1978): 149–59.

———. "Christliche Papyri VII." *APF* 27 (1980): 251–58.

———. "Die Bedeutung des Griechischen für die Juden im Römischen Reich." *Kairos* 15 (1973): 123–44.

Trobisch, David. "Das Rätsel um die Verfasserschaft des Hebräerbriefes und die Entdeckung eines echten Paulustextes." In *In Dubio pro Deo*, ed. D. Trobisch (Heidelberg: Wiss. theol. Seminar, 1993), 320–23.

———. *Die Entstehung der Paulusbriefsammlung: Studien zu den Anfängen christlicher Publizistik*. NTOA 10 (Freiburg: Universitätsverlag; Göttingen: Vandenhoeck, 1989).

———. *Paul's Letter Collection: Tracing the Origins* (Minneapolis: Fortress, 1994). Also published as *Die Paulusbriefe und die Anfänge der christlichen Publizistik* (Gütersloh: Kaiser, 1994).

———. "The Council of Jerusalem in Acts and Paul's Letter to the Galatians." In *Theological Exegesis: Essays in Honor of Brevard S. Childs*, ed. Chr. Seitz and K. Greene-McCreight (Grand Rapids, Mich.: Eerdmans, 1999), 331–38.

Tucker, Gene M. "Prophetic Superscriptions and the Growth of a Canon." In *Canon and Authority: Essays in Old Testament Religion and Theology* (Philadelphia: Fortress, 1977), 56–70.

Turner, Eric G. *The Typology of the Early Codex* (Philadelphia: University of Pennsylvania Press, 1977).

Uhlig, Siegbert. "Ein pseudepigraphischer Actaschluß in der äthiopischen Version." *Oriens Christianus* 73 (1989): 127–36.

van der Valk, H. L. M. "On the Edition of Books in Antiquity." *VigChr* 11 (1957): 1–10.

van Haelst, J., ed. *Catalogue des papyrus littéraires juifs et chrétiens* (Paris: Publications de la Sorbonne, 1976).

van Unnik, W. C. "De la regle Μήτε προσθεῖναι μήτε ἀφελεῖν dans l'histoire du canon." *VigChr* 3 (1949): 1–36.

———. "Ἡ καινὴ διαθήκη—A Problem in the Early History of the Canon." *Studia Patristica* 4; *TU* 79 (1961): 212–27; reprinted in *Sparsa Collecta* (Leiden) 2 (1980): 157–71.

Vielhauer, Philipp. *Geschichte der urchristlichen Literatur: Einleitung in das Neue Testament, die Apokryphen und die Apostolischen Väter.* 2nd rev. ed. (Berlin: De Gruyter, 1978).

Vogt, Hermann Josef. "Die Geltung des Alten Testaments bei Irenäus von Lyon." *Theologische Quartalschrift* (München) 160 (1980): 17–28.

Vögtle, Anton. "Die Schriftwerdung der apostolischen Paradosis nach 2Petr 1, 12–15." In *Offenbarungsgeschehen und Wirkungsgeschichte* (Freiburg: Herder, 1985), 297–304.

———. "'Keine Prophetie ist Sache eigenwilliger Auslegung' (2Petr 1, 20f)." In *Offenbarungsgeschehen und Wirkungsgeschichte* (Freiburg: Herder, 1985), 305–28.

———. "Petrus und Paulus nach dem Zweiten Petrusbrief." In *Kontinuität und Einheit, Festschrift für Franz Mußner*, ed. P.-G. Müller and W. Stenger (Freiburg: Herder, 1981), 223–39.

Wachtel, Klaus, and Klaus Witte, eds. *Das Neue Testament auf Papyrus: II. Die Paulinischen Briefe*, Teil 2: *Gal, Eph, Phil, Kol, 1 u. 2 Thess, 1 u. 2 Tim, Tit, Phlm, Hebr.* ANTF 22 (1994).

Waddell, W. G. "The Tetragrammaton in the LXX." *JThS* 45 (1944): 158–61.

Wanke, G. "Bibel, I. Die Entstehung des Alten Testaments als Kanon." *TRE* 6 (1980): 1–8.

Warns, Rüdiger. "Untersuchungen zum 2. Clemens-Brief" (Ph.D. diss., University of Marburg, 1985).

Weber, R. *Sancti Cypriani Episcopi Opera: Ad Quirinum, ad Fortunatum.* CCL 3 (Turnhout: Brepols, 1972).

Wehnert, Jürgen. *Die Wir-Passagen der Apostelgeschichten: Ein lukanisches Stilmittel aus jüdischer Tradition.* GTA 40 (1989).

Weiss, Bernhard. *Kritisch exegetisches Handbuch über das Evangelium des Johannes.* 7th ed. KEK (1886).

Wendel, Carl. "Bibliothek." *RAC* 2, supplement (1954): 231–74.

———. *Kleine Schriften zum antiken Buch- und Bibliothekswesen.* Ed. Werner Krieg (Köln: Greven, 1974).

Wendland, Heinz-Dietrich. *Die Briefe an die Korinther.* NTD (1965).

Wengst, Klaus, ed. *Schriften des Urchristentums: Zweiter Teil: Didache (Apostellehre), Barnabasbrief, Zweiter Klemensbrief, Schrift an Diognet, Eingeleitet, herausgegeben, übertragen und erläutert* (Darmstadt: Wissenschaftliche Buchgesellschaft, 1984).

Wenham, John. "The Identification of Luke." *Evangelical Quarterly* (London) 63 (1991): 3–44.

Wessely, C. "Literarischer theologischer Text Nr. 26." *Studien zur Paläographie und Papyruskunde*, (Leipzig) 12 (1912): 246.

Westcott, Brooke Foss. *A General Survey of the History of the Canon of the New Testament.* 6th ed. (Cambridge: Macmillan, 1889).

Wettstein, Jacobus. *Novum Testamentum Graecum* (Amsterdam: Dommerian, 1752; reprint, Graz: Akademische Verlagsanstalt, 1962).

Wevers, J. W., ed. *Septuaginta: Deuteronomium* (Göttingen: Vandenhoeck, 1977).

Widmann, Hans. "Herstellung und Vertrieb des Buches in der griechisch-römischen Welt." *Archiv für die Geschichte des Buchwesens* 8 (1967): 564–640.

Wilamowitz-Moellendorf, Ulrich von, K. Krumbacher, J. Wackernagel et al., eds. *Die griechische und lateinische Literatur und Sprache.* 3rd ed. (Leipzig: Teubner, 1912).

Wilcken, Ulrich. "The Chester Beatty Biblical Papyri." *APF* 11 (1935): 112–14.

Williams, A. Lukyn. "The Tetragrammaton—Jahweh, Name or Surrogate?" *ZAW* 54 (1936): 262–69.

Wills, Lawrence M. "The Depiction of the Jews in Acts." *JBL* 110 (1991): 631–54.

Windisch, Hans. *Die Katholischen Briefe.* 3rd rev. ed. Ed. Herbert Preisker. HNT 15 (1951).

Winter, Paul. "Some Observations on the Language in the Birth and Infancy Stories of the Third Gospel." *NTS* 1 (1954–55): 111–21.

Yadin, Yigael. *The Ben Sira Scroll from Masada* (Jerusalem: Israel Exploration Society, 1965).

Zahn, Theodor. *Geschichte des Neutestamentlichen Kanons*, vol. 1: *Das Neue Testament vor Origenes* (Erlangen: Deichert, 1888–1889); vol. 2: *Urkunden und Belege zum ersten und dritten Band* (Erlangen: Deichert, 1890–92; reprint, Hildesheim: Olms, 1975).

Zmijewski, Josef. "Apostolische Paradosis und Pseudepigraphie im Neuen Testament. 'Durch Erinnerung wachhalten' (2 Petr 1, 13; 3, 1)." *BZ* 23 (1979): 161–71.

Zucker, Friedrich. "Rezension: K. Ohly, *Stychometrische Untersuchungen* (Leipzig: Harrasowitz, 1928)." *Gnomon* 8 (1932): 383–88.

Index of Manuscripts and Ancient Sources

MANUSCRIPTS

New Testament manuscripts listed only on pp. 28–29 are not noted.

ANCIENT SOURCES